CAPITÁN
LATINOAMÉRICA

SUNY series in Latin American Cinema
———
Ignacio M. Sánchez Prado and Leslie L. Marsh, editors

CAPITÁN LATINOAMÉRICA

SUPERHEROES IN CINEMA, TELEVISION, AND WEB SERIES

VINODH VENKATESH

Cover image: Bastián Cifuentes Araya (Instagram: periodistafurioso). Photography of protester dressed as El Chapulin Colorado in Santiago, Chile, October 21–22, 2019.

Published by State University of New York Press, Albany

© 2020 State University of New York

All rights reserved

No part of this book may be used or reproduced in any manner whatsoever without written permission. No part of this book may be stored in a retrieval system or transmitted in any form or by any means including electronic, electrostatic, magnetic tape, mechanical, photocopying, recording, or otherwise without the prior permission in writing of the publisher.

For information, contact State University of New York Press, Albany, NY
www.sunypress.edu

Library of Congress Cataloging-in-Publication Data

Names: Venkatesh, Vinodh, author.
Title: Capitán Latinoamérica : superheroes in cinema, television, and web series / Vinodh Venkatesh.
Description: Albany : State University of New York Press, [2020] | Series: SUNY series in Latin American cinema | Includes bibliographical references and index.
Identifiers: LCCN 2020018283 | ISBN 9781438480152 (hardcover) | ISBN 9781438480145 (pbk.) | ISBN 9781438480169 (ebook) Subjects: LCSH: Superhero films—Latin America—History and criticism. | Superhero television programs—Latin America—History and criticism. | Internet television—Latin America—History and criticism.
Classification: LCC PN1995.9.S7 V36 2020 | DDC 791.43/652—dc23
LC record available at https://lccn.loc.gov/2020018283

10 9 8 7 6 5 4 3 2 1

For Venkatesh Ramakrishnan

Contents

List of Illustrations — ix

Acknowledgments — xi

Introduction — 1

Chapter 1 Mexican Origins — 15

Chapter 2 Urbanization and Its Discontents in *El Man, el superhéroe nacional* — 75

Chapter 3 Allegories of Trauma and Transition in *Mirageman* — 105

Chapter 4 The Superhero and a Death Foretold: *Chinche Man* in San Pedro Sula — 145

Chapter 5 YouTube, Parody, and Neoliberal Critique in *Capitán Centroamérica* — 171

Post Data: "Un pibe . . . un boludo más . . . nos vino a salvar" — 213

Notes — 223

Works Cited — 245

Index — 255

Illustrations

Figure I.1	Batman as a belligerent gringo in Latin America.	9
Figure 1.1	The silver-masked icon.	20
Figure 1.2	Faith as a defining superpower.	35
Figure 1.3	The asexual superhero.	36
Figure 1.4	More powerful than a locomotive!	44
Figure 1.5	Superheroines become super sidekicks.	50
Figure 1.6	Fighting crime in a bikini.	52
Figure 1.7	Situating Kalimán in an exotic space.	58
Figure 1.8	An iconic costume for an iconic superhero.	70
Figure 1.9	El Presidente Dictador (the dictator president).	73
Figure 2.1	El Man, a patriotic superhero.	77
Figure 2.2	Faith as a distinctively local superpower.	89
Figure 3.1	Trauma resurfaces in a jarring memory from the past.	118
Figure 3.2	Forensic clues in the moment of action.	119
Figure 4.1	Axiographic schema in the opening minutes of the superhero genre.	159
Figure 5.1	There are no heroes in the streets of Central America.	179

Figure 5.2	Parodic aesthetics and powers.	185
Figure P.1	Zenitram and Argentina in crisis.	217
Figure P.2	Fictionalizing the lay-hero in *Capitán Menganno*.	219

Acknowledgments

The ideas developed in this book originated in an undergraduate Mexican and Central American culture and literature course I taught in fall 2014. Since it was my second time teaching SPAN 3464, I wanted to expose my students to something beyond the canon, and spent hours poring over YouTube and other streaming sites to find original and grassroots content. I stumbled upon the webisodes of *Capitán Centroamérica*, and was encouraged by my students' response to the character and his antics; I was particularly taken by the connections we were able to make with other themes and texts covered in the semester.

A year later I was granted tenure at Virginia Tech, and received an email from the Provost's Office stating that they would purchase a book for the library to celebrate my accomplishments: "You might wish to designate something in your field of research, or, because we know that our faculty read widely, you might want to select something in another field of science, art, literature, or technology." I picked Liam Burke's edited collection *Batman*. Going over the essays in this anthology, and many others afterwards, I slowly carved out a space for connecting superhero studies with my own research interests. This led to an article, which then was developed into the broader ideas present in *Capitán Latinoamérica*.

There are many people to thank who have supported me through their guidance, camaraderie, and suggestions over the past few years. I am incredibly grateful to all my colleagues in Modern and Classical Languages and Literatures for their support and friendship. I am particularly thankful to my colleagues in the Spanish Program.

Special thanks to Samanta Ordoñez Robles, Santiago Rozo, Carlos Evia, Mauro Caraccioli, Veronica Montes, David Dalton, Susan Larson, Ruth Grene, Olivia Cosentino, Rita Martin, Joana Jaime, Oswaldo Estrada,

Juan Carlos González Espitia, Cristina Carrasco, Birgitte Bonning, Jeffrey Uhlmann, Craig Ferguson, Julia Simpson, Alexis Ballvé, and Grant Gearhart for sending me links, videos, and pdfs, and recounting anecdotes of watching superhero media when we have been able to talk at conferences or over a meal. Their excitement and knowledge of superheroes (in Latin America) undoubtedly enriched this book.

I am immensely grateful to the creators and producers of many of these superheroes for entertaining my emails, tweets, and Facebook messages. Thanks to Nicolás López and Steffi Lutz at Sobras International Pictures, the production and communications team at PuyA! Studios (formerly Puyaweb), Harold Trompetero, the production team behind *Capitán Menganno*, and the production team behind *Zambo Dende*. A personal thanks goes out to Súper H, Elmer Ramos, for answering all my questions. I am also incredibly grateful to Bastián Cifuentes Araya (@periodistafurioso on Instagram) for allowing me to use the photograph of a modern-day Chapulín on the streets of Santiago during recent protests; the image goes to show just how important the superhero is in our collective consciousness.

Many thanks are also in order to my family. My love for superheroes is shared and nourished through conversations and trips to the cinema with my siblings, Sabitha and Vishnu. As kids, Vish and I would dress up as Spiderman while brandishing our Thundercats swords, fighting off imaginary villains as a dynamic fraternal-twin duo in Bangkok, lending credence to the notion that superheroes are malleable and "culturally and contextually dependent" (Denison and Mizsei-Ward 4). Watching the latest superhero blockbuster during Thanksgiving has now become a tradition with Sabitha. In Melilla, many, many thanks to Joaquín, Mari Carmen, Kiny, Chica, Alberto, Luis, Yaya, Julia, Blanca, and Clara. Most importantly, I am thankful for having wonderful parents, Narayini and Venkatesh. They have been role models and pillars supporting all I do. As cliché as it is (especially in a book about superheroes), they are my true superheroes.

This book would not have been possible without the support of those who have lived it on a daily basis. I am immensely thankful to my partner in crime, my *media naranja*, Mari Carmen, for her strength and encouragement. Her unwavering love and laughter have nurtured and sustained me in this journey. I must also thank Don Duende, el Marqués de Pitiminí, for patiently waiting for me to take him out on walks. Many thanks to the developers of FIFA and PES for providing intense but needed writing breaks.

I also want to thank my editor at SUNY Press, Rebecca Colesworthy, for her unwavering commitment to the project from the very first email I sent her. Her professionalism, guidance, and encouragement have made all the difference. Many thanks as well to Eileen Nizer, Ann Valentine, and Gordon Marce. The reports from the two anonymous readers greatly improved the manuscript—I am thankful for their suggestions, comments, and critique. I am also incredibly grateful to have the support of Ignacio Sánchez Prado and Leslie Marsh, who were from the very beginning enthusiastic about including this project in their series.

An early version of chapter 3, "Capitán Latinoamérica: Affect, Bodies, and Circulations in the Superhero Genre," originally appeared in a special dossier I edited with María del Carmen Caña Jiménez titled "Affect, Bodies, and Circulations in Contemporary Latin American Film" in *Arizona Journal of Hispanic Cultural Studies* 20 (2016). I am grateful to the editors for giving me permission to use a version of that essay here.

Introduction

In the past two decades, superhero films based on comic book characters have grossed some of the highest ticket sales in US and worldwide box offices. As Martin Zeller-Jacques points out, "Since the turn of the Millennium, Hollywood-produced superhero movies have dominated U.S. and global box offices. This cycle of films, beginning with *X-Men* (Brian Singer, 2000) and continuing to the present day, has provided three of the ten highest grossing films of all time . . . [and] earned a new cultural respectability for superheroes" (195).[1] In many Latin American markets, recent Hollywood action films, many of which are of the superhero genre, have topped individual weekend and yearly sales; in Mexico during 2012, 2013, and 2016, for example, the highest grossing films per weekend belonged to *The Avengers*, *Iron Man 3*, and *Captain America: Civil War* respectively.[2] In the latter year, the top three spots were occupied by films from the Marvel and DC cinematic universes.[3] The years 2018 and 2019 have unsurprisingly been dominated by Marvel's *Infinity War* and *Endgame*. In other words, audiences to the south of the Rio Grande are now lapping up the muscled bodies, ample cleavage, computer-generated special effects, and repetitive narrative structures that have now become the standard bearer for Hollywood. One may even say that the superhero has become a colonizing genre, a vector of cultural imperialism that has quietly overrun local markets.

Such crossover commercial success in Latin American markets comes as no surprise, given the historical and cultural ubiquity of these figures in print and film media and their rapid circulation to global viewer- and readerships from their very beginning in the mid-twentieth century. What may be questioned, however, is the relative lack of local comic book superheroes that have made their presence felt on the screen. Latin

America, after all, has a rich tradition of comics and superheroes. These include such characters as El Aguila Solitaria, Súper Cóndor, Patoruzú, Supercifuentes, El Santo, Kalimán, Capitão 7, and Sónoman that have all graced the pages of Latin American comic book production, and to much commercial success, their issues often being sold across the Spanish-speaking world. Yet perhaps no other superhero is as well-known or as exported as El Chapulín Colorado, who has even influenced the US imaginary of the archetype, as evidenced by the parodic Bumblebee Man in *The Simpsons*, and Marvel's Red Locust (the superhero persona of Fernanda Ramírez) who made her debut in late 2017.

Given these market conditions and cultural substrates, we may ask why, then, the lack of adaptations in recent cinema, or even original superheroes making their blockbuster debut on the screen and competing with ticket sales of *The Avengers* and *The Justice League*, especially in a (inter)national cinemascape overrun by the genre. This lack in commercial cinema is especially significant given the serial success and ubiquity of Latin American superheroes in a variety of media, such as *El Chapulín Colorado* (television, 1972–79) and wrestler-superheroes such as El Santo (film, animated film, 1950s–) in Mexican and then Latin American markets. It is remarkable, since some of the most internationally renowned Mexican directors—who often wear the mantle of "Latin America" in global discussions on film—have successfully either made traditional superhero films (Guillermo del Toro—*Hellboy*, *Hellboy 2*, *Blade 2*) or films in which the cultural capital of the superhero is highlighted (Alejandro González Iñárritu—*Birdman*). But this absence is not only to note in multiplexes and streaming sites that now often substitute for the experience of going to the movies; perhaps more remarkable is the lack of any mention of a Latin American superhero flick in Rayna Denison and Rachel Mizsei-Ward's recent anthology on global superheroes, *Superheroes on World Screens* (2015), where contemporary characters from India, England, Australia, Thailand, Japan, and Korea are featured.[4]

All this is not to say, however, that there are no contemporary Latin American superheroes coexisting in the mediascape dominated by Marvel (and, to a lesser extent, DC) characters. There is indeed a broad spectrum of characters who have erupted onto the local and regional stage in recent years that have gained a popular and cult following with audiences in the know, and with casual browsers of social media and YouTube that click on a viral video of a parodic Capitán Centroamérica or Chinche Man. These characters are at times adaptations of comic book heroes (such as O Doutrinador and Zambo Dende), and at other times original superheroes born in the moving image, circulated through cinema and serial mechanisms and outlets that speak to an audience saturated in the US hegemony of the genre. (There are even characters created for specific purposes, though they fall outside the parameters of this book, such as Susana Distancia, a superheroine at the forefront of the Mexican government's tardy efforts to encourage social-distancing in the face of the COVID-19 pandemic.) As I will show in the following pages, the Latin American superhero is very much alive in popular media and film, and it demands a critical study that situates it within a broader examination of cultural output and critique.

The literature to date on contemporary Latin American superheroes on the screen is scarce, perhaps in part due to the relative lack of productions and the genre's association with exploitation, popular, and low-budget cinema. Several scholars, such as Ariel Dorfman and Armand Mattelart, David William Foster, Héctor Fernández L'Hoeste, and Juan Poblete, have made important inroads into the analysis of print comics and superheroes, an important precursor of the filmic genre.[5] Tangentially, Frederick Luis Aldama's *Latinx Superheroes in Mainstream Comics* (2017) is also an imperative touching stone, as the manuscript pores over a vast print archive of the superhero genre to establish just how embedded Latin/o American subjects and identities are within the field. Regarding the presence of the Latin American superhero in film, a useful point of departure is Carlos Aguasaco's work in *¡No contaban con mi astucia! México: Parodia, nación y sujeto en la serie de El Chapulín Colorado* (2014), where he examines the parodic character of the series to argue that the television show is a metonym of the failed development of the nation (and, more broadly speaking, Latin America) in the latter half of the twentieth century. Aguasaco's detailed analysis of parody as narrative mode is fundamental in understanding the broader regional archetype, as parody often is the foundation on which many of the Latin American superhero narratives today are erected.

Another thread to follow is the work on the Mexican wrestler films of the 1960s through the 1980s. Monographs by Robert Michael Cotter, Doyle Greene, and Raul Criollo, Xavier Nava, and Rafael Aviña provide a methodical compilation and analysis of characters such as Neutrón, La Sombra Vengadora, Mil Máscaras, Blue Demon, and Superzán, and how they galvanized a popular audience into buying into their fantastical confrontations with werewolves, vampires, and extraterrestrials. These studies—which I address in detail in the following chapter—importantly, align the oeuvre of films with a distinct Mexican body of cinema, instead of establishing points of contact with the broader field of superhero studies, perhaps explaining the absence of Latin American superheroes within global discussions of the movie genre.

Keeping this in mind, *Capitán Latinoamérica* contextualizes and analyzes recent superhero-themed cinema, television, and web series produced in Latin America, within a broader conversation on the boom of the superhero genre in global cinema. Through an analysis and commentary of features and series from Chile, Colombia, El Salvador, Honduras, Mexico, Brazil and Argentina, I argue that contemporary Latin American superheroes are an amalgam of regional archetypes (namely, tropes of the famed Mexican *luchador* and the parodic mode of El Chapulín) and North American blockbuster characters from the DC and Marvel universes.[6] In addition to poetically and aesthetically being a hybrid of Latin and Anglo identities, Latin American superheroes, importantly, channel specific local anxieties that already dominate the cultural horizon of their respective national contexts; that is, these local superheroes (though global in lineage and circulation) participate in cultural, social, political, and economic conversations *in situ*. In Chile, for example, *Mirageman* rehashes and works through issues of the Pinochet dictatorship and its traumatic aftermath, while in *Chinche Man*, issues of neoliberalism and gang violence in Honduras are the principal thematic nodes. In *El Man*, in turn, the rapid urbanization of Colombia (and its relationship to drug cartels) is the central concern of the parodic protagonist, whereas corruption, cynicism, and the political machinations of the state feature in the television and web series of *Capitán Centroamérica*. While these superheroes may superficially be characterized by their low budgets and kitsch aesthetic, they do, upon closer examination, problematize the complex issues facing contemporary Latin America. This analytic strategy follows Aguasaco's interpellation of the archetype with broader concerns (though not necessarily centered on the notion of superhero as metonym), thus reading the superhero beyond the frontiers of the narrative and diegesis, and onto an intricate cultural terrain populated by a variety of sociopolitical actors and issues.

Through the study of superheroes across media platforms and narrative modes, I argue in *Capitán Latinoamérica* that contemporary Latin American superheroes are digital natives, their origin stories firmly rooted in the Internet and smartphone age, and use tech and web platforms to connect to their engaged public in a democratic fashion. They are truly bottom-up heroes; that is, they arise and emanate from the populace in times of greatest need, demonstrating that the "hero" in the superhero can be anyone and everyone, readily available to the common person through a quick email, text message, or video call. In doing so, Latin American superheroes importantly—unlike their US counterparts—often challenge the politicoeconomic status quo, instead of defending, as Umberto Eco has argued, the structural tenets of injustice that are often smoothed over in archetypal Anglo narratives. American superheroes, after all, are known for maintaining the status quo even while apprehending the villain, as villainy is constrained to succinct ruptures of the legal fabric, leading Richard Reynolds to observe that "the ideological import of the superhero is to inflict a sense of powerlessness and resignation on readers. . . . A key ideological myth of the superhero comic is that the normal and everyday enshrines positive values that must be defended through heroic action . . . the superhero is battling on behalf of the status quo" (236–37).[7]

The Latin American superhero, however, is, significantly, an agent of change, a point of critical inflection and introspection, a narrative genre that probes and questions the (social, political, and economic) status quo, quite unlike the ontologically inert and impotent North American trope that superficially masquerades as a hero of the subaltern, all while maintaining in place the principles of savage capitalism and US geopolitical hegemony.

In broad strokes, their bodies, stories, and powers are strongly local, both in terms of issues and themes and in reference to their genetic antecedent, namely, the dyad of El Chapulín-El Santo, that made the first forays of the region into a global superhero mediascape. Regarding the former, Latin American superheroes often rely on parody to critique systems of power and control, deploying the genre and its powers to undermine autocratic and overbearing regimes. In terms of the latter, these superheroes harness the fact that the greatest Latin American superhero effectively did not have any real superpower besides his mask, honor, and faith (especially in the earlier films), suggesting that good character and strong physical aptitudes are enough to truly become a superhero for the people. In fact, many of the superheroes analyzed in the following pages lack a true superhuman power. This may be because of their archetypal antecedents (which I examine in the following chapter), or simply because the superhero tends to come from humble origins, an everyman that due to circumstance dons a mask and costume to intervene when the Law proves futile. Secondly, their narratives are also often heavily inflected by US-Latin American relations; that is, the Latin American superhero often arises out of the impossibility *and* rejection of translating the North American figure to the reality of Latin America. This is no surprise, as El Chapulín often notes that he is the local superhero that the people yearn for, unlike Super Sam, who barges in, imposing his own will on a public that wants nothing to do with him, not unlike US incursions into the territories in the post–World War II stage.[8] In other words, these superheroes, their supervillains, and their narrative arcs meditate on both palpable local issues and transnational debates, often characterized by the politicoeconomic relationship between the Northern hegemon and local territories.

An illustrative example of this is found in Enchufetv's two YouTube skits titled "Superhéroes en Latinoamérica." It may seem odd at first that our discussion of superhero films begins in a medium that is not the typical feature film, but this concern is quickly mitigated by the fact that superheroes have never been exclusive to a particular platform, or, as Denison and Mizsei-Ward remind us, "the superhero is . . . an emphatically transmedia phenomenon; or, at very least, needs to be conceptualized as a genre whose wide-ranging manifestations are hard to pin down to an original or even dominant source" (4). The production conditions of Enchufetv itself, furthermore, may give us clues as to the lack of superhero films—seeing themselves strapped by possibilities in commercial television and film (mediascapes that prefer importing and dubbing successful US productions), the creative voices behind the YouTube channel decided to self-produce skits and shorts and upload them directly to the digital streaming site ("Humor ecuatoriano"). Since 2011, the channel has garnered over 18 million subscribers and 3 billion views, while their Facebook page has over 10 million followers, with the largest audiences residing in Colombia and Mexico.[9] The fact that these streaming videos garner significant audiences beyond the country of production (Ecuador) establishes them as useful references in conceptualizing a "Latin American" superhero genre.[10]

The skits in question that interest us are "Superhéroes en Latinoamérica" (2015) and "Superhéroes en Latinoamérica 2" (2015), both of which were filmed in Colombia and at a moment where the international mediascape was dominated by various superhero characters and films. The first skit opens with a green screen with white text, a replica of MPAA screens that display the following text: "The following preview has been approved to accompany this feature" (for web trailers this is modified to "the following preview has been approved for appropriate audiences").

"Superhéroes en Latinoamérica," however, begins with no such warning or note. Instead, we are greeted with the following epilogue: "The following sketch is only for us to laugh at our beautiful and complex idiosyncrasies. If you wonder why the 'gringo' superheroes speak like Latinos, it's because the accent quickly sticks. Warning: you were an unwanted baby. PS: subscribe, it's free and your mom will never find out" ("El siguiente sketch es únicamente para reirnos de nuestra hermosa y compleja idiosincrasia. Si se pregunta por qué los superhéroes 'gringos' hablan como latinos, es porque el acento se pega rápido. Advertencia: no fuiste un bebé deseado. PD: suscríbete, es gratis y tu mamá nunca se va a enterar").[11] There are several issues that merit comment here: the acknowledgement of "our beautiful and complex idiosyncrasies" points to the cohesion of a singular "latino" identity, one that allowed for the marketability and popularity of El Chapulín decades before to a transnational audience; and that the superheroes featured in the skit are translocated "gringos" who have quickly picked up local characteristics, without having shed their gringo identities. The title of the skit further evokes the notion that superheroes are imports and not autochthonous characters or tropes. That being said, they are imports that have been resemanticized through local idioms and issues. The parody of the green-screen credits adds to this, as the creators rework an ever-present image into a point of comedic inflections.

The skit begins with the page-flipping intro credits that global audiences have come to identify with the Marvel media universe. This is the next step in parody, as we are presented with the familiar, which will then be exaggerated for comedic effect, not unlike the opening credits of *Capitán Centroamérica*. By (re)using a format perfected by Marvel, the skit situates itself within a global genealogy of the superhero, yet by modifying the images within the montage, it also successfully indicates to the viewer that what is to come is similar yet different, a global archetype or narrative with now distinctively local accents. A female newscaster greets us, informing the viewer and viewing public that the US government has decided that superheroes are a danger to public security and that they are now being exiled, and will be transferred to "a place where their destruction will go unnoticed . . . Latin America" ("un lugar donde su destrucción no se note mucho . . . Latinoamérica"). Between the newscaster noting their exile and the government's decision to move them, a soft dissolve transitions to a shot of the newscaster on a screen, and the camera pulls out, showing the image on a small television set in a workplace (which we soon discover is security at a Latin American airport). This detail, at the very beginning of the skit, may seem innocuous, but we must remember that films in the genre tend to begin with important "origin" information, or scenes that somehow explicate the poetics of the particular hero and his or her becoming super.

The opening sequence of "Superhéroes en Latinoamérica" after the zoom out follows with a security guard calling superheroes a "stupidity" ("pendejada"). The guard's dismissive attitude towards the superhero may perhaps be a reflection of why there has been no serious and nonparodic superhero film in the region, yet it may also signal the audience's perception that the antics and powers of archetypal superheroes would never work in a reality that is not Metropolis or Gotham. Guillermo Helo's recent feature-length film, *Niñas Araña* (2017) (whose plot has nothing to do with superheroes), alludes to this, as the protagonist comments at the very end that Spiderman would never survive in the Santiago that she inhabits. In fact, US superheroes rarely venture away from their North American skylines, and when they do, they only tend to go to Europe (see *Avengers: Infinity War* or *Spider-Man: Far from Home*).

Returning to the skit, a character with blatant similarities to Wolverine attempts to pass through security but is met with blaring alarms from the metal detector. When he tries to explain that his skeleton is infused with adamantium—a fictional, nearly indestructible alloy—the guards sarcastically ask him if he will regenerate from the anal probing they are about to perform as part of their security protocol.

There are two important notes to glean from this short introductory scene, as a sort of blueprint for contemporary films in the genre: first, the use of parodic devices and satire, and the allusion to the tensions between the North and South, evokes a connection to the poetics of the Chapulín, as an ontoformative reference in any Latin American attempt at a superhero; and second, the focus on the superhero's masculinity as a point of negotiation and demythification. Addressing the former, the skit calls our attention to the portrayal of "Latin America" as a Cold War backwater of the United States; a forgotten space where the rule of law (Western and international) does not apply. In regards to the latter, unlike the North American referents that were ontological to masculine codes of the time (see the aesthetics and etymology of Superman, for example) the superhero when reterritorialized in the Latin American cultural sphere is not immune to *albures* (puns) and emasculatory exchanges, no longer protected by the cape and musculature of the costume but, instead, a self-reflexive coda of masculinity that can be questioned, disarticulated, and refashioned.[12]

El Chapulín—as I will comment in the next chapter—often infantilized and feminized Superman and Batman, so it should come as no surprise that the purportedly masculine North American superhero is undressed as comically and misogynistically inadequate.

The confluence of these two issues is developed in subsequent scenes when we see how ineffective these Anglo superheroes are in Latin America. Batman is a drunk who doesn't speak Spanish, while Spiderman cannot swing freely from skyscraper to skyscraper, as there are none in this metonymic space that is Latin America; when he does manage to sail through the air, he gets caught up in the labyrinth of power lines running across the urban ceiling. "Superhéroes en Latinoamérica 2" portrays similar moments of contact between the narratives and heroes from the North, and the local conditions in which they must now operate as *deportados* or deportees. Captain America, for example, is confused with El Santo by a young boy and his mother seeking a photographic memento. When he informs them that he is not the famous Mexican luchador, but Captain America, the mother quite rightly wonders if the flag on his iconic shield is that of Chile or Puerto Rico. The skit plays with the aesthetics of this character to harvest a critique of US geopolitics, as the Captain explains that America is the United States. The mother and son quickly retort that America is the entire continent, and that only the US with its bloated sense of self-importance would go so far as to claim the whole for itself.

These two short skits, with over 36.5 million views between them, provide an important substrate for contextualizing recent productions.

Figure I.1. Batman as a belligerent gringo in Latin America.

Importantly, the two videos suggest that the contemporary Latin American superhero is self-reflexive both of the genre's principal traits and of its relationship with archetypal figures from the North American archive. The presence and transmission of the videos through freely available web platforms also further the notion that the contemporary Latin American superhero is often born from popular mediums and channels, and not through big-budget, top-down productions. This characteristic, in turn, explains my broadening the corpus to include television and web serials, as to simply cordon off filmic productions would do a disservice to the state of the superhero in contemporary cultural production. In fact, as I explore in the study of *Chinche Man* and *Capitán Centroamérica*, Latin American superheroes are dynamic, genre-transgressing characters and narratives that move seamlessly across production mechanisms and circulatory networks, engaging local and diasporic viewers across mediums and devices.

Every superhero needs an origin story, and *Capitán Latinoamérica* is no different. In chapter 1, I examine the first Latin American superheroes who appeared in television and film, namely, the Mexican *El Chapulín Colorado* (television, 1972–79) and *El Santo* and a cohort of other wrestlers (1950s onwards). I begin this chapter by outlining the presence of these tropes in contemporary media, before moving to a study of several cult films featuring El Santo and other wrestlers such as Blue Demon. I lay out the characteristics of the wrestler-as-superhero trope, paying attention to the constructs of ideology, gender, and politics and how they are conjugated in a variety of films that also include characters initially crafted as superheroes (and not wrestlers) and female superheroes. Included in this discussion is a tracing of the filmic archive to a print medium, wherein I argue—through ideas at the nexus of comics and film studies—that the Santo films are really adaptations of a comic book oeuvre, and are thus not altogether different from similar US adaptations that successfully made the jump to the moving image. I also map out the relationship between the luchador and films featuring Kalimán, one of the very few comic book heroes that is adapted to the cinema. Next, I analyze *El Chapulín* and its recourse to parody as a narrative and aesthetic mode to portray the superhero. I focus on the powers that this hero lacks, linking the trope of the parodic superhero to issues of gender hegemony and political critique. The chapter concludes with a speculation that the Santo and Chapulín genealogies come to a close in the 1980s and 1990s as a symptom of economic crises and the transformation of the Mexican economy and everyday life under the purview of neoliberal policies.

Chapter 2 begins the case-study section of this project, wherein I examine contemporary superhero moving images within particular sociocultural contexts. In this section, I analyze Harold Trompetero's *El Man, el superhéroe nacional* (2009) within the horizon of Colombian cultural production. Trompetero's protagonist follows the superhero-as-parody archetype favored by El Chapulín, featuring a taxi driver, Felipe, who dons yellow, blue, and red spandex (representing the national flag) to become El Man, the defender of the poor and disenfranchised in Bogotá. He fights against an old neighbor, Federico Rico, who with an ill-gained fortune wants to displace Felipe and his neighbors from their homes in the historic center of the city. The film's parodic mode runs in stark contrast to critically acclaimed Colombian cinema that has focused on issues of violence and drug cartels, but the narrative details of the plot reveal a thematic focus that scholarship has not fully explored, that is, the impact of urbanization in everyday life. Linking *El Man* to other films produced since the 1990s, I argue that the notion of space, specifically urban space, needs further exploration and problematization. The chapter has two analytic foci, namely, the effect of parody in the construction of gender in the superhero and the film's thesis on urban renewal and spatial politics, and how these evoke an invisible violence that is sometimes ignored in favor of the spectacular.

Chapter 3 analyzes Ernesto Díaz Espinoza's *Mirageman* (2007) as an allegory of the Pinochet dictatorship and the transition to democracy in Chile. Starring famed Chilean martial artist, Marko Zaror, the film oscillates between kitsch and a dynamic realism to conceptualize the effects of the dictatorship on the psyche of individual Chileans and the collective social body in the late twentieth century. The protagonist, Maco, is traumatized after witnessing the murder of his parents and the rape of his younger brother, Tito, who now is catatonic in a psychiatric facility. A chance encounter that results in saving a television reporter during a home invasion leads Maco to adopt the persona of Mirageman, a crime fighter for the layperson in twenty-first-century Santiago. Parting from theories of allegory vis-à-vis politics and trauma, I argue that the film is a cogent meditation on the effects of state terrorism on the social psyche. Centering my analysis on the development of Maco into a superhero, and Tito as he recovers from the originary trauma of the rape, I suggest that *Mirageman* relocates legal and social debates of the transition to democracy within a genre film that may otherwise be viewed as lighter fare. I conclude the chapter with a section on the protagonist's mask and its ability to generate affective intensities in the viewer and other diegetic subjects. I extrapolate this argument to a wider corpus of superhero films, arguing that the mask as sartorial accoutrement is emotively and narratologically significant in the crafting of any superhero tale.

Chapter 4 relocates the reader to San Pedro Sula, a city in the north of Honduras that has earned the unflattering moniker of the most violent city in the world due to the proliferation of gang and drug violence in the city. *Chinche Man* (2015) originates in an urban space where unmitigated murder and impunity are an everyday occurrence. Making his debut first in a television skit, then YouTube video, and then finally a feature-length film, Chinche Man is—like Mirageman—a superhero who defends the rights and livelihoods of citizens downtrodden by drug cartels and police corruption. In this chapter, I correlate details of the film's plot with the murder of the superhero's creator, Igor Padilla, on January 17, 2017. I argue that the sanitized violence of the film (where not a single character is killed onscreen) and the recourse to parody as a narrative mode functions as a salient allegory of the sociocultural milieu of the extradiegetic world—as a sort of chronicle of a death foretold—that saw the targeting of Padilla and other members of his creative staff by local gangs. The chapter includes an analysis of the creation of the character in a television skit, and the use of YouTube as a social media platform to generate popular interest in the project that then coalesces into a film. The chapter concludes with a commentary of Súper H, a real-life superhero who—wearing a luchador mask and the jersey of the country's national soccer team—uses Facebook as a platform to engage the community of San Pedro Sula in social work and to mount a critique of controversially elected president, Juan Orlando Hernández.

In chapter 5, I examine *Capitán Centroamérica*, a production of the YouTube channel Puyaweb based in El Salvador. As in previous sections, I analyze the origin, construct, and politics of the title superhero, in addition to the narrative development of the character vis-à-vis an antagonist, which in this case is organized crime. First, I detail the character's engagement with parody as a narrative mode, contextualizing the protagonist as a variant of Marvel's Captain America, and then examining the superhero's divergent engagement with political ideology. I then study the web series (2011), its emission platform (YouTube), and how this impacts its circulation both within the political frontiers of Central America and its diasporic communities in the United States. I engage with scholarship on mass media, YouTube, and mobile technology (specifically, the idea of "spreadable media") to inform this section. My analysis then shifts to the television show, which first aired on national TV in 2013 and was then exported to streaming platforms that cater to a US market in 2017. In the television adaptation, the producers expand the storyline to include more characters and explain the origin story of the Capitán. I analyze the changes that take place in the adaptation to the weekly format (versus the on-demand nature of YouTube), and then anchor both productions and the superhero within current debates in contemporary Central American cultural production.

The book ends with a brief conclusion wherein I mention other films and series that I have not analyzed here or that are currently in production. In tracing the advent of the superhero from origin texts to contemporary manifestations that move across mediums, narratives, and borders, *Capitán Latinoamérica* echoes Denison and Mizsei-Ward's contention that the superhero today is "part of wider cultural negotiations between globalizing media exchanges and local histories and tastes," and that "the superhero's meanings are culturally and contextually dependent . . . [and] often subject to local reinterpretations and remodeling" (Denison and Mizsei-Ward 4). Latin American superheroes, importantly, are unique and merit further study in that they are not simply deployed to defend the status quo, but rather are fashioned and mobilized to critique the contemporary and to lay bare the injustices of systems already in place.

Chapter 1

Mexican Origins

Every superhero needs an origin story (or two or three if a reboot is in order), and *Capitán Latinoamérica* is no different. When the humble taxi driver is asked to don the mask and uniform of the superhero in *El Man*, he is compared to Gandhi, Jesus, Che Guevara, and El Chapulín. When Mirageman storms the streets of Santiago to kick ass and take names, the newspapers call him a Chilean Chapulín. When a somber Ráfaga explains the mission of Nafta Súper in *Kryptonita*, an antagonist tries to belittle him by calling him "Chapulín." When Chinche Man first appeared as a character on television, the only phenotypical indicator of his superness (as his physique is lackluster at best) was the luchador mask he wore to hide his face. Similarly, Alfonso Sahagún Casaus's El Alambrista is a superhero who defends the rights of undocumented migrants crossing into the United States from Mexico in *El Alambrista: The Fence Jumper* (2005) and *El Alambrista: La Venganza* (2014). His costume is a cape and a mask in the colors of the national flag that he wears while wrestling in the ring and while fighting vigilantes who seek to create a legion of monsters from the unsuspecting migrants. Yet it is not solely fictive contemporary superheroes that link their identities to earlier characters or types taken from a Latin American popular imaginary: the Honduran superhero-cum-social worker, Súper H, wears the shirt of *la selección* in addition to a wrestler's mask adorned with the five stars of the national flag. When I asked him why he wears a wrestling mask, he replied that wearing it made him "want to fight for a better Honduras" ("querer luchar por una Honduras mejor"); he also added that the idea came from watching his favorite superhero, El Santo, fend off werewolves, vampires, and robots.[1]

The examples above demonstrate that should the contemporary Latin American superhero attempt to trace his or her DNA through one of the many swab-by-mail services that promise your genotypical history, he or she would discover at least three distinct heritages. First, and as is the case with most global superheroes, our Latin American superbeings would display vestiges of their Anglo forefathers. Either inspired from print or celluloid artifacts, contemporary Latin American superheroes often emulate, deconstruct, or resemanticize US and Hollywood heroes, taking the DC and Marvel juggernauts as their base-text, reformulating their aesthetic, axial, and political qualities to conjugate the local.[2]

Second, a large percentage of their DNA would be traced to the wrestler El Santo (and a cohort of other fighters such as Blue Demon and Mil Máscaras), who featured in films from the late 1950s onwards. Aside from providing an aesthetic model to follow (the distinctive mask, the beefy physique), these wrestler-superheroes provide an axial model for the contemporary superhero as an *hombre de bien*; that is, his primary superpowers are his honor, wisdom, and faith. This is evident in characters such as El Man, Chinche Man, and even Capitán Centroamérica in his final incarnation, as their superhuman strength and speed are often subsidiary to their unimpeachable moral character. The latter is often the one true superpower, replacing physical and psychic strengths, or the ability to conjure nature's elements: to be virtuous and fair is more powerful than anything else, suggesting that the didactic element in these films is less fantastical and more explicit, as any viewer could (in theory) become said hero.

Finally, their DNA results would show close affinities with the parodic ethos of El Chapulín Colorado, the star of a homonym television show that aired from 1973 to 1979. Sartorial, aesthetic, and narratological parody are at the core of the majority of contemporary superhero productions, which encourages both a critique of the extradiegetic world, and an examination of North-South relations (that is, of the dialectic between hypo- and hypertext). As El Chapulín showed millions of viewers in its initial run and reruns, parody can be an effective and popular mechanism for reading the world.

There are several points of contact between these two superheroes. Both characters were originally produced in Mexico, birthed from a distinct sociocultural milieu and mediascape that was propitious for the creation and dissemination of popular characters based on the North American character type and narrative genre of the superhero. Mexico, after all, was the center of commercial Latin American cinema during its Golden Age from the 1930s to 1960s, and was not only home to famed directors and film stars, but also steadfast in its development of genre film.³

Importantly, the cinematic ecosystem of the Mexican Golden Age transcended national borders, becoming the cinema par excellence in the Spanish-speaking world as its features and stars were exported globally.⁴ The spreading of Mexican cinema stimulated a correlative osmotic nature, where the industry was quick to adopt production and narratological conventions of its Northern neighbor—it was a contact zone between Anglo US cinema and a Latin American cinema. It is therefore unsurprising that the superhero of contemporary Latin American moving images finds his first steps within the Mexican mediascape.

That being said, the superhero tends to appear at moments of crisis, when the sociocultural telos is at its most fragile and the political zeitgeist is one of polar contradictions. Superheroes dominate the collective imaginary when normal heroes no longer suffice to give us a sense of stability. Superheroes galvanize the popular spirit when the axial and ideological pillars that sustain our daily lives come into question.⁵ Latin American superheroes are no different (as we will see in later chapters), and the early Mexican superhero boom follows this hypothesis, as the genre appears and gains massive popularity during two distinct crises. First, the Santo and company films appear at the very end of the Golden Age, at a moment when the Mexican film industry entered a crisis stage due to antiquated and unsustainable funding structures and increased competition from Hollywood in a post–World War II global and ideological market for cinema (Ramírez Berg 37). The Santo films (along with other popular genres such as the *fichera* genre) were churned out like *churros* to compensate for the economic woes of a once-strong industry (Schroeder Rodríguez 116), appealing to a popular urban audience that was not always reflected in the Golden Age oeuvre.

Second, the superhero-wrestler genre and the parodic Chapulín emerge at a politicoeconomic crux, when the Mexican Miracle was in full swing. The Miracle describes a period of approximately three decades when the economy—due to the successful implementation of import substitution industrialization and the proliferation of the petroleum industry—was on a perpetual rise. A thriving economy brought about significant demographic changes, including growth in income per capita, improved health and education metrics, and, importantly, rapid urbanization (Alba and Potter 47).⁶ The positive trajectory of the economy was, however, contemporaneous with the rise of an antiauthoritarian sentiment characteristic of a global ennui in 1968. In Mexico, students in the capital organized protests and strikes demanding increased civil liberties and a more transparent and democratic government (the ruling Partido Revolucionario Institucional had been in power since the end of the Revolution). Their requests for change were met with impunity, as the military and police of president Gustavo Díaz Ordaz (and his secretary of the interior, Luis Echeverría Álvarez) commandeered an indiscriminate massacre on October 2 in the Plaza de las Tres Culturas in Tlatelolco. The ensuing government cover up only served to highlight the episteme of crisis that Mexican civil and intellectual life had entered, albeit while enjoying unprecedented economic success.[7]

In sum, the cinematic and televisual Mexican superhero is birthed in a moment of polyvalenced instability, characteristic of the genre's genesis and proliferation across national and temporal frameworks. The genre takes on multiple roles during the crisis episteme (including a narrative representation and hashing out of conflicting political positions), though its principal impulse is to maintain a status quo under siege. I begin this chapter with a study of several cult films featuring El Santo and other wrestlers to lay out the characteristics of the wrestler-as-superhero trope, paying attention to the constructs of ideology, gender, and politics and how they are conjugated in the genre. In doing so, I am interested in delinking the character from a purely luchador and mexploitation genealogy and to instead suture him to the superhero genre proper. In doing so, I am not suggesting that the wrestler-as-superhero film is mutually exclusive from the luchador genealogy that Doyle Greene, Robert Michael Cotter, Raúl Criollo, José Xavier Návar, and Rafael Aviña have so expertly traced. Rather, my aim is to understand El Santo primarily as a superhero analogous to US heroes that demonstrates idiosyncrasies based on the cultural specificity of his place of origin. This, in turn, would explain his being source material for contemporary Latin American superheroes that are not wrestlers. I follow this section with an exploration of other characters that were not necessarily linked to the world of wrestling, including female superheroes and characters that were more superhero than wrestler, before studying the *Kalimán* series that successfully adapted a popular radio and print hero to the screen. To conclude, I analyze El Chapulín and its recourse to parody as a narrative and aesthetic mode to portray the superhero. I focus on the powers that this hero lacks, linking the trope of the parodic superhero to issues of gender hegemony and political critique, focusing specifically on US-Mexico relations. In this section, I contrast the hypervirility and exaggerated physique of the luchador vis-à-vis the superhero-as-parody trope of El Chapulín, to demonstrate how these polar opposites conjugate the semantics, aesthetics, and ideology of the contemporary Latin American superhero character.

El Santo as Superhero

No other image or icon is as quickly identified by a global audience with Mexico and its collective identity than that of the masked luchador; at times, all we need is the mask itself sans body, a vague outline of a face with exposed eyes that semanticizes an entire history.[8] And perhaps no other mask is as iconic as the silver one worn by Rodolfo Guzmán Huerta in a career that spanned five decades. Born in 1917, El Santo began his career fighting under his own name, as a *rudo* or heel, in 1934 just after wrestling was imported as a sport and spectacle to Mexico by Salvador Lutteroth.[9] Like others in the sport, the wrestler went through a series of personas to settle on "El Santo" in 1942.[10] The name at first was paradoxical, as the wrestler continued in his character as a *rudo*, but then slowly evolved as he gained a mass-media presence by starring in comics produced by José Guadalupe Cruz. First appearing in 1952, Cruz's *El Santo, el Enmascarado de Plata* was a massive hit (Lieberman 5; Rubenstein 572).[11] These comics "used photographed still images and captions to tell a story much like the drawn panels in traditional comic books and comic strips" (Lieberman 5). They were not *fotonovelas*, that is, comics composed of live-action photographs arranged to tell a story, but rather used the technique of *fotomontaje* that combined photographs and drawings in hybrid format that transgressed the idioms of veracity and fantasy employed by the strictly photographic or drawn (Wilt, "El Santo" 206). Importantly, the print medium "offered the first construction of Santo as the hero of the Mexican people, endowed with superior intelligence, morality, and almost superhuman powers" (Lieberman 5). The transmogrification of the *rudo* to comic book superhero (thus effectively inserting the wrestler figure and El Santo within a genealogy and genre of the superhero comic book) "manufactured the popular image of Santo as a superhero fighting the forces of crime and evil threatening Mexican society, and also served as a basis for the Santo movie formula" (Greene 51). Importantly, the comic book hero was not a wrestler now placed in crime-fighting scenarios, but was an altogether different protagonist that benefited from the aesthetics and popular consciousness of *lucha libre*.[12]

Figure 1.1. The silver-masked icon.

The plot of Cruz's comics was simple and recyclable: a layperson (usually either a lower-class boy or middle-class woman) facing some sort of calamity is widely ignored until a wise acquaintance tells them to get help from El Santo (Rubenstein 573). The wrestler would listen to them in his urban office, and then go off and fight the crooks (sometimes real, other times supernatural). In between, of course, he would also wrestle in stock images taken from real Santo fights. The comics effectively place the wrestler within a recognizable narrative and visual genre that borrows heavily from the superhero comic, replacing a working-class wrestler who earned the ire of the public when purposely flouting the rules of the ring with a sleek superhero that evoked characters from US comic books. As Anne Rubenstein notes, "El Santo wore a suit . . . and usually appeared at the beginning of a new story working alone, behind a desk, in an office. He used new 'scientific' gadgets to help him, a conspicuous display of higher education" (573).

Though Rubenstein is correct in asserting that this Santo climbs the social ladder, as he is now educated and distinctively middle class (though in later films he will live in a mansion and drive a snazzy sports car), I want to add that the Santo we see in the comics is a wrestler molded to the trope of the superhero. Like US counterparts, he is an urban hero, uses cutting-edge (though some would argue impossible) technology, and comes to the rescue of the people no matter how small or trivial their affliction may be. He has a distinct identity and persona that separate him from others within the diegesis (though he does not have a secret identity like Superman or Batman—that being said, not all superheroes lead a double life, take for example the X-Men). Like his counterparts, he occupies a social role that is capable of real, powerful change; though not a journalist (Superman, Spiderman), philanthropist (Batman), or scientist (Iron Man, the Hulk), El Santo's job as a wrestler is deeply powerful within the Mexican context, as the fighter in the ring is not solely there to entertain, but rather to "invoke a series of connections" with deep political ramifications (Levi xiii).

The wrestler, in other words, is not simply a charlatan in a leotard (as the audience knows that the matches are fixed), but rather a public actor within the ring-as-theater paradigm that Heather Levi underlines as so important in considering wrestling within Mexico's popular and political imaginary. In this line of argumentation, the wrestler is the embodiment or agent of critical ideological dyads within the political and social sphere, responsible for bringing to life abstract and macro processes to a live audience.[13] The wrestler, thus, is a political figure, capable of playing out the theater of real-life within the syntax of the ring. In other words, the Santo of the comics (and then film) "allowed Mexico to find in him a cultural leader" ("permitió que México encontrara en él un líder cultural"; Illescas Nájera 51). In all this, we must also consider that the wrestler transcended the ring, or as Juan Villoro persuasively argues, "the justice meted out by the wrestlers in three rounds without a time limit is too tempting to be corralled within the twelve ropes of the ring" ("la justicia que los luchadores imparten a tres caídas sin límite de tiempo es demasiado tentadora para permanecer entre las doce cuerdas"; 16). In this vein, Levi's reading of wrestling as performance is expertly parlayed into a discussion of the rise of social wrestlers that never saw the mat of a ring, but who took on important political projects (xii). She includes in this discussion such characters as Superbarrio, Ecologista Universal, Mujer Meravilla, SuperAnimal, SuperGay, and Superniño (128).[14] These characters are evidence of the cultural, political, and social function of the wrestler-type and its configuration as a popular superhero.

El Santo's meteoric popularity did not simply stop, however, at the comics; he was a television star in lucha libre's boom during the Alemán presidency, as wrestling was broadcast to a national audience that could now share in the drama of the bouts.[15] Wrestling's (and El Santo's) presence on the screen, however, was quickly curtailed by a controversial broadcast ban that saw the sport relegated to specific areas of the country's growing urban space where an audience could attend a live match.[16] But the television ban was not successful in removing the masked wrestler from the popular imaginary and from ideational constructs of the nation; if anything, it had an opposite effect, as it spurred alternative strategies for producers and media moguls to capitalize on the positive (cultural and affective) associations with the luchador. Important in all this is that while television did provide a new circulatory mechanism for the emission of lucha libre to a broader audience, it still "barely penetrated the homes of the popular classes" (Hegarty 21). In fact, there would be another stream that would be even more advantageous for the character and genre to gain mass appeal: the cinema.

Before we begin to look at the films that featured El Santo and to understand the character as a superhero, it behooves us to first understand what a superhero is. Superheroes are everywhere: they dominate the posters and ticket sales at multiplexes; adorn t-shirts and other items at clothing and shoe stores; grace the boxes of cereal and other foodstuffs at supermarkets; are the protagonists of some of the most accomplished (and also frustratingly difficult) video games ever made; and appear as spokespeople for a wide variety of products and services.[17] They move across media platforms, national borders, and digital/analog divides, occupying the interstitial fluid of cultural memory between human generations of the past centuries and the present. Given the ubiquity of the type and genre, it is surprising that there is no universal definition of the superhero, leading Robin Rosenberg and Peter Coogan to note that though "everyone knows what a superhero is . . . everyone seems to have a different answer" as to its definition (xvii).[18]

Peter Coogan poses that the superhero is an evolution of the hero-type originating in ancient Greece, and is

> a heroic character with a universal, selfless, prosocial mission; who possesses superpowers—extraordinary abilities, advanced technology, or highly developed physical and/or mental skills (including mystical abilities); who has a superhero identity embodied in a code name and iconic costume, which typically expresses his biography or character, powers, and origin

(transformation from ordinary person to superhero); and is generically distinct, i.e. can be distinguished from characters of related genres (fantasy, science fiction, detective, etc.) by a preponderance of generic conventions. Often superheroes have dual identities, the ordinary one of which is usually a closely guarded secret. ("The Hero" 3)[19]

The difficulties in definition arise when readers quickly point out the existence of one or many heroes that do not strictly adhere to this or any other definition, leading critics such as Coogan and others to insert a variety of exceptions and caveats. Defining the superhero requires an adept and adaptive strategy. This is seen in Marc DiPaolo's definition: "Superhero narratives . . . involve colorfully garbed heroic icons that demonstrate uncanny strength, intelligence, supernatural powers, and near-infallibility" (2). He nuances the principal characteristics of the type by adding that they "may be a result of their divine or mythical origins . . . ; alien heritage . . . ; or magic" (2), and that "there are other superheroes . . . who are unremarkably 'human,' but are made supremely powerful by access to advanced technology, or, . . . through spending years mastering fighting techniques and honing detective skills" (2).

The superhero can be one and many things, but is always more than strictly human; a superhuman character with a recognizable and marketable persona (that is othered within the diegesis, that is, other characters *recognize* the figure as a *super*human) whose principal narrative struggle is the survival and betterment of their non-super peers in the face of everyday crime or some great cataclysmic moment.[20] Superheroes are a conglomeration of divergent and convergent ideologies, acting out and working through some of the most palpable issues facing their contemporary societies. Their actions in fighting crime or saving the damsel in distress from the grasps of the supervillain are ethical interventions that permeate the extradiegetic universe of reception. Importantly, the superhero is a litmus of the reigning politicocultural zeitgeist, a popular and attractive expression of issues and hypotheses already in play.

An important addendum to this definition is that the superhero is, above all, born and bred in the US of A. Coogan and others argue that the superhero as a genre and character was inaugurated on April 18, 1938, with the publication of *Action Comics* #1 featuring Jerry Siegel and Joe Shuster's Superman. (Some readers, however, may disagree with this assertion, as characters such as Patoruzú [Argentina, 1928] precede the publication.) The rise of the superhero is invariably tied to the rise of the United States as a global political and cultural superpower in the twentieth century, working hand in hand with foreign and domestic policy and propaganda as a purveyor of American values and worldviews (Kohut 20). Perhaps there is no better known essay on this assertion than Umberto Eco's "The Myth of Superman" (1972), which counters the superficial reading of superheroes as protector-types by posing instead that Superman (in particular) embodies specific (North) American virtues. Eco argues that the character rejects a direct confrontation with structural problems that cause social injustice, focusing instead on micro battles that allow for instantaneous ethical satisfaction. In doing so, there is "an implicit acceptance and defense on the hero's part of the tenets of capitalism and bureaucracy, such as property ownership, legality, and due process. In sum, Superman is ideology" (Peaslee 37).[21] Rosenberg and Coogan further argue that the superhero evolves as an ideological kin of the Western, the genre that previously dominated box offices and international markets for Hollywood (xvii). Comparing the two, they outline how both genres "depict an 'epic moment' when civilization is threatened but the forces of savagery—whether represented as Indians or outlaws in Westerns or villains in superhero stories—are defeated" (xvii). The evolution from Western to superhero occurs as a result of a changing geopolitical climate: "Whereas the violence in Westerns was in service of containment (trying to keep the 'Reds' on the reservation, as with the Truman Doctrine and the West's attempt to limit communist expansion), the violence in superhero stories arises as a last resort (as with the Powell doctrine after the Cold War), engaged in by the superhero because of the implacable threat posed by the supervillain" (xvii). In other words, the superhero takes over from where the Western left off, providing a narrative space and metaphor for the playing out of US political aspirations and fantasies.[22]

But superheroes, as we well know, are no longer exclusive to the United States and its culturescape, but rather have taken on original and hybrid shapes and narrative arcs across world cultures. Rayna Denison and Rachel Mizsei-Ward argue in the introduction to their anthology *Superheroes on World Screens* that "many national cultures have created (or re-imagined) superheroic figures, and the world of superheroes now contains many icons whose histories borrow from local folklore, myths, and legends" (3). If the genre's seeds were first planted in the United States (in comics, then television and film), they have now matured as a "transnational genre, one with myriad sub-categories and disparate local originating myths, producing texts aimed at a wide range of audiences in a range of cultural milieus" (4). In a series of nine essays that cover a variety of lines of inquiry (including production, circulation, and thematic analysis), it is telling, however, that the Latin American superhero never makes an appearance.

The absence of a Latin American superhero in the anthology is surprising, given the proliferation of contemporary characters in movies, television, and web serials today, and, more importantly, the popularity of their tropic ancestors in the Mexican mediascape of the mid- and late twentieth century. El Santo and Chapulín, after all, were international superstars, appearing in dozens of feature-length films, television episodes, and comic strips, and translated and aired to a global audience. The profile of El Santo as a pop culture icon is particularly significant—when T. Fikret Uçak made his now-classic *3 Dev Adam* (1973), a low-budget Turkish film with an amalgam of superheroes (a successful crossover before *Avengers: Infinity War*), he chose a character (very) loosely based on Spiderman as the supervillain, and a tag-team of Captain America and El Santo as the good guys. In Uçak's worldview (and in the diegesis of *3 Dev Adam*), El Santo was at the same level of prestige, superness, and recognition as his American counterparts, thus demonstrating on a global level how the wrestler transcended a national mediascape to embody the position of the superhero to a world audience.[23] El Santo may have been a well-known *técnico* to the urban audiences who were lucky enough to see him live, but in the popular imaginary (and to a broader media audience across the globe), he was for all intents and purposes a superhero. In this fashion, El Santo embodies Denison and Mizsei-Ward's idea of "the superhero as a global phenomenon that is locally inflected, transnationally distributed and transculturally exchanged" (16)—there is no better example of this than his role in fighting off a bastardized Spiderman halfway around the globe.

El Santo—both the specific character, and the cinematic genre and industry his popularity spurred forward—was the first cinematic Latin American superhero to captivate popular audiences and to coalesce as an icon that could move across media, borders, and genres akin to North American luminaries from the DC and Marvel universes. Critical reception of El Santo and his films, however, has tended to favor a categorization along the lines of mexploitation and wrestling-themed genealogies.[24] This is readily evident in the titles of Robert Cotter's *The Mexican Masked Wrestler and Monster Filmography*, Doyle Greene's *Mexploitation Cinema: A Critical History of Mexican Vampire, Wrestler, Ape-Man and Similar*

Films, 1957–1977, and Raúl Criollo, José Xavier Návar, and Rafael Aviña's *¡Quiero ver sangre! Historia ilustrada del cine de luchadores*. While at first glance it is true that his films and those of others merge into a recognizable genre that may best be described as a "masked wrestler" cinema or "cine de luchadores," I want to suggest that it may be productive to rethink the character and the films as originating of a Latin American superhero type—one that will circulate and germinate posterior adoptions of the superhero in specific sociocultural situations outside the strictly Mexican context.

In this gesture, I am not arguing that these films are not mexploitation or luchador films, but rather that we may conceptualize the latter (and mexploitation when it does feature a superhero wrestler) as a subcategory of the superhero genre; this is not a zero sum move, as there are productive reasons for keeping them disparate from a global genre as is the superhero, as doing so allows for an explanation of the trajectory of a national Mexican cinema. For the purposes of *Capitán Latinoamérica*, however, I believe it is important to collocate El Santo and company within the superhero genre, especially given the clear allusions to the character and trope by contemporary mass media superheroes from across the continent. In doing so, I want to extricate these films from the dark side of the cinematic archive that they have been relegated to, to bring them out of the ghetto of genre and exploitation film that they have been labeled as.[25]

My recategorization follows Doyle Greene's defense of the wrestling films as important artifacts for understanding a vertiginous period in the cultural, demographic, and political history of Mexico.[26] Greene first provides an overview of the critiques of the genre, before moving that "such a blanket condemnation . . . completely ignores any cultural function these films may have served" (7). Instead, he argues that "one should consider that Mexican horror films *very much* reflected the concerns and problems of contemporary Mexican society in highly complex ways" (7; emphasis in the original).[27] Like the superhero genre, these films reflect and renegotiate the complex, implicit, and structural issues facing society.[28]

My naming of the wrestler as a superhero is not particularly original: David Dalton calls El Santo "an authentically Mexican, mestizo superhero" (29), while Cotter, Greene, and Kerry Hegarty also refer to the wrestler as a superhero in their respective studies. The website for the Morelia International Film Festival, furthermore, has a feature on "Mexican Superheroes in Film" ("Superhéroes mexicanos en el cine"), and includes wrestlers Blue Demon and El Santo alongside the comic book adaptations of Chanoc and Kalimán. This list is significant in that it places the wrestler films alongside superheroes that did make the jump from print to film; it bears mentioning, as I go over in the introduction, that Mexico and Latin America has a strong history of print superheroes. What I want to glean from this is that El Santo of the silver screen is really a comic book character, a superhero in the comics sharing many of the character and narrative traits of local and international superheroes, that was then adapted to film. This jump is, again, not a revolutionary gesture, as the films themselves speak to their source material, as moving images clearly inspired by the comic book genre and format: as Cotter succinctly states, they are "onscreen comic books" (3).

The films starring El Santo, Blue Demon, Mil Máscaras, and others share many of the characteristics of the comic book hero and genre, such as:

> their episodic narrative structure, with the flow of scenes resembling the organization of comic panels more than the standard narrative arc structure; their basic, expository dialogue, articulated slowly, as if in speech bubbles; the awkward juxtaposition of character to setting . . . ; . . . their incessantly recycled formulas and rapid production rates . . . ; and, of course, their completely fantastical nature (though in this regard the movies cannot compare to the comic books, in which Santo uses a jet pack, wrestles a giant octopus, and sees his leg grow back mysteriously after being bitten off by a crocodile). (Hegarty 9)

In fact, we may categorize the luchador films under what Liam Burke calls the comic book film adaptation, a type of film that now dominates Hollywood. Burke provides an overview of films that were adapted from print source material (including comics and graphic novels).[29] He comments on the points of confluence and inflection between source and adapted media, highlighting the fact that a common denominator among both is the nature of the principal characters. He argues that "comic books are built on succinct signifiers" (100), and that this is often and easily translated to genre films. This is clearly evident in the Santo and other luchador films, where the wrestler is always a stand-in for the good, while the monster/mad scientist/ghost from the colonial past is semanticized as the bad or evil, thus setting up a facile confrontation between the two that is ethically experienced, read, and digested by a popular audience. There is no character depth in the films, and, like comic books, the viewer/reader can quickly make axial associations that allow for a didactic reading.

There is another important caveat to glean from Burke's identification of comic book adaptation. He notes that genre cinema is characterized by its "oscillating about a baseline of reality with the verisimilitude of the piece becoming most exaggerated from physical laws during the moments that characterize the genre" (the singing and dancing that characterizes the musical, or the completely unbelievable convergence of serendipity in the romantic comedy, for example), but that "for the comic book movie heightened reality is a generic motif" (104). In regard to El Santo's film, Villoro again puts it quite clearly: "If fiction demands that disbelief be suspended, the cinema of luchadores annihilates it with a flying kick" ("Si la ficción exige que se suspenda la incredulidad, el cine de luchadores la aniquila con una patada voladora"; 18).[30] The inverisimilitude of the films is not solely chalked up to low production budgets, but is indeed a salient characteristic of the broader genre. Like comic book adaptations across the globe—and, more specifically, within the superhero adaptation—the suspension of belief required in luchador films is a generic motif that both signals the source text and sutures the characters to the specific genre. While it may be easier to believe the CGI images and characters in big budget productions, these special effects are—like the cardboard disk that is supposed to be a UFO—moments of phenomenological and epistemological inflection, where the viewer is invited and must acquiesce to believing the unbelievable to somehow make sense of the events unfolding before them.

In other words, the foundational material (in terms of characters, style, and narrative) of the films is not the live wrestler in the ring per se—though of course these films build off the popularity and celebrity of the luchador—but rather the luchador-cum-superhero who appeared in print media, who experienced unbelievable events on a weekly basis fighting off criminals and monsters, and who was read by hundreds of thousands of readers.[31] The comics, after all, transformed the *rudo* Santo to the hero who helped the downtrodden and poor—El Santo only became a superhero through his crime-fighting adventures in print that contrasted with the persona he had developed in the ring up until that point. Based on Keith Rainville's work, Hegarty notes that many elements of El Santo's films such as his "sports car, his secret hideout full of gadgets, the scientist who needs his help, his collaboration with law enforcement, the damsel in distress and the femme fatale—were already established in José Guadalupe

Cruz's comic-book series" (8). Hegarty parlays this observation to pose that "the films would have had a familiar appeal for the large sector of the mass audience who read comic books" (8). David Wilt adds that "unlike most celebrity tie-ins designed to capitalize on an individual's existing fame, the Santo comics and movies materially enhanced and altered his public image from a tough-guy professional wrestler popular chiefly with aficionados of that sport, to a heroic multimedia superhero with a much broader fan base" (200).

The opening credits of *El hacha diabólica* seem to support this thesis, as they instruct the viewer to consider that "this production is based on a fantastic story and does not take place in a particular place, therefore all the characters are imaginary and fictitious" ("esta realización está basada en un cuento fantástico y no se desarrolla en ningún sitio preciso, por lo cual todos los personajes son imaginarios y ficticios"). The Santo who will fight the supernatural supervillain is the Santo of the popular comic books, albeit a Santo born from the *cuadrilatero* (ring).

This is not to say that the films were a straight adaptation of popular comics, but rather moving images inspired from the ethos of the print genre.[32] The fact that Cruz used *fotomontaje* is critical in our evaluation of the interstices between print and film. David Wilt poses that "the realism of *fotomontaje* was its selling point: although the images were manipulated, sometimes extensively, they were still intrinsically more 'real' than a cartoon drawing" (210). This "led to an almost subliminal perception of 'reality' on the part of readers" (211). In sum, the fantastical nature of the movies was indeed "rooted in a photographic pseudoreality" (211). The ontology of the comic book raised the import of the character beyond a simple agent of the law; when he saved the damsel in distress or a young boy tormented by demons, he became a superhero, a "representative of Good versus Evil incarnate" (Wilt 213).

The origin of the films from a tried and true format is a survival strategy for an industry in decline (not unlike Hollywood's churning out of superhero movies, and sequels and prequels from well-established franchises such as Star Wars and Jurassic Park in the last few years to cope with fewer viewers going to the movie theater, preferring instead to stream films and binge watch series at home). The costs associated with these films, and the fact that they could be churned out quickly and efficiently with a recognizable plot formula made them a profitable substitute for the cinema of the Golden Age.[33] The latter had entered a crisis stage due to several factors, including a change in Hollywood's model of export, a decline in state financing, and the rapid decline and instability of intrinsically unsustainable variables within the equation of a national cinematic industry. In its wake, Charles Ramírez Berg notes that Mexican cinema moved to three distinct models: prestige, problem, and popular films (6–7). Unmistakably, the Santo films fall into the latter category, which were the most widely seen and commercially successful films of the post–Golden Age period.

The boom and ubiquity of the wrestling-superhero films also occurs as a result of a separate trajectory, which is the translation of the Hollywood serial genre to the Mexican cinemascape.[34] I say translation because there was no true serial genre in Mexico, but rather films that were shot in the episodic nature of the serial and that "display[ed] the spirit of the serials" (Cotter 20). They include *El enmascarado de Plata* (1952), and the *Sombra Vengadora* (1954) and *Huracán Ramírez* (1952) series.[35] These films predate the appearance of El Santo's first feature, *Santo contra el cerebro del mal* (1961), though the title of *El enmascarado de plata* seems tailor-made for the wrestler. In fact, the creator of the comics, José G. Cruz was behind the project, which had clear allusions to the successful comics, but Santo passed on the film (El Médico Asesino starred instead).[36] *El enmascarado de plata* is the first film in a long genealogy to introduce the idea of a wrestler transformed into action star, fighting off crooks and villains in and outside the ring (the *Tormenta* films of the early 1960s are another great example). It is similar to the Huracán Ramírez series, which featured a wrestler character created specifically for the screen. This is not a crime-fighting movie per se, but rather a sports films that starred a wrestler character who took on criminals such as the gangster El Príncipe. Importantly the popularity of Huracán Ramírez demonstrated to an industry in decline that the wrestler as hero was a viable formula for ticket sales; the wrestler did not necessarily have to be a real-life athlete, as the masked-wrestler trope had already galvanized the popular imaginary of the country.[37]

The Sombra Vengadora films are also a vital point of departure in understanding the cinematic ecosystem ante El Santo. Like Huracán Ramírez, the hero was not based on a real wrestler but specifically created for the films, "complete with fancy cape and buccaneer boots" (Cotter 26). The character wears the archetypal mask, aligning himself with the luchador figure, but also sports a cape and fights crime, evoking the superheroes of the North who had already made their presence felt in mass media. He is an amalgam of hero tropes, mixing the performative and social characteristics of the wrestler with the fantastical traits of the superhero. Like Huracán Ramírez, Sombra Vengadora is a superhero built on the cultural substrate of lucha libre.

There is another character that bears mentioning in this swath of films: Neutrón. The superhero starred in three films produced in 1960 (after the production but before the release of Santo's first two films). Like the two characters described above, he was made specifically for film, and was more a superhero and less an actual wrestler. The films were clearly inspired by the serial format, as each was divided into three distinct parts, thereby providing a base template for the luchador-as-comic-book-film adaptation genre. Neutrón was played by Wolf Ruvinskis, a Latvian-Argentine wrestler who found a home fighting the likes of El Santo and Médico Asesino in real life matches. Neutrón is a "classic superhero cast within the lucha libre mold" (Greene 53), but unlike El Santo, Blue Demon, and others, he is not an actual wrestler, but rather a "freelance superhero" (Cotter 156) like La Sombra Vengadora. Neutrón presented audiences with the classic superhero foes of North American comics and moving images; instead of solely fighting off common criminals and Mafioso gangs, he takes on supervillains in the shape of mad scientists and communists, and earth-shattering threats such as the atomic bomb.

The character expanded the repertoire of ethical possibilities in the genre, bridging the local trope of the wrestler with the defining characteristics of the superhero genre proper, such as the presence of an arch villain. Returning to Coogan's definition of the superhero, Neutrón (like La Sombra Vengadora) successfully reproduced the genre-specific traits that Superman first developed in the 1930s in the print media, that is, the conventions of *"mission, powers,* and *identity"* ("The Hero" 3; emphasis in the original). Neutrón's identity was a secret, crime-fighting character highlighted by the wrestling mask; his powers were his strength and fighting skills; and his mission was a prosocial saving of society from the threat of the supervillain. The mission factor is a defining element of the superhero, distinguishing the character from other hero types. Importantly, the superhero's mission "is to fight evil and protect the innocent; this fight is universal, prosocial, and selfless. The superhero's mission must fit in with the existing, professed mores of society, and it must not be intended to benefit or further the superhero" ("The Hero" 4). This ethos—where the luchador becomes a popular hero defending the wellbeing of the layperson and society as a whole—will mature in the Santo films, as "whether facing an international terrorist gang, . . . a flock of buxom female vampires, or the mummies of Guanajuato ... [wrestler superheroes] fought for the common good and always won ... the narrative of the luchador promised a vision of stability, an incorruptible hero immune to the ravages of time" (Levi 190). The luchador-superhero does not defend the interests of a particular organization, government, or social group, but rather fights evil for the sake of it, protecting the layman and woman from any multitude of villains who are often bad for the simple sake of being bad.

Neutrón would go on to star in two more films in the mid-1960s, thus coexisting with El Santo in the early years of luchador cinema. In effect, El Santo's movie career begins to take shape within a movement in place, a shift in commercial cinema characterized by the likes of Neutrón, Sombra Vengadora, and Huracán Ramírez that were already in circulation and dialogue with the popularity of comic books, serials, and science fiction, and that visibly borrowed from the established superhero genre from print and moving images. The shift was also inflected with the aesthetics of trendy US superhero television shows such as *Batman* that popularized the print superhero to a mass audience (Cotter 101). Cotter further argues that characters such as Neutrón successfully jumped over to television via reruns, and that in the early years of the luchador genre "he may have been as recognizable as Santo" (156). All this is important in understanding the genesis of the luchador character as one taking place within a broader surge in popular superheroes made specifically for the moving image, as characters meant to take on the ideological and cultural baggage of the trope for a general audience. The genesis also takes place during the late 1950s, when "Mexico's social, cultural, and political systems" were falling apart (Ramírez Berg 6); the popularity of the superhero is unsurprising if we consider that its primal drive is towards stasis, a stability that was nonexistent outside the cinema halls.

But there are important nuances to this origin moment: El Santo did not play the wrestler who moonlighted as a superhero (or vice versa?) in the early films. In *Santo contra el cerebro del mal* and *Santo contra hombres infernales*, that is, the two films that distinctively overlap with the Sombra Vengadora and company corpus above, the character is a sort of international man of mystery à la James Bond (but with a mask) who fights crime. To note is that both films were Cuban-Mexican coproductions, and made no pretenses of where they were shot. Like so many other luchador films that feature extensive long shots of the city or other locales, these films are characterized by setting shots of prerevolutionary Cuba. Other details emerge that set these films apart from the later filmography of El

Santo. In the former (released in Mexico in July 1961, though made in 1958), for example, he is simply known as "El Enmascarado," perhaps in deference to the fact that his real-life persona was still that of a *rudo*.[38] His role is relatively minor, and he shares masked-hero duties with Incognito (played by Fernando Osés, who also starred as La Sombra Vengadora). In the latter film (released in December 1961, though made at the same time as *El cerebro*), Santo plays a sort of accessory to the police as they infiltrate a gang of Cuban drug smugglers. Again, he plays an unnamed masked character who does not wrestle or enjoy any of the narrative protagonism that we will see in later films.

The concluding scene at the airport of both films (there are several scenes that are shared) is of significance in tracing the development of El Santo as superhero—in both, a police officer asks his chief: "Why do they cover their faces? What is their nationality?" ("¿Por qué cubren sus rostros? ¿De qué nacionalidad son?"). The interrogative here is a hallmark of the superhero genre (in print and film), as again, the superhero is only super when diegetic characters recognize him or her as such (one only needs to think of the early observers identifying the Man of Steel as a bird or plane, before settling on Superman). By posing a question about their identity, the scene sets the character apart from other do-gooders in the film, enshrining the character with the aura of the superhero. This is made clear in the chief's answer: "They are citizens of the world, their duty has no borders. They hide their identity behind masks to do good for humanity" ("Son ciudadanos del mundo, su deber no tiene fronteras. Cubren su identidad tras máscaras para hacer el bien a la humanidad"). Note in the response the defining characteristics of the superhero, that is, the (secret) identity and the prosocial mission to help all (his powers are extrapolations from the conclusion as the character's actions were decisive in defeating the villains).

The first two films in which El Santo appears were relatively unsuccessful at the box office, and failed to properly situate the character within a cinematic imaginary as a superhero akin to Neutrón or La Sombra Vengadora.[39] This all would change with the production of four films in 1961 that were screened in quick succession from mid-1962 to mid-1963: *Santo contra los zombies*, *Santo contra el rey del crimen*, *Santo en el hotel de la muerte*, and *Santo contra el cerebro diabólico*. Repeating the catchy title format of *Santo contra* (which clearly evoked the serial genre and established some sort of continuity for a general audience), these films refurbished the "citizen of the world" into a recognizable luchador-superhero who could attract mass audiences to the cinema. Additionally, they established the chief qualities that will come to characterize the remaining entries in his oeuvre, namely, the inclusion of real or staged wrestling matches (that often opened the narrative or were key moments where the wrestler fights the villain), the use of high-tech gadgets, the creation of a top-secret space from which the superhero operated (another convention of the genre), and his partnership with the police to fight crime and other supernatural maladies (Hegarty 14).

These four movies (which overlap with the success of the Neutrón films) definitively transformed the on-screen Santo into a fulltime, *Mexican* superhero, and the off-screen wrestler into a *técnico*. The transmediatic relationship here is of particular interest, as unlike other superheroes that were fashioned between, say, film and print, or film and television, El Santo established a symbiosis between his on-screen persona, the print superhero, and his off-screen performance in the ring. The tripartite nature of the character is truly unique and would ensure his durability and ubiquity across borders and through generations more than any of his superhero contemporaries that were originally as successful. El Santo is the apotheosis of the luchador as superhero, a cultural hybrid of the prototypical Hollywood hero with decidedly autochthonous characteristics.[40]

The superhero quickly became an industry-leading character, moving from production studios and directors as a franchise that would guarantee economic success (not unlike the way studios have had to vie for characters in the twenty-first-century Hollywood superhero boom). In 1964, El Santo signed to work with Luis Enrique Vergara, and starred in two (of a total of four) films that are now considered classics in the genre. *Atacan las brujas* is shot as three parts that are then united as a feature film (released in 1968), evocative of the serial genre and its episodic nature. The film is the first in the wrestler's oeuvre that will be a remake of an earlier film—*Santo contra las mujeres vampiro* (1962)—with witches substituted for vampires. The plot is, to put it kindly, bizarre and limited: a young woman, Ofelia, dreams that she and El Santo are to be sacrificed by a coven of witches to Satan, led by Mayra, who was in turn sacrificed by a hysteric populace some three hundred years ago. Ofelia wakes up from the dream and is told by her boyfriend Arturo that Santo really exists (they are seemingly acquaintances, though this is not explained in the film). We learn that Ofelia was left a property in the will of her parents that will become hers after she lives in it for a year. The deceased parents' secretary, Elisa Cárdenas, is the one who delivers this message, though we find out later that the real Elisa died 15 years ago. Mayra impersonates the secretary, apparently to gain access to Ofelia as an offering to Satan. The film consists of Santo coming to Ofelia's aide and fighting off Mayra, Medusa, and the other supernatural threats, as he "protects the weak and the helpless" ("protégé a los débiles y a los desamparados") (a universal, prosocial mission).

While the plot lacks depth, there are some thematic points that merit mention. First, the viewer cannot escape the role of religion in the film, which comes as no surprise, since the principal antagonist is a minion of the Devil. In fact, we could even say that Santo's real superpower in this film (and in early movies of his career) is his faith. In the opening dream scene, he scares off the witches tormenting him and Ofelia by standing in the shape of a cross—the shadow he casts is kryptonite for the worshippers of Satan. In a climactic scene where he takes on the witches and their henchmen, he brandishes a large cross that causes them to burst into flames. After defeating them, the cross also helps him cure a stabbed Arturo. (Catholic) Faith as a superpower should not be a surprise in a cultural terrain where religion has played a central sociocultural and political role. It is a superpower that transcends time, evident even in the postmodern age; El Man in Colombia is helped by angelic spirits in his moments of need.

Figure 1.2. Faith as a defining superpower.

Another detail that deserves recognition is the sexuality of the superhero. We must remember that the first Anglo superheroes, such as Superman and Batman, demonstrated what John Shelton Lawrence and Robert Jewett call "sexual segmentation" (43), that is, they are asexual in costume but are permitted to have love interests in their nonhero lives. While El Santo has a love interest or girlfriend in several contemporary films of the 1960s (and in future features), the amorous knot in *Atacan las brujas* is created by Ofelia and Arturo, and not the superhero (this plot point is also seen in *Santo en el museo de cera* [1963]). The superhero's asexuality is symptomatic of broader social change that saw tension between sexual liberalization and more conservative thought, reflective of Héctor Fernández L'Hoeste's observation that "despite the sexual revolution—or precisely because of it—Latin American cultural products of the 1950s and 1960s habitually upheld an ersatz puritanical air, trying to cling to society's vanishing grasp of the normative" (66). This characteristic of the superhero in *Atacan* will be discontinued in later Santo and other superhero films, but reminds us of the vestiges of a zeitgeist within the cinemascape, exemplifying how the superhero trope is effective in providing a litmus of cultural flow.

This quality of the superhero figure and genre is further noted in the spatial associations and displacements present in the film. The inherited house is located in a dingy, rural area, leading Ofelia to exclaim at

Figure 1.3. The asexual superhero.

the very beginning of the film that she wants to go back to the city and leave behind the "house of witches" ("casa de brujas"). While large and habitable, the house has no electricity and evokes a living space of yore, prior to the modernization of infrastructure and industrialization. The urban-rural dialectic will play out in several of the superhero's films, and represents a shifting ethos that correlates with drastic demographic changes.[41] These changes, that is, the massive urbanization of the country's population during the years of the Mexican Miracle, present critical issues for the national cinema in terms of genre, style, and distribution. The cinema of the Golden Age attempted to address this transformation, creating, as Carlos Monsiváis argues, a mythological matrix constituted of archetypal characters that created a moral tableau that clearly delineated an ethical triumph of good over evil (117–22). In Monsiváis's thesis, the representational system aligned "the rural, the traditional, the mestizo, and the catholic" with the good, while "the modern, the urban, and the secular were perpetually cast as moral antagonists" (Hegarty 6).

This moral universe, however, was didactic, top-down, and disconnected from the social reality of the urban masses, created by an elite class that relegated the popular to the spatial/cultural/ideological outskirts of a national Mexican essence. El Santo's films thus take on a metaheroic role, "invert[ing] the populist discourse of the films of the Golden Age . . . which resigned the urban masses to poverty and suffering" (Hegarty 13). The wrestler as superhero bridges the social life of the city (through his real-life exploits in the ring) with the projected and symbolic ideologies of the cinema (through the symbiosis of the print comic and the films), thus allowing "the masses to experience a true sense of triumph over the hegemonic forces that were continually threatening to marginalize their values, identity, and way of life" (Hegarty 13).[42] In rejecting the rural, Ofelia effectively aligns the superhero and the other protagonical characters with an urban ethos, one that that evades the dangers and calamities created by the supernatural demons in the outskirts.

This dialectic will play out in the very nature of the wrestler-superhero in other films, as the aesthetics of the movies "foreground the modern, the glossy, [and] the urban" (Hegarty 12). In *El hacha diabólica* (1964), for example, Santo drives a fancy sports car, uses ultra-modern devices such as a time machine, and hangs out at the ritzy Hotel Regis. He is an urban superhero, far removed from the antiquity and supposed backwardness of the rural space that tormented Ofelia. But that does not mean that he and his acquaintances are now free from the threat of the spooky; in fact, all that which was rejected in *Atacan* now reappears and continues to haunt the character in the urban space, suggesting that the symbolic workings of the wrestler-hero are always in motion and never at rest, evocative of the necessary perpetuity of ideological work in the cinema.

The film is of note in the character's oeuvre as it conjoins many of the character traits that will provide the ontology of the wrestler-superhero genre moving forward. The plot is more complex and complete than earlier films such as *Atacan las brujas*, *Santo en el museo de cera*, and *Santo contra los zombies*: the action begins in the colonial era (1603; like many other Santo films, there is a stitching together of some past action with a present threat) as the modern wrestler's ancestor (also known as El Santo) is entombed by a procession of holy men. His coffin bears a large cross, evoking the religious allusions in earlier films that saw the hero cast as a beacon of Catholic righteousness (or *cristiana humildad*). The character was a nobleman, of the upper social and economic class, whose burial is unceremoniously interrupted by a masked man with an axe vowing vengeance. The action cuts to the present day, where the nobleman's descendant continues wearing the mask and defending the virtuous, albeit now within the *cuadrilatero*. The protagonist makes his way to the ring, wearing a cape (which we will later discover is indestructible) in addition to his mask. The cape serves a dual sartorial purpose in that it is characteristic of both the luchador and superhero archetype. The fact that it has special powers in the film suggests that El Santo is not solely a wrestler, but also a superhero akin to the North American superheroes that were already circulating in print and film media in Mexico at the time.

The opening lively match between Santo and Lobo Negro is interrupted by the same masked axeman, who, in a present-day eerie form, is impervious to bullets fired by the police. He attempts to kill El Santo, but then vanishes when he is foiled by the wrestler. In the subsequent scene, the diegetic characters and the audience come to realize that the antagonist is somehow more than human—a supernatural superfoe that stands in ethical opposition to the *técnico*—as he does not appear in photographs taken by a journalist standing ringside. To note is the superhero's close relationship with the police and the press, as a sort of third pillar upholding justice and virtue in contemporary urban society, not unlike North American analogs who work closely with either or both institutions.

In the following scene, El Santo leaves the ring with his attractive girlfriend, Alicia; he is no longer the third asexual wheel, but rather leads a normal amorous life typical of a successful cosmopolitan man.

Open heterosexuality and a strong masculinity are, after all, fundamental ontological qualities of the (Latin American) superhero, and find their roots in earlier nationalist texts and moving images.[43] We even see El Santo remove his mask to give her a kiss! He does this after confessing to her that he feels that he is in love with someone else, a mysterious woman that he cannot definitively identify. In the next scene, a sleeping superhero is surprised by the axeman, but manages to fight him off. The villain disappears into thin air, but leaves behind the axe. With the help of a wise man—Dr. Zanoni—Santo discovers that the axe dates from 1603, and that his own mask has a secret design attributed to an ancient wizard by the name of Abraca. In this scene, the specter of his ancient love Isabel appears, directing the hero to defeat the axeman so that they may be together again. Unlike *Atacan* that saw the hero come to the aid of an innocent bystander (in Ofelia) in a prosocial act characteristic of the superhero genre, the mission in *Hacha* is punctuated instead by a diachronic melee that signifies a broader ethical engagement between good over evil; an engagement that easily extrapolates onto the axial and political arrangement of the narrative. In other words, though the tension may seem personal in the film, it is really a communal conflict that serves to strengthen the cultural heroism of the luchador as a signifier in the contemporary fashioning of a collective identity.[44]

Santo and Zanoni travel to the seventeenth century via a time machine to present to the audience what is one of the very few origin moments in the Santo portfolio. They observe how the axeman's desire for Isabel is thwarted by her own desire for a silver-masked noble. The villain kidnaps her but is defeated by the nobleman and the forces of the Inquisition—he is sentenced to burn at the stake (in a scene that will be recycled in other films) but escapes at the very last minute by transforming into a bat. He gains his superpowers through the demon Arimán, an allusion to the destructive spirit in Zoroastrianism that grants him infinite wealth and powers in exchange for his soul. The demon here is not the Satan of Catholic lore or the European monsters seen in other films, but an exotic creature whose esoteric origins generate a sense of mystery to the narrative. That being said, its actions are not altogether alien to the viewer; like the Satan character in other films, it functions as a narrative antithetical position to the superhero who defends the good.

Returning to the present day, Santo is tasked with finding Isabel's remains and defeating the villain (who has also murdered Alicia and Zanoni [who we find is the magician who originally gifted El Santo with special powers]). The final battle between the two characters takes place in an eerie colonial house, where the hero defeats the axeman by unmasking him. The decisive action points to another point of contact between the superhero genre and wrestling, that is, the power of the unmasking moment in defeating a character. As I will discuss in later chapters and with a multitude of characters, the action of removing the mask is the ultimate action of defeating a superhero, a trope repeated in print and filmic interpretations. It plays a similar role in the ring, as in unmasking, the wrestler "loses the illusion of being more than human" (Levi 117). In wrestling (and, I would argue, the superhero genre) "the fact that anonymity and the charisma of mystery can be irrecoverably lost gives [the mask] a heightened value" (Levi 118).

The film ends with a victorious Santo (though now alone, as Isabel's spirit has been freed and Alicia has been killed) vowing to stand for justice and righteousness (and other corollary traits such as faith, chivalry, humility, and honor—all traditional "pure" values). The scene evokes the spirit of the character as a prosocial trope that we will see develop over several decades of films, as a cultural symbol that will galvanize an immense national (and international) audience trying to make sense of the social, economic, and political changes of modern society. Importantly, the essence evoked in this and other early Santo films established the character within the mold of the superhero as a paradigmatic cultural referent. As Hegarty succinctly puts it, "El Santo was the perfect 'leader' to guide the country's masses through the realm of urban cultural modernity, in that he enacted and reenacted a struggle in which ancient wisdom and contemporary savviness combined to cast Mexico's traditional cultural values in a winning role" (12). In essence, El Santo is (modern) Mexico and (modern) Mexico is El Santo; the national ontologically inextricable from the birth and life of the superhero.

There is another plot point that bears analyzing, that is, the relationship between the past and present. This dialectic is at the core of the superhero genre: every hero needs an origin moment that traumatizes them into transformation; every hero fights to avenge some sort of historical wrong that gives them purpose and a mission. In the case of El Santo, the colonial past often casts inflections on the contemporary figure. In *Atacan*, it is the Inquisition that sets off the spirit of the axeman to avenge his lost love. In *El mundo de los muertos* (1969), it will be the same institution and set of beliefs from the ante Independence period that will torment the modern hero. We may read this tension—that is, the interpellation of the past and present, and how this dialectic may inform an identitarian position—as a symptom of a broader debate on *mexicanidad* established in cultural and intellectual circles, and that was at a height in the 1950s.[45] The film teams up El Santo with Blue Demon, albeit here not as the sidekick that we will see in other films, but as a tormented spirit caught in purgatory and under the orders of Satan (although he is really a good guy).

Blue Demon is perhaps the second most iconic wrestler in the luchador genealogy. Like El Santo, he began his career as a *rudo* but then transitioned into a *técnico*. This change, however, took place before his film debut.[46] Though he appeared in bit roles in two films from the early 1960s, it is only in 1965 that he is given a starring role in *Demonio Azul*. He would act in several other films in the late 1960s, many of which were carbon copies of Santo features, and would team up with the *enmascarado de plata* beginning in 1969. To note, however, is that in some films (including *El mundo*) and in real life, the characters were not necessarily allies but rather antagonists. A contemporary audience knew of this, and it surely added spice and humor to the scenes between the two dressed in suits (masks on, of course), using radio watches, and driving sports cars on the way to apprehending the supervillain du jour.

El mundo de los muertos recycles the principal plot point of a victim of the Inquisition being reborn in modern times to seek revenge against El Santo and all that he represents. The film begins in 1676 at a moment when the Church took it upon itself to extinguish what it considered heresy (interestingly, it is devil worship that earns its ire in the film, and not indigenous beliefs that were stamped out by the clergy, perhaps adding to the invisibilizing of indigeneity in Mexican cultural production). We see four men being burned at the stake (as was the axeman in *Hacha*), while their leader, Damiana, looks on from a distance. She asks Satan for help, who sends as an emissary Blue Demon whose spirit he has kept as a prisoner. Santo's ancestor confronts her after she kills his love interest, and she is condemned to burning.

Fast-forward three centuries and the narrative takes up the adventures of the modern superhero that audiences have grown to love. He is an accomplished wrestler, man of justice, and urban heartthrob with a car and girlfriend to match. His partner, Alicia, however, is a reincarnation of Damiana (as are other characters in the present, who are played by the same actors playing those from the past). Her body is occupied by the spirit of the high priestess, resulting in a supernatural tête-à-tête between the superhero and the forces of Satan (including Blue Demon!). Santo predictably vanquishes his foes, the film ending with a shot of a church steeple and a voiceover declaring the wrestler as a man of faith.

El mundo de los muertos stars the familiar cast of wrestlers, zombies, buxom women, and satanic disciples, but also presents the audience with heuristic challenges.[47] If the hero is a man of faith, then how are we to reconcile the priest laughing in glee as Damiana is killed? Furthermore, a viewer with a basic knowledge of the country's history would create quick associations between the purging of the Satanists and the massacre of indigenous bodies, epistemologies and beliefs, leading to a critical impasse between the religiosity of the past and the present, and, importantly, their reconciliation.[48] After all, the scenes in the present take place in a recognizable space, as the director (Gilberto Martínez Solares, in this case) splices in long aerial setting shots of the city, firmly situating the crime-fighting exploits of the masked man in Mexico City proper. The end of the film gestures towards two conclusions: first, that faith is a vital, axial pillar of Mexican society, and that the superhero embodies it as he does other qualities that are symbolic of a populist ethos for a nation in flux (and a cinema-as-representational system in crisis); second, that the wrestler in the present is quite different from the smiling (Spanish) priest of the past, as he is reactive to threats and does not simply burn for the sake of burning. In other words, he is a defender of the national, post-revolutionary status quo of *mexicanidad*, and not one to impose a new hegemon, as was the case of the colonial powers during the seventeenth century.[49]

The haunting trope of the past reappearing in the present as an ontological threat will be repeated in several films from the genre, further suturing the corpus of films with a global superhero genre that indeed relies on a similar temporal schism to establish ethical binaries and boundaries (Coogan, *Superhero* 82). While superheroes are born and bred from a historic moment of origin—which interweaves itself in the present in random and dynamic patterns—the supervillain is also a product of the past: his or her "grandiose self-aggrandizement arises from a sense of victimhood, originating in a wound that the supervillain never recovers from" (82). Damiana, Dracula, the axeman, and the rest, all follow this trajectory. But it is not always a colonial antagonist that rears its head as a threat to the national. In other films such as *Santo y Blue Demon contra Dracula y el Hombre Lobo* (1972) or *Santo y Blue Demon contra Dr. Frankenstein* (1973) (among many others), it is a menace from the Old Continent that will loom over contemporary Mexican society. The villains in both these films and their aim of creating a mindless society evoke Western European fascism (which contrasts with the threat of communism in Anglo films of the genre and epoch). To note in this type is that the past here is very recent, and permeates the narrative as an immediate threat. But it is a threat nevertheless, and relies on the same, repeated tropes from the colonial-era witches and demons. In this regard, the luchador films effectively play out a central narrative arc in the superhero genre, but adapted distinctively for the Mexican case. As Greene puts it, "By expressing a strong distrust of *the past* and its traditions, [the] films often celebrate modernity and social progress, glorifying technology, urban life, and cultural sophistication in a country undergoing rapid economic progress and modernization in the post-WWII era" (22). The past (and not tradition, as Lieberman convincingly argues [14]) and an inability to look toward the future is at the root of any malaise. It is this forward-looking gesture towards a modern, just, and viable future that successfully situates the Santo films at the foundation of a Latin American superhero.

Superzán, Las Luchadoras, and Other Superheroes in the Mexican Archive

While El Santo will be the fulcrum on which an entire genre, industry, and social imaginary will be built, there are also other Mexican productions that are stepping stones in lending nuances to a nascent Latin American superhero genre.[50] The two Superzán films, for example, come to mind—*Superzán el invencible* (1971) and *Superzán y el niño del espacio* (1972)—as they showcase a wrestler-character who has superhuman powers (beyond the superhuman strength and *sabiduría* that Santo deploys in all his films).[51] The first clear allusion to the superhero genre appears in the very name of the character, the moniker alluding to "an amalgam of Superman and Tarzan" (Cotter 162). The hybrid name is not a reflection of any single trait of the superhero: though he does fly like Superman, he has nothing in common with Tarzan. Rather, the naming appeals to popular characters already inhabiting the mediascape (in print and moving images), allowing for an audience to easily situate the character within a genre. Superzán bears similarities to La Sombra Vengadora and Neutrón that predate him by a decade in that the character is a made-for-movies superhero and not a wrestler transmogrified to celluloid. In fact, he tried to embark on a career in the ring but was never successful.

A second allusion appears at the very beginning of *Superzán el invencible*. A band of crooks ties a defenseless woman to the train tracks. Their motives are unexplained (evil for the sake of evil is a narrative trope in the superhero genre), just like the parallel appearance of three aliens somewhere in rural Mexico. Amid the cries for help from the damsel in distress, the camera cuts to a figure flying over the landscape below. He arrives on the scene, swiftly defeats the bad guys, and stops the train with his bare hands. A voice-over informs the audience that before us is "Superzán the invincible. Endowed with superpowers, he fights for justice and the wellbing of the good people" ("Superzán el invencible. Dotado de superpoderes, lucha por la justicia y el bienestar de la gente buena"). The viewer would be correct in feeling a sense of déjà vu after watching the first few minutes of the film play out, as Superzán basically copies the iconic montage of Superman's powers. Whether in the form of comic book covers, cartoons, the television series, or movies, the Superman franchise has recycled the one-two sequence of the superhero flying in to save the day and stopping a train with his brute strength. Superman, after all, is, as the classic voice-over instructs us, "faster than a speeding bullet . . . more powerful than a locomotive"; Superzán will not fall short of such lofty expectations, demonstrating from the very beginning that he is on par with the North American Man of Steel.

Figure 1.4. More powerful than a locomotive!

The film is self-reflexive of its hybrid (luchador and Superman, that is, local and foreign) character, as in an ensuing scene in a carnival the camera lingers on the figures of a merry-go-round. The seats are not the typical horses or ponies but rather cartoon characters such as Donald Duck, evoking Ariel Dorfman and Armand Mattelart's critique of US imperialism in *Para leer al Pato Donald* (1971). This seemingly insignificant detail in *Superzán* is, however, essential if we are to understand the flow and hegemony of North American media and ideology within the Latin American/Mexican mediascape.

Dorfman and Mattelart argue that superheroes from the adventure-strip genre live "in a world of order governed by the law of order" ("en un mundo del orden regido por la key del orden"; 140). They, furthermore, "cannot deviate from the norm, are irreducibly good and concentrate all the divine power of order in their body and mind, having no conflict with the world or with themselves" ("no pueden desviarse de la norma, son irreductiblemente buenos y concentran además todo el poder divino del orden en su cuerpo y su mente, no tienen conflicto con el mundo ni consigo mismos"; 140). Like Eco's reading of Superman (published a year later), Dorfman and Mattelart agree that the superhero is a bastion of the status quo, as "his crusade of moral rectification . . . is a restoration of his harmonious and immaculate world. By expelling evil, the world is cleansed and they can go on summer vacation" ("su cruzada de rectificación moral . . . es una restauración de su mundo armónico, inmaculado. Al expulsar a la maldad, el mundo queda limpiecito, y ellos pueden veranear"; 140). In this line of argument, the reader (or viewer) self-identifies with the hero, as he has a dual identity of "the quotidian" ("lo cotidiano") and the "supreme and powerful" ("supremo y poderoso") resulting in an axial and epistemological trajectory wherein "the only movement is from the everyday to the superior and back, but never within the world of the habitual" ("el único movimiento es desde lo cotidiano a lo superior y de vuelta, pero nunca dentro del mundo de lo habitual"; 140–41). This line of flight (and return) bears detailing, as it understands the superhero as a genre of the extreme, a condition replicated in the luchador-from-comics films, as their suspension of belief is a static quality that upends any semblance of verisimilitude. Though they are punctuated by wrestling scenes (that are either real or simulated for the particular film), the narrative and axial crux of the plot revolves around the unreal and supernatural that is extraneous to "el mundo de lo habitual."

Dorfman and Mattelart argue that unlike the superhero genre (of which Superzán is clearly an expression), Disney characters "reject the crude and explicit schema" ("rechaza[n] el esquematismo burdo y explícito"), though "the ideological background is undoubtedly the same" ("el trasfondo ideológico es sin duda el mismo"), that is, the perpetuity of a capitalist vis-à-vis US ethos. Disney, instead, "colonizes the everyday world, in the reach of man and his common problems" ("coloniza el mundo diario, al alcance del hombre y sus problemas comunes"), unlike superheroes who rely on a "projection of fantasy beyond the everyday" ("proyección de la fantasia fuera del mundo diario"; 141). This is the derivative reading the viewer is to glean from the setting shot of the carnival, as it situates the superhero within a semiotic and ideological topography that is already overrun with tensions and conflations between local and US culturemes. Superzán should not be read as an intrusion of a North American Anglo culture onto the local space that the film metonymizes, but rather as a symptom of a colonization already in place, as evidenced by the unquestioned and omnipresent Disney character.

The plot of the film is not unlike that of the Santo movies, in that the superhero is called upon to intervene in a critical moment where the real-unreal, human-superhuman collide. But the film is not a simple calque of its contemporaries, though there are commonalities that cannot be ignored. The unreal element is not a werewolf or vampire, but rather the arrival of extraterrestrials. Unlike the alien bodies that will feature in later Hollywood productions, the ETs here don moonsuits, leaving to our imagination their anatomy. They do, however, possess advanced technology in the form of their transportation and rays that freeze any living thing that they aim at. They befriend a young boy and enlist his help, as one of them has gone missing. Amid all this the carnival goes on as Los Campeones Justicieros arrive. They are allies of the protagonist, but are only wrestlers and cannot fly (though Superzán will lose this superpower in later movies). Of interest in the carnival scene is the five-on-five match between Los Campeones and a set of *rudos*, as Superzán watches from the audience. He does not enter the ring for the diegetic and nondiegetic audiences' entertainment, or bring the antagonist into the fight as El Santo was fond of doing; by remaining outside, the character underlines his identity as superhero over luchador, avoiding any such confusion that could take place if he were to enter the *cuadrilatero*.

During all the festivities (of the wrestling, singing, and a beauty pageant), a band of gangsters (dressed the part as mafiosos that would be just at home in Chicago) strikes. Superzán is made aware of the heist with the help of his own advanced technology and his sidekick (an Afro-Mexican character called Johnny) from a high-tech lair in a skyscraper (presumably in a city, away from the rural landscapes of the carnival *pueblo*). He flies in and defeats the criminals—we also learn here that he, like the Man of Steel, is bulletproof.

While all this is going on, the aliens continue to look for their colleague but are soon met by a band of distrustful villagers who take it upon themselves to lynch the outsiders. They pick up torches, sticks, and a bottle of liquor to hunt down the moonmen. Just as they are about to descend upon them, Superzán shows up to save the day. They find the fourth ET in a church and leave in their spaceship, not before paying due homage to a statue of Christ.

Superzán el invencible is worth highlighting in this lineage of films because it broadens the scope of mexploitation cinema to include characteristics of the classic superhero genre. Superzán flies, is bulletproof, and does not moonlight as a wrestler (though his Justiciero buddies do wrestle to appease the audience). He has a sidekick, a secret lair, and has a prosocial mission that benefits all for the sake of doing good. The very opening scene in the train tracks (plus the Disney detail) effectively sutures the character and film to a foreign genre, translating the Anglo superhero (character and genre) to a very local context. The film does, however, reproduce some of the narrative and symbolic elements of the Santo films, such as the spatial hierarchies of the urban and rural; it is, after all, the urban superhero (and his technology vis-à-vis modernity) that saves the extraterrestrials from the rural mob. Religion is also upheld as a core (though narratologically peripheral) tenet of modern Mexican society, as the aliens recognize the symbolism of the church and its God in the very ending of the film before they depart for outer space. The racial elements of the urban-rural dialectic are also of interest, as the dark skin of the villagers stands in contrast to the otherwise whitened cast of mexploitation cinema.[52] The didactic message—a mainstay in the superhero genre—here is clear: don't be like the Luddite, backwards villagers; instead, embrace modernity and all that it may bring, as even the aliens may share in our values and culture. Importantly, the aliens here do not serve "as metaphors of Cold War politics and Atomic Age fears" (Greene 19), as we will see in Hollywood films of the era, but rather as metonymic entities of a modernity within reach as Mexico enjoyed the advancements of its economic miracle.[53] The bad guys in the film, that is, the characters the audience should not emulate, are the mob whose distrust of all that is modern blinds them.

There are several other characters and films that merit consideration aside from Superzán in this tracing. The films starring the luchadoras are of special interest, as they held in the spotlight female protagonists who fought crime like their male counterparts, and brought to a wider audience the notion of the *chica moderna* that began to take shape in the cultural imaginary of twentieth-century Mexico. The modern woman was urban, educated, and employed, and chose to wear contemporary clothing that sartorially aligned her with the modernizing ethos of contemporary Mexican identity in the 1960s and 1970s. She often lived alone, eschewed early marriage and maternity, and was economically self-sufficient akin to her North American sisters who felt the blessings of socioeconomic emancipation in the postwar years. The luchadora films emulate this social change in presenting female wrestlers that fight off threats from the netherworld while engaged in stylized holds and throws in the ring for the libidinal satisfaction of the audience in and outside the film.

Las luchadoras contra el robot asesino (1969) is a contemporary of some of the most renowned numbers of the genre, but is noteworthy in that it quickly adapts the narrative schematic of the wrestler film to one starring female protagonists. The film was directed by René Cardona, who was behind several Santo films and the original *El enmascarado de plata*. Gender roles and tensions were, after all, at the center of El Santo's film, as it comes as no surprise that their theme of modernity "also extends to gender attitudes and the shifts in gender relations" that were "the products of the fundamental changes in Mexican society in the post–world war two period" (Lieberman 11). It is natural then that the wrestler-superhero trope should also include female characters who could partake in the crime-fighting, nation-building antics of the genre.

Las luchadoras contra el robot asesino is the fifth film in the field to star female leads.[54] Female superheroes are nothing new (though rather absent in contemporary Latin American moving images); one only need to peruse the long history of print characters (and their filmic adaptations) to arrive at the conclusion that though women have often only occupied peripheral positions in the genre (see, for example, the damsel in distress trope tied to the train tracks), there are important characters that have come to define the archetype. The film repeats many of the plot points seen throughout the genre, such as wrestling matches inserted into the narrative, a superhero who works with the police, and a mad scientist type who plays the role of the principal villain.

The antagonist here is Orlac, a brilliant if misguided scientist who is bent on converting human beings into mindless robots.[55] He makes the mistake of kidnapping and killing another scientist, Professor Reina, who happens to be the uncle of Gaby Reina, the tag-team partner of Gema Nelson, a renowned wrestler who—according to the ringside announcer—has had much success in Central and South America. The uncle is a stand-in for the older male in the genre that links the present and past (see earlier Santo films), providing a sort of connective tissue between a collective heritage—that may or may not be rejected—and the advent of modernity. An example of this is seen early on, when he insists that Gaby should get married (he, ironically, is a bachelor or *solterón*). The luchadoras, however, are there to challenge gender roles and conventions. Unlike the daughters of other scientists (who are housewives), they live alone and attend to traditionally male duties such as painting the house and other handyman tasks. They literally and figuratively wear the pants in their household.

The setup, climax, and denouement of the film is unexceptional, as the good guys predictably triumph over the machinations of the villain. What is of interest, however, is how this happens. While male superheroes often partner with the police, it is their intellect and strength (and sometimes divine intervention) that overcomes the adversary. In the case of *El robot asesino*, however, the female superheroes become almost sidekicks to the male detectives who succeed in neutralizing Orlac and his latest creation, Elektra, a female-wrestler and robot amalgam who stands in axial and erotic opposition to the luchadoras. Elektra is not only a cyborg but also a foreign threat, as she is introduced as the reigning US champion in opposition to Gaby, who is the Mexican champion.

The policemen are Arturo and Chava, who in addition to assisting the luchadoras also fawn over them in and outside the ring. In the climax, the two duos wrestle with Orlac and Elektra. The latter fends off the luchadoras in the ring, but then tangles with Arturo as the female heroes look on. She manages to free herself from him and tries to escape with Orlac as they climb a metal platform. Arturo races up the scaffolding to confront her, but is quickly defeated as the luchadoras look on. Hanging by the edge of his fingers from a walkway, Arturo is saved when Chava picks up a rifle and takes aim at the villains. When he realizes that Elektra is bullet proof, he is instructed by Gaby to aim at the remote-control device that Orlac uses to control her. The creature plummets to her death as the mad scientist looks on, promising eternal vengeance, a vengeance that is cut short when Chava buries a bullet in his back. The bad guy falls to the ring, joining his creation in a macabre portrait of the vanquished.

What strikes the viewer in this energetic and dramatic montage is that it is the male detective who takes on the villain as the protagonists are unable to nullify her within the rules and regulations of lucha libre. It is clear that though they occupy the tropic position of the wrestler-superhero, las luchadoras are not super enough and must rely on decidedly nonsuper policemen to do their muscle work. Arturo is of visual and thematic importance, as in addition to adopting the principal axial role in the narrative—in that he is set against the principal villain—he is also juxtaposed to an antithetical sidekick. Chava is quite unlike the macho, svelte, and handsome Arturo (played by heartthrob Joaquín Cordero); he is skinnier, balding, and has a long nose. Played by the comedian Héctor Lechuga, Chava is a countertype to the masculine ideal embodied by Arturo.[56] Their combination, that is, the macho and nonmacho, defeats Orlac and Elektra, though we must acknowledge that it is Gaby's intellect that manages to find the Achilles heel of the villain.

Figure 1.5. Superheroines become super sidekicks.

In sum, it is the male duo that disentangles the challenge posed to the status quo in a film supposedly headlined by female wrestlers, leaving the viewer to wonder who the real superheroes are in *Las luchadoras contra el robot asesino*. El Santo and Blue Demon (and even Superzán!), after all, maintain the apical narrative role in their super endeavors, leading us to question the viability of female superheroes within the cultural horizon of twentieth-century Mexico. Perhaps there is credence to Greene's affirmation that "one can ultimately suggest that the space made for the luchadoras in these films does not empower them in Mexican society, but rather exploits them as objects of voyeuristic-fetishistic pleasure for men" (107), an observation that gains momentum if we are to consider other films from the subgenre.

La Mujer Murciélago (1968) is another Cardona flick, and is a liberal adaptation of the Batman television series and films that were popular at the time. Like other entries in the genre, it combines the superhero archetype with the Mexican ruse of the wrestling element, presenting a masked character who takes on diabolical villains in and outside the ring. La Mujer Murciélago is very much like Gema and Gaby in *Las luchadoras*, but is different in that she has a masked identity that is a wholesale rip off of Batman and Batgirl, albeit the bodysuit is substituted with a skimpy bikini. The antagonist this time around is a Dr. Williams, who seeks to extract the pineal fluid from excellent physical specimens to make a man-fish hybrid that will allow him infinite power.[57] He first tries his experiments with macho wrestlers, but ultimately fails as their extracts are unstable, as the wrestlers do not survive the experiment. The police get wind of his machinations when a body washes up on the beaches of Acapulco, and we learn that similar cases have occurred in Macao and Hong Kong, thus lending an international air to the villain. He then decides that a female wrestler is what is needed, and proceeds to track down the protagonist. What follows does not require much imagination: a sexy La Mujer Murciélago (played by the Italian actress Maura Monti) comes to the aid of the police and fights him and his creation (the man-fish hybrid, Pisces), ultimately succeeding against the *contra natura* threat of genetic experimentation.

La Mujer Murciélago is an enviable superhero, described by the police as "a wonderful and extremely rich woman who lives in the capital. . . . Her fortune has put her in the service of justice, fighting tirelessly against evil. . . . Endowed with rare qualities, in a short period of time she mastered all sports. . . . And beneath a mask and the nickname of

Figure 1.6. Fighting crime in a bikini.

the Mujer Murcielago she became an extraordinary wrestler" ("Una maravillosa mujer inmensamente rica que vive en la capital. . . . Su fortuna la ha puesto a servicio de la justicia luchando incansablemente en contra del mal. . . . Dotada de unas cualidades poco comunes, en corto tiempo logró dominar todos los deportes. . . . Y bajo una máscara y el apodo de la Mujer Murciélago se convirtió en una extraordinaria luchadora"). All this is revealed in a kitschy montage complete with groovy music and caveats of her spearfishing, wrestling, and taking on gangs of criminals. She fulfills by all accounts the tenets of the superhero, deploying her identity, powers, and mission to the benefit of society at large. The message is clear: she is a superhero who moonlights as a wrestler and not vice-versa, wrestling simply being another activity that she has mastered in her education.

While at face value the film suggests an empowering narrative for the female superhero, the concluding scene swiftly disqualifies any such notions. The unmasked heroine relaxes with a drink accompanied by two detectives. She explains to them how she artfully managed to defeat Dr. Williams and the monster not through brute strength, but by logic and guile. As the detectives (and the audience) marvel at her craftiness and intellect, the camera cuts to a close shot of the worried protagonist looking at something off camera. She screams and exclaims "A mouse!" ("¡Un ratón!") before jumping into the arms of the two men (who quickly brandish their guns, should the fish-monster strike again). She clings between them, genuinely frightened and exhorting "Please kill it!" ("¡Mátenlo por favor!"). The ending credits music comes on, and the two detectives laugh and pose a homosocial retort ("Women, eh" ["Mujeres, eh"]), as the superheroine has been reduced to a gendered stereotype. Their chummy sexism permeates the celluloid frontier, as the positioning of the men and the protagonist includes the viewer within the diegesis, suggesting that we too should be in on the "joke" that women are always going to be women, even if they have fancy gadgets and a superhero persona. The fact that this occurs at the very end of the film, and not earlier, also provides the viewer with the takeaway that gender equality is not on the cards for this viewing. In other words, La Mujer Murciélago may be a crime-fighting superhero, but the end of the film reminds the viewer that she (like las luchadoras) is still a woman that cannot escape the sexist overtones, the voyeuristic-fetishistic male gaze, and the gender determinism of society. Importantly, her crime-fighting does not pose a threat to the (gendered) status quo, ironically reaffirming her tropic position as a superhero.

Adapting Kalimán

As I note earlier, not every superhero in the Mexican movie archive is a cheap copy (La Mujer Murciélago, for example) or a conjugation of the luchador figure. There were some noteworthy examples of characters—who like their North American counterparts—made the jump from successful print comic to the film medium. As David Wilt notes, "Nearly two dozen live-action feature films were adapted from Mexican comic books between the late 1950s and the mid-1980s" (200). Perhaps the most noteworthy of these are the Kalimán films (though the Chanoc films are also of interest, the character is not a bona fide superhero), as they ported a popular radio and print superhero into what would be a megabudget blockbuster for the time.

Kalimán checks all the boxes for the superhero trope, and is, additionally, a prototype of the cross-media phenomenon that is the superhero today. The character made his debut as a radio series on September 16, 1963, on Radio Cadena Nacional in Mexico City, in what was the Golden Age for Mexican radio.[58] Such was the popularity of the superhero that its creators, Rafael Navarro Huerta and Modesto Vásquez González, modded the character and his adventures to the comic format: the first Kalimán comic appeared in 1965 and was widely distributed by a series of companies in Spanish-speaking America well into the 1990s. In 1994, *La Leyenda de Kalimán* appeared as a book (and not a weekly serial), and gave readers a new storyline. The publishers released two other volumes that compiled several storylines in an anthology format that was poorly received. Attempts were made in the late 1990s and the first decade of the 2000s to resuscitate the print character but these proved unfruitful. Included here was the manga-style comic *Kalimán Regresa* that was meant to cross web, print, videogame, and film platforms, adapting the character to the mediascape of a globalized twenty-first century. A website for this endeavor still exists (www.kaliman.mx), but the site is nothing more than a video proclaiming the character as a superhero. For all intents and purposes, Kalimán the character has entered an extended period of hibernation, which may or may not be interrupted by the changing cultural dynamics of global superhero production and circulation.[59]

Several critics to date have studied Kalimán, including David William Foster, Harold E. Hinds, Roshni Rustomji, Luz de la Rosa, and Héctor Fernández L'Hoeste, though their research has tended to focus on the print and radio history of the character. They have convincingly read the character vis-à-vis theories of orientalism, postcolonialism, and gender studies, leaving no doubt as to the import of the character and the comic book (as a medium) in the cultural history of Mexico.[60] What interests me, however, are the two film adaptations that were made in the 1970s, and how they enter into conversation with the established genre of the Mexican (Latin American) superhero film that was pioneered by the wrestler-superhero model, especially since Kalimán "is, quite probably, the most popular and profitable superhero in Mexico and Latin America, with the possible exception of El Santo" (Fernández L'Hoeste 57). What are the principal characteristics of the filmic hero and how may these be seen in the evolution of the contemporary Latin American superhero genre?

I am here referring to *Kalimán, el hombre increíble* (1972; also known as *Profanadores de tumbas: Kalimán, el hombre increíble*) and *Kalimán en el siniestro mundo de Humanón* (1976), both directed by Alberto Mariscal. But before we discuss each film, it bears reviewing the basics of the original character. Kalimán is a superhero whose mysterious origins, exotic name, and muscular appearance create a sort of enigma that captivates the reader. He is the seventh generation of the goddess Kali. Fernández

L'Hoeste notes that he is from a remote kingdom called Agharta, and that he was rescued from a basket floating on a river, abandoned by his birth parents. The Rajah of the kingdom of Kalimantán and his wife adopt the young baby, but his fate is not yet secured as an enemy of the monarch—wishing for there to be no successor—tosses the child into a river. The young child, now called Kali, is found by a man (Krishna) and his son (Ali) in the Indian jungle. They take him under their wing, and the young boy will, under their tutelage, and that of others, mature in skills, wisdom, and powers in a life journey that will take him all over Asia.

Kalimán, importantly, is a superhero of the world, and not a character birthed from a particular national context, as was the case of Santo in the comics. Covadonga Troncoso Navarro adds that "many people believe that Kalimán is Mexican, but they are wrong. He is a demigod and, as such, does not have a nationality" ("mucha gente cree que Kalimán es mexicano, pero están equivocados. Él es un semidiós y, como tal, no tiene nacionalidad"; cited in Zubieta). In line with this observation, Fernández L'Hoeste affirms that Kalimán is "not particularly Latin American," but is "a cultured, rational individual who uses his impressive physical and mental powers to assist fellow human beings in distress"; he is a "refined individual, cognizant of martial arts, Oriental philosophies, linguistic proficiency, remarkable erudition, and Western know-how" (58). The character possesses a variety of powers, including the ability to shape-shift, telekinesis, and telepathy (with humans and animals), in addition to strength (though his real powers are those of the mind). Readers may draw apt comparisons to another cult figure of the time, the Incredible Zovek, a magician and escape artist that starred in two superhero films, *El increíble Profesor Zovek* (1972) and *Blue Demon y Zovek en la invasión de los muertos* (1973). Like Kalimán, Zovek relied on mystical arts and oriental(ist) wisdom, though his films did engage more explicitly with the luchador genealogy.

I would add that Kalimán is not particularly Asian, but is rather an amalgam of impressions of *el lejano oriente*, as he is the product of a series of stereotypes and imaginations that are not grounded in reality. The first detail is of course the idea of a kingdom of Kalimantán; there is no such place in India! Kalimantan is actually the Indonesian portion of the large island of Borneo (the other part of the island belonging of course to Malaysia). Perhaps the creators were confusedly thinking of Bali, an Indonesian island that does have a large Hindu tradition and population. The kingdom of Agharta is also a fictional creation, a product of the nineteenth-century European mind that was addicted to all things exotic. The father-son duo that rescues the young child is also an impossibility, if we are to equate their names with two conflicting religions (Krishna = Hinduism, Ali = Islam). His travels to and education in Tibet, China, the Middle East, and other locales reflects an orientalist projection, where the Asian is associated with mystical knowledge and physical training.

Perhaps the greatest contradiction in the character is his white skin. Fernández L'Hoeste argues that Kalimán is "a mishmash of ethnic markers, facilitating the reader's confusion and the re-affirmation of many stereotypes" (61). Kalimán's phenotypical and ontological qualities are not an accident or coincidence, but rather posit the superhero in a central axis around which Mexican popular culture could create an imaginary wherein the nation (and its readers) would be aligned with a sociocultural bloc that systematically reproduced an orientalist discourse. In other words, "Through [Kalimán], Mexico legitimates its role as part of the Western world. . . . When his creators envisioned the hero, they were . . . proclaiming the fact that Mexicans could also be Orientalists. They could share the prepotent, arrogant attitude of the European (and U.S.) gaze and partake in its benefits" (62). Fernández L'Hoeste convincingly argues that this is to create the representation of Mexico as an industrialized, Western state that was ready to embrace the world as an economic powerhouse in the height of the late 1960s and 1970s. Kalimán, like all superheroes, is ideology, but with an angle towards the inside and the outside (unlike the Santo films that coalesced an internal agenda of modernity and *lo mexicano*). He is a "model of Mexican honor" (Hinds and Tatum 43) and "appeals to positive Mexican self-images and represents a national model to counter the foreign one" (Foster 16).

Kalimán, el hombre increíble is based on the superhero's very first adventure, *Profanadores de tumbas*, which previously appeared in radio and comics. The plot is centered on the lost tomb of the pharaoh Tut-Kamon and the various groups seeking its location. Among these is a professor and daughter (of Anglo origin), a German explorer, several local Egyptian bands, and Kalimán, who—in Egypt, looking for signs of extraterrestrial life—enters the escapade when he rescues the professor and his daughter Alicia from a group of bandits. The plot develops the attempts of the various groups to find the secret tomb, and involves the superhero demonstrating several of his powers: in an early scene, he causes an artificial eclipse; in others, his superior strength overpowers villains; while later in the movie he uses his powers of feigning death, gaining the upper hand against his adversaries. A superhero film is never complete without the fantastical (even beyond his superpowers), which is personified here by the character Mateo who we learn is an alien that is charged with protecting the tomb from looters. We learn that the ruins were in fact built by aliens centuries ago, and that the supernatural mummy Oetam that protects it is indeed also from another planet. The irony of aliens building the pyramid is not lost, as it rehashes a repeated Western fantasy that has at its core the racist belief that ancient Egyptians lacked the technology to actually build the pyramids. This belief is ridiculous, especially since the construction of ancient Greek and Roman structures is never questioned, but alas, they were the forbearers of Europe, and not of backward Africa. The plot point is especially ironic given that the ancient Aztecs built pyramids in Mexico! Or were the aliens also involved in those constructions? The film ends with the superhero defeating the Bedouin antagonists and the aliens, escaping just in time with his accomplices as the tomb caves in as a bomb detonates.

Aside from presenting the character and his powers, the film moreover provides an origin moment for the incorporation of the superhero's sidekick, an Egyptian boy named Solín, a descendent of the pharaohs. Solín is young but crafty, his guile being a defining characteristic. He, like Kalimán, is of noble heritage, but "both reject the wealth they are born into" (Fernández L'Hoeste 58), distinguishing the Mexican duo from other man-boy tag teams such as Batman and Robin, whose superness was directly related to the immeasurable depth of the Wayne treasure chest. Humility, after all, is ontoformative to a national ideal (as was the case of the Santo films), and is at the core of both Kalimán and Solín, especially when juxtaposed to the riches flaunted by foreign characters.

The opening seconds of the film are perhaps the most interesting, as they are composed of a composite close shot of structures of Egyptian architecture superimposed onto the superhero's blue eyes framed by his distinguishing white turban. The shot sutures the character and his body to the exotic, decentering the viewer momentarily to a land quite unlike the national, but nevertheless to an ideational space very much concerned with constructs and tropes of a national imaginary (given that the character is readily recognizable to a popular Mexican audience). In a move that I have not seen repeated in any other superhero film, a somber voice-over declares, "I, Kalimán, authorize the actor Jeff Cooper to play me in this part of my life that takes place in mysterious Egypt. My decision to allow this young actor to physically and psychologically play me is based on his integrity as a person and his dedication to the study of the human mind" ("Yo, Kalimán, autorizo al actor Jeff Cooper a interpretar este pasaje de mi vida que tiene lugar en el misterioso egipto. Mi decisión de permitir a este joven actor tomar por la corporea y psicológica de mi persona se basa en su integridad como individuo y su dedicación al estudio de la mente humana"). The image then cuts to the professor, Alicia, and a collaborator, Dr. Zarur Tagore, discussing their efforts to find the tomb, as the plot proper unfolds.

While other entries in the comic book film adaptation genre may signal the source text through the format of the credits or the style and aesthetics of the film, Mariscal's film deploys the unorthodox strategy of having the title character directly address the viewer. To note in this is that the speaker in the voice-over is not the filmic superhero, but rather the radio character, that is, the original Kalimán. The quick, opening voice-over is a foundational lead into the film, as it links the moving image directly to the sound format, providing a familiar voice for the viewer already acquainted with the character. For the uninitiated viewer, the voice-over is less recognizable, but nevertheless signals that what is to come is not

Figure 1.7. Situating Kalimán in an exotic space.

an isolated character and story but rather an iteration of a successful superhero franchise. That being said—and like popular Hollywood films today—you can watch and enjoy *Kalimán, el hombre increíble* by itself, but can also connect the viewing experience to the narrative archive of the character.[61]

A corollary of the voice-over is that it severs the moving image from the epistemics of the radio show, posing that the film is, instead, a fictive representation of a "chapter" of the life of the hero. By noting that what we see is a fiction of otherwise implied to be real events, the voice-over suggests that the radio Kalimán is indeed an actual character and not a figment of fiction. The film, therefore, is acknowledged as an adaptation of the radio story and the character, losing the semblance of an aura of authenticity and veracity that was attributed to the trusted voice of the radio. I am not arguing that the radio show was meant to be received as a set of real adventures, but that the voice-over sets a hierarchy of fiction wherein what is to come is a filmic adaptation or version of a story that the viewer is already familiar with.

Kalimán, el hombre increíble was a big-budget film, shot on location, and with an international cast. It brought a loved radio and comic character to the silver screen, the apotheotic format of any superhero worth his or her salt, as it allowed for greater distribution, popularity, and financial success. The production details of the film stand in stark contrast to the superhero-luchador flicks of the 1960s and 1970s, which came as no surprise, as the original character was created as an "alternative to what conservative Mexican sectors identified as the increased vulgarization of their culture" in 1960s churros films; "in contrast, *Kalimán* represented an attempt to produce for the masses with concern for a higher quality and, regressively, a return to a nobler, more honorable role model—above all, within the traditionally moralizing scope of the middle class" (Fernández L'Hoeste 62).[62] The voice-over adds to the overarching ethos of the series and character, as it emphasizes that any defects we may perceive in terms of production value, acting, and editing are the result of the adaptation between mediums, the limitations of film technology, and adaptation between the reality of the radio and the fictive recreation of the cinema.

If the first Kalimán film addressed mummies and the supernatural (which were a staple in luchador films), then the second properly took on the other standard Mexican supervillain: the egomaniacal madman wanting complete mind control of the human race. Directed by Mariscal and starring Cooper, *Kalimán en el siniestro mundo de Humanón* was also partly filmed on location in Brazil. There is no opening voice-over here, as Kalimán the radio star takes for granted that the viewer has already seen the first movie and knows that Jeff Cooper has been given permission to play the titular role. Likewise, the film does not delve into any origin moments (as was the case of Solín in the first film), instead playing out a story that is adapted from "Cerebros infernales," a classic Kalimán story. The lack of an origin moment or narrative in the film is not surprising if we consider that even though both films are adapted from specific adventures (the first film adapting "Los profanadores de tumbas," numbers 1–10 of the comics), *Humanón*'s plot is lifted from a much later adventure, "Cerebros infernales," appearing in numbers 344–87.

Readers and viewers are assumed to be so familiar with the character that no time is wasted in introductions or character development; like the most popular films starring El Santo and company, we jump straight to the machinations of the villain and the crime-fighting antics of the superhero. In fact, if it weren't for the exotic locales and higher production budget, one could even confuse *Humanón* for a luchador film (though there are no gratuitous ringside cameos).

The plot is even wilier than the first film, as Kalimán and Solín attend a parapsychology conference in Brazil where they find that Kalimán's old friend, Dr. Rabadam is now dead. Instead, they are greeted by his supposed widow, Xiomara (who wears a half niqab covering a scar left when Humanón threw acid on her face—even when wearing a bikini—evocative of the stereotypical Arabian princess), and Dr. Ferrao, another luminary of the world of parapsychology.[63] The superhero is then targeted by Humanón, a super villain bent on experimenting on human life and creating the Perfect-Humano. Dressed in a red robe and hood, emblazoned with the sign of an atom on his cape, Humanón threatens the world at large by wanting to transform all humans into zombies that are "freed beings . . . all equal" ("seres liberados . . . todos iguales"). Like the villain in *La Mujer Murciélago*, his contra natura intentions demonstrate a complete disregard for human life (and the soul) and threaten the fabric of civilization.

Humanón is a striking criminal because he coalesces the fear of communism and the Left at large into a singular character/caricature. While the Santo films often portrayed the foreign antagonist as a purveyor of a fascist ideology that was antithetical to the spirit of revolutionary democracy that was propagandized in post-revolutionary Mexico, *Humanón* materializes the foreigner as a mind-controlling Commie.[64] Ironically, Communism and the threat of nuclear warfare (as symbolized by the atom, though there is no mention of a nuclear bomb in the film) is at the axial core of the film while the Cold War entered a period of détente. Perhaps the fear is not of macropolitical tensions, but rather of the politicocultural affront posed by youth counterculture and the student Left in Mexico, and the subsequent massacres in 1968 (and 1971).[65] The superhero, after all, sustains the status quo, and no greater test of the stasis of Mexican political life was the challenge mounted by throngs of politically committed students demanding real change and the fulfillment of the original ideals of the Mexican Revolution. It is timely that a superhero—and especially a staunchly conservative superhero as was Kalimán—faces the threat of the Left and leftist thought.

This is done through an almost comically pathetic portrayal of the Left through stereotypes and dog whistles that leave little for the audience to actively analyze or decipher. When Kalimán enters Humanón's jungle hideout, he is met by a henchman who proclaims that "thinking is not allowed" ("no está permitido pensar"). The majority of the villain's mindless goons are also caricatures of the indigenous peoples of the Amazon, fueling the idea that Humanón and all that he stands for is anathema to the Mexican national, mestizo project and any positive iteration of a common identity.[66] The message to the audience is crystal clear: to align oneself with the red, mind-controlling villain (and his barbarous lot of zombies) is to align oneself with everything that stands in the way of a modern, Western, nation-state.

Humanón concludes with the triumphant protagonist saving the world, as the bad guy falls prey to his own creations and self-destructs, an easy metaphor for the political didacticism behind the exposition, climax, and falling action of the film. A quite stupendous explosion sees the hero and his companions escape to safety as they make their way back to the civilization of Rio de Janeiro. The spatial demarcations of the film, that is, the urban-rural divide, are analogous to similar dyadic shots seen throughout the luchador series of films, as the vertical, white, and prosperous modernity of Rio is contrasted with the horizontal, colored, barbarity of the jungle. Returning to the city is a triumphant act, pointing the viewer in no uncertain terms towards the "correct" side of the political spectrum. The hero punctuates this missive when he exclaims "It's all over" ("Ya terminó todo") as they make their way back to the city. The sexual tension between the two (though more on her side, as Kalimán is remarkably chaste, as are most of the superheroes from the Mexican archive) reaches a tipping point, as the hero removes her veil, uncovering her scarred mouth and jaw. She then removes this second mask to show that she was always beautiful (an awed Solín exclaims, "Wow! You much very beautiful, Xiomara" ["¡Wow! Eres mucho muy bonita, Xiomara"]). The camera pauses and alternates between the superhero and his damsel, in a shot/countershot dynamic that highlights their Caucasian features with the jungle as backdrop. Their white, heterosexual alliance—as opposed to the monstrosity of Humanón and his indigenous henchmen—is privileged as a model to emulate.[67] Any rendezvous between the superhero and the lead female, however, is left to the viewer's imagination, as the film ends with Kalimán and Solín leaving on a plane, on to new adventures, wherever they may be.

The two Kalimán films demonstrate an evolution of the Mexican superhero film from its origins in the luchador genre to a multinational, big-budget production based on well-known radio and print characters. While the archetypes of the villains stay the same, the hero is a measured, traditionalist bastion of Mexicaness, not to be confused with the extravagant and "vulgar" hero of the masses that fights baddies in and outside the ring. For the most conservative quarters, the films ease the stigma of Mexican cinema as a churro factory populated by fantastical events and cheap special effects. It goes without saying that the status quo is maintained as an image of Western modernity is forwarded as a model to follow. Importantly, Kalimán's primary adversary is not the threat of the past (as it stands in the way of modernity), but rather contemporary politicosocial shockwaves produced in 1968 and afterwards. The exotic-but-White superhero—a symptom of internal colonization as Fernández L'Hoeste would argue—is tasked with mending the political thread of a country at the brink of political action and repression; a country that is met with a superhero that fails to avenge those massacred by their very own government. The reiteration of "It's all over" ("Ya terminó todo") suggests that if repeated as a mantra, one would suddenly be able to move on from the paradigm-shattering events and deaths that were produced in the climax of the film and in the climax of student protests. Alas, maybe that is too much to ask of the superhero, who within his archetypal confines is only really tasked with buttressing the structures of domination and inequity that are at the core of injustice.

No Contaban Con Su Astucia

Perhaps no other superhero is as universally known and loved by Latin American and Hispanic audiences as Roberto Gómez Bolaños's El Chapulín

Colorado. Unlike the wrestlers who often straddled genre boundaries, El Chapulín is cut from the same cloth as archetypal thoroughbred superheroes, perhaps explaining why he is the primary reference when the contemporary Latin American superhero is mocked (see *Mirageman*, *El Man*, and *Kryptonita*). Dressed in a characteristic red leotard and yellow shorts that mark his decidedly nonmuscular body, the Red Grasshopper appeared in over 256 episodes of a homonym television show that aired in more than seventeen countries between 1973 and 1979.

Like El Santo, an entire book could be dedicated to the character and series, tracing thematic lines across episodes and seasons.[68] But El Chapulín is of interest to us due to two main factors: the series is the first to establish itself consistently in the medium of television—seen by millions across the Spanish-speaking world on a weekly basis—and it situated the Latin American superhero within the narrative mode of parody. Films starring El Santo, Superzán, and Las Luchadoras were not parodic, though definitely cheesy due to their low production value and special effects. These two qualities set El Chapulín apart from its predecessors, and establish a narrative tradition for the Latin American superhero that will be retaken in future characters such as *El Man* and *Chinche Man*.

El Chapulín first appeared in a sketch in the comedy program *Los supergenios de la mesa cuadrada*, whose format was comprised of supposed letters from the public that the panelists then answered and debated. In an episode from November 1970, one such letter asks, "If the fearsome vampires really exist, how can you fight them?" ("¿Si en verdad existen los temibles hombre vampiros, cómo se les puede combatir?"). The vampires could of course be substituted with any of the baddies from Santo's films such as the mummies from Guanajuato, werewolves, or Martians (showing how pervasive the wrestler-superhero genre was in popular culture). The resounding answer is El Chapulín Colorado—and not a luchador—and thus was born a cultural phenomenon that persists to the present day.

Each episode is divided into a set of disconnected sketches that feature the protagonist in mundane situations. He is beckoned to help the layperson surmount everyday inconveniences or challenges, quite unlike the traditional superhero and his mission of universal justice; El Chapulín never fights Satanists bent on destroying modern civilization and rarely encounters alien invaders. The show is profoundly intertextual, building a referential network across genres such as the Western, science fiction, and musicals, and across literary works such as Don Quijote, Romeo and Juliet, Don Juan Tenorio, and El Conde Lucanor (Aguasaco 97). With a set of allies, and against a recurring group of antagonists, *El Chapulín*'s comedic value is appealing to a multitude of audiences across national and temporal boundaries.

Employing a theoretical framework built around the ideas of Marx, Laclau, and Althusser, Carlos Aguasaco argues that—on a broader level—the series "is an allegory of the level of development of the so-called 'national projects' in Latin America" ("es una alegoría del nivel de desarrollo de los llamados 'proyectos nacionales' en Latinoamérica"; 23), and that, "as a cultural product, the series represents a historical document of the state of the Mexican national project in the 1970s. Due to its place of enunciation, that is, as being a discourse coming from a position of hegemony, it serves within the structure in the process of ideological definition necessary in the consolidation of a national project" ("como producto cultural, la serie representa un documento histórico del estado del proyecto nacional mexicano en la década de los setentas. Por su lugar de enunciación, es decir por ser un discurso hecho desde una posición hegemónica en la estructura sirve, obviamente, en el proceso de determinación ideológica necesario en la consolidación de ese proyecto"; 141). In other words, the critic situates the production of the series at the tail end of the Mexican Miracle, that is, juxtaposed to the palpable issues of uneven development and prosperity that came as a side effect of rapid urbanization and industrialization.

The 1970s were a critical period in Mexican history. While the economy initially boomed, economic maladministration and a speculative climate created an unstable fiscal base characterized by foreign debt and capital flight. Some stability was gained from a renewed petroleum sector, but this too would later be an Achilles' heel in the eventual *década perdida* as an overreliance on oil and its price fluctuations would effectively tank the economy. The aftershocks of Tlatelolco were still felt, and were indeed amplified by a subsequent massacre of students on Corpus Christi in 1971.[69] Political tensions, a call for more civil liberties and increased electoral transparency were met in 1976 by the farcical election of José López Portillo who ran unopposed, winning 100% of the vote. The election of the PRI candidate demonstrated to Mexico and the world just how broken the political system was.

Commenting on the legacy of 1968, Roger Bartra signals that while "the revolution never arrived," the "ferocious efficiency of the repression of Tlatelolco was not able to stop those same wounds of defeat from receiving the seeds of a slow political transition. The authoritarian system was indeed injured, but the political putrefaction process lasted for twenty years" (136). The metaphor of decay is apropos, and combines well with Aguasaco's linking of the series to an economic paradigm that similarly lacked a sense of wholeness. In other words, the social, political, and economic paradigms from which El Chapulín emerges are of fragmentation, that is, they are best described as either in decomposition (as would be in the political theater) or as a sort of patchwork (in regards to socioeconomic developments).

Aguasaco further argues that El Chapulín materializes at a moment when the protectionist economy dissolves and Mexico enters a global(izing) stage (70). After all, no other country had so quickly hosted two premier international events, that is, the Olympics in 1968 and the football World Cup in 1970. But this is not necessarily steady footing, as it is well known that globalization is not a monolithic or unidirectional force, but rather a process characterized by tensile forces, multivariate calculations, and polydirectional lines of flight. Local cultural practices and artifacts do not simply disperse into a universal semiotic cloud of signs, iconographies, and narratives that smoothen cultures across the globe, but rather comingle and mutually interact with free-floating components of the global, cultural assemblage. Just as the Santo mask enters a global-cultural hierarchy—evoking a Mexican essence across a multitude of tableaus—it does not collapse within itself as a local reference in a long history and tradition of lucha libre. In other words, the global and local coexist in a perpetual tussle for visibility and dominance, even if the macro needle seems to point towards the global winning out.

The national cinema industry also underwent seismic changes in this period, as the government of Luis Echeverría Álvarez (López Portillo's precursor) maximized state support of film (which had been increasing since the 1960s). A generation of filmmakers bloomed during this period, including Jorge Fons and Jaime Humberto Hermosillo, and Mexico's reputation in the international circuit returned to glory as several films enjoyed critical acclaim. These advances, however, were tempered by several factors, including new policies enacted by López Portillo that hamstrung any structural changes by disinvesting the government from the industry. He also installed his sister, Margarita, as head of the Dirección General de Radio, Televisión y Cinematografía, who increased government censorship of films. Gains made in art, festival, and politically motivated cinema did not, furthermore, translate into box office sales, which, as Ramírez Berg and Ignacio Sánchez Prado signal, was dominated by Hollywood.

In fact, it is the ubiquity of Hollywood at the movies, and, by extension, North American television shows and pop culture icons in other arenas of consumer consumption that heavily factored into the poiesis of Gómez Bolaños's superhero. Looking back at the show, Gómez Bolaños comments that the character "was a critique, as Cervantes did so with Don Quijote, a critique of the excess of the chivalric novels of his time. In my time there is an excess of Supermen and Batmen and things like that; I wanted to frame a critique on the Mexican or Latin American level, that is, with little money, resources, and sensational inventions, weak, stupid . . . but very brave" ("era una crítica como hizo Cervantes con el Quijote, una crítica al exceso de novelas de caballería que había en su tiempo. En mi tiempo hay un exceso de Supermanes y Batmans y todas esas cosas; y yo quería hacer una crítica a nivel mexicano o latinoamericano, es decir con muy poco dinero, sin recursos, sin inventos sensacionales, débil, tonto . . . pero muy valiente"; Aguasaco 65). The excess of these Anglo superheroes is a symptom of Mexico's coming out on the global stage, as cultural artifacts and signifiers flow through the osmotic pores of the ideational frontier of the national, calling into question the very structure of the state. It is this tension, the dynamic dialectic between the global and local, that births El Chapulín. Unlike the wrestler-superhero films that copied Hollywood villains and plots that were then given a local flavor (see the monsters and villains in Santo films, or the protagonist of *La Mujer Murciélago*), El Chapulín surfaces in opposition to and in dialogue with its North American referents, as a delimited resistance to US cultural hegemony. While El Santo was a calque of similar Hollywood films—or mediator "between native culture and foreign hegemony" as Hegarty would argue (24)—El Chapulín is a direct adversary.

But El Chapulín is not the first parodic superhero in this global-local genealogy, even if he is the most popular one. Predating the appearance of the character in *Los supergenios* is El Aguila Descalza, a character created by Alfonso Arau and Héctor Ortega in comic books that appeared weekly in 1968, and that was later adapted to a homonym movie produced in 1969 and screened in 1971. The film is the first in Arau's star-studded career (which include *Como agua para chocolate* [1992]), and won various awards at the 1972 Ariel ceremony, including Best Actor, Best Screenplay, and Best Film. No other superhero film before or after *El Aguila Descalza* has gone on to win Mexico's most prestigious film award.

Starring Arau himself as the print protagonist, the reader learns (from the inside front cover of the comic) that he is "influenced by the superheroes from the comics that he avidly reads" ("influenciado por los superhéroes de las revistas de historietas que lee con avidez"), and that he invents "a modern Quijote, a secret character, through which he can heroically fight against evil and injustice" ("—cual moderno Quijote—una personalidad secreta, a través de la cual combate heroicamente el mal y la injusticia"). El Aguila will fight enemies "that embody our myths" ("que encarnan a nuestros mitos"), such as La Divina Garza, the Three Kings, and La Malinche, but also characters popular with comic book readers, such as La Mujer Araña and Nazis (that will be caricatured in *El Chapulín*). In the opening panels of the fourth issue of the comic, the reader is asked, "But, would you ask yourselves: Who is 'El Aguila Descalza'? WHO? WHO?" ("Pero, se preguntarán ustedes: ¿Quién es 'El Aguila Descalza'? ¿QUIEN? ¿QUIEN? [sic]"). Here, Arau and Ortega, like Gómez Bolaños later, link the local character to a global phenomenon, but also echo El Chapulín's financial limitations: "Is he but a poorman's Batman?" ("¿Es acaso el Batman de los pobres?"). The answer, like El Chapulín, is an autochthonous hero, one that can effectively operate within the constraints of everyday life in Latin America. He is decidedly not "a poorman's Batman" but "¡EL AGUILA DESCALZA!"

Arau and Ortega call to our attention the insufficiency of the North American hero in coping with the reality and uneven development of Latin America (as seen in *Niñas Araña* and the Enchufetv skits) in the following page, as the hero and his sidekick, "the amazing dog" ("el perro maravilla"), come to the rescue, swinging over rooftops from a rope a la Spiderman. The kinesthetic archetype, that is, the superhero traversing the urban space without the structural and systemic constraints of city planning and carefully delineated streams of movement, is only utopic in this Latin American city, as in the next panel, both characters smash into a wall (the sidekick exclaims, "I snurt my hout" ("Me hociqué el reventón"), that is, "I hurt my snout," evoking El Chapulín's iconic "¡Que no panda el cúnico!," a misspelt "Don't panic!" Perhaps superheroes can only fly or swing around a properly developed city, and not one stymied by poor construction. The metaphor of movement is clear, as unimpeded circulation is impossible in the under and unevenly developed microcosm of the national. Instead, the superhero mounts a bicycle, and "rides through the streets . . . at supersonic speed" ("cruza por las calles . . . a velocidad supersónica"). In the next panel, we see that "as good comic book heroes, they use the chimney to enter a building" ("como buenos héroes de historietas, se valen del tiro de la chimenea para entrar en el edificio"). Such tactics may work for superheroes in the fetishized domiciles of Metropolis, Gotham, or New York, but not in the polluted megacity of Mexico, as the two characters emerge coughing and with soot-darkened faces.

The mode of parody is clear in these opening pages, as the superhero reflects and refracts archetypes and tropes normalized in the North American genre, but rendered farcical at best when transposed to the local. The movie adaptation stars Arau as the superhero and supervillain, lending a sly wink to the early masked-hero movies that saw characters go through a rigmarole of masks and identities. The film juxtaposes Jonathan Eaglepass, a gangster from Chicago (who resembles the villains in the Superzán film), and Poncho, a working-class youth who moonlights as the superhero. The plot is simple and punctuated by various slapstick sequences and shots of Christa Linder in underwear: the Mafioso comes to Mexico to take control of a factory owned by Poncho's *patrón*, Don Carlos, that is really a front for drugs. El Aguila intervenes, saving his love interest (the boss's daughter) and the factory from the crooks, but in the end finds himself pursued by the police as the chief suspect.

The character is a solid adaptation from the comics, following the trope of the superhero as a bungling fool that achieves justice in spite of his own actions, a model that Gómez Bolaños will perfect along several seasons of *El Chapulín*. El Aguila's costume is more eclectic than the yellow leotard and shield in the shape of a heart; he wears a striped Nexaca soccer jersey over a leotard, a bullfighter's cape, work gloves, and a baseball cap worn backwards that doubles as a half-mask. As the comic specifies, "Each one of these gadgets, in addition to the giant brass buckle that sports his shield—an eagle with human feet—evoke different periods of his life, where he was, successively: a footballer, a wrestler, a bull fighter, a machinist, a baseball player and, finally, a superhero" ("Cada uno de estos adminículos, así como la fajilla con gigantesca hebilla de latón en la que aparece su escudo: un águila con pies humanos, recuerdan diversas épocas de su vida en las que pretendió ser, sucesivamente: futbolista, luchador, torero, maquinista, beisbolista y finalmente, superhéroe").

While the character bears resemblances to El Chapulín in terms of aesthetics and poietics, it bears highlighting that El Aguila (in the film and in the comic books) takes on missions that are more in line with the Santo films; that is, he is not a superhero mired in the humdrum of daily life, but rather intervenes in opposition to a villain with malicious designs. Arau, indeed, highlights this link, as several Santo comic books can be spotted in the film. El Aguila, then, soars not only from the adaptation of Batman and company to the Mexican condition, but also from the superhero-wrestler genealogy. In doing so, the film situates both local and global archetypes within a broader semiotics of the superhero, in a gesture that will be recycled in contemporary Latin American moving images. In saying all this, I want to suggest that the archetype followed, and eventually defined by, El Chapulín continues a poietic trend seen in the earlier El Aguila, a successful strategy in transposing the superhero genre to the Mexican and Latin American context.

Gómez Bolaños refines many aspects of the archetype, slowly perfecting a figure that will appeal to a broad audience that stands the test of time. Among these techniques we find the use of a standard Latin American Spanish that avoided regionalisms or a specific dialect (Aguasaco 232), and plot points crafted around universal figures (such as a housewife, judge, policeman, etc.). The sartorial parody present in El Aguila is further codified into an iconic costume, whose elements and outline were easily recognizable and exportable, paralleling the silver mask in its semantic potentials.

The principal elements of parody in *El Chapulín* lie in its refraction of North American tropes. The opening lines of every episode, for example, introduce the character as "more agile than a turtle; stronger than a mouse; more noble than a lettuce, his shield is his heart" ("más ágil que una tortuga; más fuerte que un ratón; más noble que una lechuga, su escudo es un corazón"). The cadence and syntax immediately remind us of the Superman intro ("faster than a speeding bullet . . . more powerful than a locomotive")—that was evoked and literally transcribed in the action in Superzán—but here the female voice resorts to parody, straightaway delineating the narrative mode of what is to come. The opening credits montage highlights his physique and buffoonery, guiding the viewer in reading the character as a distortion of the archetypal figures made familiar in print, cinema, and television. This, when combined with the inane missions in each sketch, effectively parodies each component of the definition of the superhero (costume, mission, and identity).

But these (implicit) elements are not the only parodic strategies employed in the series, as the character will explicitly compare himself with his North American counterparts. To do so, he often resorts to *albures* and other sexist jokes that "establish a new hierarchy . . . that places that Latin American male at the top of the structure" ("establece una nueva jerarquía . . . que pone al macho latinoamericano en la cima de la estructura"; Aguasaco 90). When he is not making snide and

Figure 1.8. An iconic costume for an iconic superhero.

homophobic remarks about Batman and Robin, or feminizing jokes about Superman's underwear-on-the-outside, El Chapulín resorts to infantilizing them (Aguasaco 91), again situating himself above the Anglo referents in a new and subversive hierarchy. In doing so, the character suggests that Batman and Superman are not macho enough to deal with the realities of Mexico/Latin America, again reinforcing the untranslatability of these characters to the local.

Taking stock of the entire series, we can see how Linda Hutcheon's observation that "parody is doubly coded in political terms: it both legitimizes and subverts that which it parodies" (*Politics* 101) plays out. This is evident in the gender roles and stereotypes inherent in the genre, which El Chapulín only exacerbates when he employs homophobic and sexist puns; *El Chapulín* in fact does not collapse or deconstruct the principal tenets of the superhero, but only reinforces them amid his tomfoolery.

There is, furthermore, no unequivocal investigation of the state elements and actors that are responsible for the underdevelopment that is pervasive in the character and his context. While the show pokes fun at the different cogs in the politicoeconomic system (such as a drunk judge in the very first episode, or the geriatric Dr. Chapatín who is a caricature of the inefficiency and corruption of the bureaucrat), there is no systemic takedown of the upper echelons of the PRI and its henchmen that brought about the civic and economic tensions of the 1970s. El Aguila, we must remember, is more critical of local characters and assemblages, as the entire plot about the factory critiques economic policies and corruption that prevented foreign ownership, while the actual name of the superhero (and his emblem) ridicules the national coat of arms (an eagle with bare human feet would be bitten by the rattlesnake). Though the lack of a specific critique of the government may be interpreted as Gómez Bolaños sidestepping censorship and making a product that was narratologically exportable, we may also argue than in doing so, the series upholds the conservative impulse in the genre; that is, the superhero addresses the symptoms but never the underlying cause of social inequity, crime, and injustice.

While treading carefully around the critique of the local, the series does, however, undertake a robust assessment of US-Mexico relations. This is metonymized in the Super Sam character, a superhero from the North who often impinges on El Chapulín's turf (even when the people he intends to help refuse, preferring a local superhero). Super Sam speaks a macaronic Spanish, wears an Uncle Sam top hat and beard, and a Superman costume that either has the emblematic "S" or a dollar sign, suggesting that his real superpower is his economic might (symbolized by the bag of money he carries with him at all moments). Aguasaco intimates that the character appears "to substitute for the impossibility of Batman or Superman appearing in the series" ("para suplir la imposibilidad de presentar a Batman o a Superman en la serie"; 91), suggesting that the character is a critique and parody not only of US policy in Latin America, but also of the superhero genre as cultural artifact. The parallelisms between the superhero body and the nation do not stop there, as Super Sam often competes with El Chapulín instead of working together, suggesting that both sets of relations are marked by "competitiveness and forced coexistence.... Super Sam is an invader who comes, armed with a bag of money, to import his ideology" ("la competividad y la convivencia forzada.... Super Sam es un invasor que viene a importar su ideología armado de una bolsa con dinero"; 91). El Chapulín as a local hero, therefore, coalesces and mounts a cultural and ideological challenge to US hegemony, all while poking fun at and parodying customs, quirks, and idiosyncrasies of the local.

Concluding Notes

The popularity of the Santo films and the airing of *El Chapulín* (though the character will continue in *Chespirito* sketches) came to a close in the turn of the decade, as volatile oil prices and structural faults in the Mexican economy gave way to the *década perdida*. The governments of Miguel de la Madrid and Carlos Salinas de Gortari implemented sweeping changes that restructured the economy and everyday life, ushering the country into the neoliberal age with the signing of NAFTA and entry into the GATT. These measures occurred amid a general climate of austerity and privatization, moving the country from a protectionist ISI economy to an open-market system that encouraged foreign direct investment.

In the cultural terrain, "the theme of crisis was definitively entrenched in the discourse of the lettered classes" ("el tema de la crisis se instaló definitivamente en el discurso de los sectores letrados"; Cabrera López 342), and saw radical changes in the distribution and consumption of the moving image. Sánchez Prado notes that the privatization of the cinematic ecosystem "led to major changes in the communities of spectatorship and in the social function of film" (6); that is, middle-class audiences who could sustain an industry—and who were estranged with the luchador and other genre films of the 1960s and 1970s—had to now be drawn back into the cinema hall. Instead of low-budget, kitschy films that had little plot depth, audiences now had to be cajoled with films that reflected what Sánchez Prado calls a neoliberal structure of feeling, attracting viewers through "displacements in the ideologies and aesthetics of cinema brought about by the economic changes in production and distribution" (6). In their wake, Mexican films turned to the romantic comedy and other genres that appealed to the middle and upper classes, while a general audience continued to consume whatever Hollywood sent south of the border. As Néstor García Canclini observes, "The relationship with the world seemed more prestigious than the local, as the media hurried to bring us what was filmed in Hollywood" ("la relación con el mundo parecía más prestigiosa que el arraigo en lo local a medida que las comunicaciones se apuraban a traernos lo que se filmaba en Hollywood"; 79).

Superhero aficionados were now enthralled with the 1980s boom of the Hollywood action film and its muscled stars, and the subsequent ubiquity of the superhero, first in the Warner Bros. Batman franchise of the late 1980s and 1990s, then in the 20th Century Fox X-Men features of the first decade of the 2000s, and the most recent blockbusters in the

Figure 1.9. El Presidente Dictador (the dictator president).

Marvel Cinematic Universe (and the DC films to a lesser extent). Superheroes in the neoliberal age are now outsourced, as the tensions between the global and local (which were at the crux of El Chapulín) have now been superficially smoothed out. If we were to solely go by gross box office performance, those calls for a local superhero vis-à-vis Super Sam have now gone mute, as Hollywood superhero films have dominated Mexican ticket sales in the last two decades.

That is only, however, a partial reading of the current status of the Mexican and Latin American superhero. El Chapulín is now freely available on demand through YouTube, while an animated version also circulates through television and online platforms. El Santo, too, was adapted to the animated format (presumably for a younger audience), appearing in a 2004 miniseries titled *Santo contra los clones*, while the life of Blue Demon was made into a television series in 2017. In popular culture, Santo and Blue Demon are still evoked as popular superheroes, ready to take on any super villain, including Donald Trump, who, in several T-shirts spied in a market—is referred to both as "the son of a bitch and his fucking wall" ("el hijo de la chingada y su pinche muro") and as "the dictator president" ("el presidente del terror") with a swastika behind him.[70] All this sets a course for the contemporary Latin American superhero that I study in the following chapters. While each arises from a specific sociocultural milieu and politicoeconomic substrate, they all express genetic traits of their Mexican ancestors to some degree or another.

Chapter 2

Urbanization and Its Discontents in *El Man, el superhéroe nacional*

The narrative and aesthetic mode of parody established by El Chapulín is pursued in *El Man, el superhéroe nacional* (2009), the fifth feature-length film by Colombian director Harold Trompetero, who also scripted and produced the movie. Trompetero has developed a comprehensive portfolio of films, television serials, and advertisements, earning awards in multiple festivals and categories. With an ensemble cast of well-known television, theater, and (comic) movie actors, *El Man* is a lighthearted comedy that translates the superhero genre to the Colombian context, a cultural horizon that has been dominated by audiovisual and literary depictions of the violence created by decades of civil conflict and the drug trade. One would initially assume that Trompetero's superhero would come out blazing against narcos from the Medellín cartel and the Fuerzas Armadas Revolucionarias de Colombia (FARC), but the injustices and enemies that interest El Man are somehow entirely different.

Trompetero's success may be read in tandem with Julián David Correa's assertion that Colombian cinema, along with other "minor" cinemas outside the relative behemoths of Mexico, Argentina, and Brazil, is currently undergoing a boom in terms of production and ticket sales (111–12). This is evidenced by the critical and commercial success of films such as *La vendedora de rosas* (1998), *La virgen de los sicarios* (2000), *Rosario Tijeras* (2005), *Los colores de la montaña* (2010), *El cartel de los sapos* (2011), and *El abrazo de la serpiente* (2015). Readers familiar with these films will recognize that violence is at their very thematic core, even if other issues (such as homosexuality and indigeneity) are tangentially explored. In this vein, Juana Suárez argues in her seminal overview that the thematics of contemporary productions may be explained by "the chronic violence that has plagued the country" (*Critical Essays* 1) since the decade-long period known as *La Violencia*. This time frame refers to a protracted sociopolitical violence and civil war rooted in the "Bogotazo" of 1948, stemming from the assassination of Jorge Gaitán, a popular candidate from the Liberal Party for the presidential elections. Súarez furthers that La Violencia is not a one-off event, but rather that there are several seismic reverberations afterwards, culminating in a generalized violence that is perpetrated by newer actors such as drug cartels. Suárez historicizes this argument by noting that "many recent occurrences in Colombia cannot be understood in isolation from certain complex events during *La Violencia*. . . . Traumas left in the wake of that period have played a crucial role in constructing the discourse of violence" (44).[1]

While this is true, especially given the cursory overview of the films just listed that have made waves in global cinema circuits, there are, however, a number of films made after 2010 that narrate "the romances and dramas of the urban middle class" ("los romances y los dramas de las clases medias de las ciudades"; Correa 113). This is evidenced in the commercial success of Trompetero's *El paseo* (2010), which spawned three sequels that broke box office records for a domestic film (Martínez Abeijon).[2] This broader trend, that is, of the popularity of comedy, can be seen as a symptom of socioeconomic shifts and their impact on the cultural landscape within Latin America as a whole (although to different extents in specific national contexts). This line of thinking follows Ignacio Sánchez Prado's assertion that comedy, and particularly romantic comedy, exemplifies the ideological and allegorical worldview of late neoliberalism (204). *El Man* can thus be lumped together with this swath of cinema that eschews serious political reflections or critiques of violence, harnessing comedy instead as a medium and mode to engage a variety of issues that linger in the background of contemporary Colombian cultural production.

The plot of *El Man* is similar to the other films explored in *Capitán Latinoamérica* in that the underdog becomes a superhero to avenge an injustice perpetuated by a metonymic social actor. The narrative unfolds in a city named Villarica, which is easily recognized as Bogotá. The (re)naming of the urban space evokes the renaming of New York City in US comics and films as a fictive yet easily identified space and milieu. The film begins with Felipe de las Aguas, a taxi driver, paying off the last installment on his taxi at a local bank. In making the final payment, he also regains the rights to his historic house that was held as collateral by the bank. Debt free and overjoyed, he and his mother are soon met by Federico Rico, a one-time neighbor who offers to buy the "sad and old house" ("triste y vieja casa") at, what he argues, is a very good rate. In addition to the cash paid out, he promises them a new unit in an apartment building he owns. Felipe's mother, however, explains that the house is not for sale, and that, even if it were, she would not exchange it for a "box of matches" ("caja de fósforos"). Felipe, however, sees an opportunity, and tries to later convince her of the many advantages of modern living. Though initially tempted by the proposition, Felipe later realizes that Federico's company (Camaleón Enterprises) is buying up all the properties in the neighborhood, and that his own is worth many times the 20 million pesos offered. An enraged Felipe returns to the barrio to see Rico's men attempting to evict the residents of a retirement home. With the help of one of the residents, El Coronel (his mother's geriatric boyfriend), he becomes El Man, and confronts Rico's henchmen. "Dressed in yellow, blue, and red—very patriotic—with underpants over his underwear" ("Vestido de amarillo, azul y rojo—muy patriota—, de calzoncillos por encima de una trusa"; Mayolo), El Man's only superpower is his religious fervor. In a narrative arc that includes a love interest (Angeluz de las Estrellas) and an older male mentor (El Coronel), El Man takes on Rico and his plans to demolish the historic district, displace its neighbors, and replace it and them with shopping malls and apartment buildings for a younger professional class of resident.

Figure 2.1. El Man, a patriotic superhero.

Trompetero explains the rationale behind writing and directing the first Colombian superhero character:

> I was fed up with the stories of drug trafficking, war and violence, and I said, why can't we make a different story about someone beautiful, a Colombian with a brave spirit. Then I started looking at the taxi drivers, the people who have to look everywhere to be able to get ahead. In the common people we find wonderful things. The story evolved until it became El Man.
>
> (Estaba mamado de las historias de narcotráfico, guerra y violencia, y dije, por qué no podemos hacer una historia diferente sobre alguien bonito, un colombiano con ese espíritu "echado pa lante." Entonces empecé a mirar los taxistas, a la gente que se las tiene que rebuscar por todo lado para poder salir adelante. En la gente común están las cosas maravillosas. La historia fue evolucionando hasta que se convirtió en El Man; Mayolo)

Note the contrarian nature of the poietics of the film; that is, Trompetero fashions El Man in reaction to the audiovisual zeitgeist of narcos and armed conflict. The film is reflexive of the broader horizon of contemporary Colombian cultural production, preferring to align itself instead with a tangent that leaves aside popular portrayals and archetypes of a national tableau.[3]

Trompetero is also cognizant of the impressions a local hero may have on a domestic viewing public. He adds, "When I proposed to film a superhero story, everybody mocked me and annoyed me by saying, Will he have a hat?, Will he have a poncho?, and I said no, inside every Colombian there is a superhero. Then I put myself to the task of taking that idiosyncrasy of that awesome man and put it there. That is why it is credible and believable" ("Cuando propuse hacer una historia de superhéroes todo el mundo se me burló y me molestaron diciendo: ¿va a tener sombrero?, ¿va a tener ruana?, y yo digo no, dentro de cada colombiano hay un superhéroe. Entonces me puse en la tarea de coger esa idiosincrasia del hombre verraco y la puse ahí. Por eso es verosímil y creíble"; Mayolo). The believable and plausible part of his answer is up for debate (and I will develop this later), but his decision to avoid idiosartorial characteristics in favor of a now-universal attire for the superhero is reflective of

Latin American superheroes adapting and evolving from North American archetypes. The leotard, cape, emblem on the chest, and underwear on the outside are unambiguous vestiges of Superman, whereas the half-face mask evokes (the also North American) Zorro.[4]

El Man is a calque (and not a copy), attired in the colors of the nation's flag and deploying original superpowers that are quite unusual, even within the global superhero universe. He does not have superhuman strength, speed, or vision; neither can he harness energy fields, control the minds of others, or manipulate the elements. The actor who plays the superhero, Bernardo García, explains:

> The Man is a guy who only has one power: faith. He is a person who is capable of believing over any vicissitude, that it is possible to change the destiny of things if we really feel that we can. He is a superhero, as there are hundreds in Colombia, only he is a guy who dared to fight against something that was not right, as everyone should do.
>
> (El Man es un tipo que solo tiene un poder: la fe. Es una persona que es capaz de creer por encima de cualquier vicisitud, que es posible cambiar el destino de las cosas si realmente sentimos que podemos. Es un superhéroe, como hay cientos en Colombia, sólo que es un tipo que se atrevió a luchar contra algo que no estaba bien, como todo el mundo debería hacerlo; Mayolo)

His faith is the only power he has, and we first see it appear in the confrontation with the henchmen evicting the seniors. Standing atop the building, he threatens the bad guys who simply laugh off the admonishments coming from an implausible joker wearing yellow spandex. But then El Man prays for divine intervention, and a swift thunderstorm pours down, lighting striking the goons employed by Rico, scaring them off and saving the day.

Trompetero's disdain for stories about drug trafficking, war, and violence and the far-fetched nature of the protagonist's powers would, at first glance, suggest that the film is a light comedy that is ethically and politically disengaged; a low-budget parody that makes no serious intervention in the cultural landscape. This reading, as the audience may suspect, is a superficial gloss of the film, as I believe the archetypes and structure of the genre suggest otherwise. The Latin American superhero, after all, arises from and engages in distinct politicoethical predicaments that outlay a cogent and cohesive engagement with issues that dominate the contemporary cultural conversation. The superhero as a force of righteousness takes on the enemy who metonymizes issues stemming from the recent history of the particular national context. While Federico and Camaleón Enterprises are neither narcos nor guerrilla fighters, they do embody the sinister mechanisms behind a late capitalist, neoliberal episteme that has brought about important spatial and demographic changes. These changes, furthermore, are localized in the nondiegetic reference of Villarica, that is, the capital city of Bogotá.

Issues of space and spatiality are a primary concern in contemporary Colombian audiovisual production. Aside from the movies I discuss throughout this chapter, a quick perusal of the music videos of some of the country's most popular singers demonstrates how these artists choose to resemanticize the spaces of Colombia from that of violence to something else. In Carlos Vives's "La tierra del olvido," the viewer is taken on a picturesque journey through some of the country's most striking rural landscapes, while in his feel-good collaboration with Shakira, "La bicicleta," the northern coastline and its joie de vivre is highlighted. Other artists have instead chosen to renegotiate the urban spaces that were the setting for some of the most violent conflicts resulting from the drug wars. J Balvin's hypnotic "Mi gente," for example, opens with gorgeous panoramic images of Medellín, and paints the city as a hip and artsy space for dancers and famed Instagram influencer Gianluca Vacchi to move to the beat. Some international artists have followed this trend, that is, of imagining Colombia along parameters that exclude violence. The most notable case is of American band Pillar Point in their video for "Dove" where Kia LaBeija, a queer, biracial, and HIV+ visual artist and dancer struts through the streets of Bogotá. All in all, it is fair to say that the spatial imaginary of Colombia is going through a radical change away from violence (even if such television series as *Narcos* and *Perdida* are resoundingly popular with global audiences).

Writing on a body of films set in the city from the mid-1990s to the mid-2000s, Suárez affirms that "a large part of the attention shown . . . derives from the transformations that were initiated by mayors Antanas Mockus (1995–1997) and Enrique Peñalosa (1998–2000). During these administrative periods, Bogotá became a type of urban laboratory for projects of cultural agency . . . and for rethinking public space"

("Decentering" 51; also see Jaramillo Morales 67). In analyzing *La gente de la Universal* (1993), *Soplo de vida* (1999), *Perder es cuestión de método* (2004), and *La historia de baúl rosado* (2005)—all noir films—Suárez focuses on the disappearance of the traditional *centro*, the historic heart of the city, in the face of economic change that precipitates the rethinking of public space in a neoliberal climate. She argues that these films, instead, attempt to reincorporate the *centro* into the human geography of the city, showing how the space's transformation is "strongly linked to corruption, extortion, and the mechanisms of powerful economies that arise outside the law" (50).

The processes of urban change seen in these films (and in *El Man*) reflects the redevelopment of the urban imaginary upwards and away from the traditional nucleus of the historic center, representative of the shift towards a neoliberal economy and model of cityspace that leads inevitably to the creation of the megacity, or, as Manuel Castells understands it, "discontinuous constellations of spatial fragments, functional pieces, and social segments" (407). Bogotá in these films is less a capital, or central administrative, economic, and political space, and more a city undergoing rapid development at the hands of global markets. This new city, in a sense, reflects Edward Soja's theorizing of contemporary urbanity, "a form and process of political governance, economic development, social order, and cultural identity that involve[s] not just one urban settlement or node but many articulated together in a multilayered meshwork of nodal settlements or city-centered regions" (13). This is evident in Federico's plans for the houses in the neighborhood: instead of being residential units in a traditional barrio born from colonial and postcolonial settlement, he intends to resurface the urban center as a conglomeration of spatial nodes characterized by commercial, residential, and administrative units. In other words, the city that Rico promises is a matrix of microcities, demarcated along class lines, within an unending sprawl that delinks the urban from the historical.

The fragmentation of the urban is the product of a long history of economic engineering and its resultant social impact in Colombia. In the 1960s, the government adopted Lauchlin Currie's notion of accelerated economic development, which "led to the extensive dispossession and displacement of the *campesino* population in specific areas of the country" (Brittain 337). Currie argued that the "removal of the 'underutilised' rural population from the countryside to the urban centres of the nation would enhance the economic development of Colombia" (337).[5] As James Brittain argues, this strategy involved the "consolidation of the accumulation process through the monopolization of agricultural centres by a few agribusiness capitalist enterprises" (342). By the 1970s, the urban population of Bogotá (and other large cities) continued to grow due to the changes in labor conditions and market demand; by the twenty-first century, Bogotá is one of the densest cities in the world, and the fifth largest in the America in terms of overall population. The capitalist project of appropriating land use and ownership provokes a massive urbanization and sprawl of the city, leading to the development of low-cost tenements, and the increasing segregation of the population in class-conscious ghettoes. With the agglomeration of commodities and their corresponding bodies and ideologies comes a resurfacing of space; when this happens in large urban cities, the affluent erect gated neighborhoods and exclusive apartment blocks. This, after, all is the narrative crux of *El Man*, as Federico wants to transform the historic neighborhood into a residential-commercial complex for the upper class, relocating the current neighbors to apartment buildings he has built elsewhere.

Though the majority of the film is shot in the same barrio, Trompetero goes on a visual road trip about halfway through the narrative. After El Man defeats Rico's henchmen in their attempt to evict the seniors, the neighbors receive a notification from the bank that the appraised value of their property has increased 300 percent. As such, they are now required to pay a higher tax rate, an absurd amount of money that is due in only a month. The mortified group realizes that this increase is the result of corruption, as the letter ends with a note to the recipient that they should consult Camaleón Enterprises for a loan or sell the property. El Coronel declares that El Man should come to the rescue (and Angeluz echoes this request), but Felipe is unconvinced. He gets in his taxi and goes for a drive to clear his thoughts. It is in this montage that Trompetero reveals the broader scope of the resurfacing of the neighborhood along Rico's insidious plans. Stopping at a gas station, Felipe sees a poor family walking along with their belongings. They are disheveled, their clothing suggesting that they are new arrivals from the countryside. Tragic music accompanies the dialogueless montage, as the camera follows Felipe in this flaneur-by-car itinerary away from his neighborhood. Next, he spies an adult woman poking away at the garbage. She is unwashed and homeless, the organic waste of others being her only subsistence. The camera focuses on Felipe's face, as he is visibly anguished by her predicament. He stops at a red light, and a young boy quickly cleans his windows. When the smiling youth comes to the driver's-side window, he scratches his stomach, indicating hunger, and our goodhearted protagonist gives him an apple. The vignettes serve not only to portray Felipe as a caring and empathic character (a requisite for any superhero seeking audience buy-in in the Latin American cinematic ecosystem) but to also demonstrate the stark results of urbanization and sprawl. These anonymous characters today may very well be Felipe and his neighbors tomorrow, displaced and disenfranchised by the economic interests of Federico and Camaleón Enterprises. The final shot of the montage is by night, as the camera now follows the taxi as it makes its way through the meandering Avenida Circunvalar in the outskirts of the city. In the background, we see the illuminated city and can identify two important characteristics: vertical growth seen by the high-rise apartments alongside the road; and the specter of sprawl evoked by the unending city lights.

Felipe returns from this detour to see that Camaleón has evicted the seniors and taken hold of the residence. Angered by this act—and presumably by the injustice he has witnessed throughout the city—he decides to retake the costume and mask and to fight Federico. I want to pause here and go back to the montage, as the final shot of the Avenida Circunvalar evokes a critical scene in another film about urban change in Bogotá: *Buscando a Miguel* (2007) by Juan Fischer.[6] While *El Man* and the films Suárez identifies pose a resistance to the decentering of the *centro*, *Buscando a Miguel* takes multilayered and polydirectional urban growth—or simply neoliberal cityspace—in Bogotá as a fait accompli, posing instead a study of how this space conjugates new social relations among its displaced residents.

The title character, Miguel, hails from a wealthy family and has his sights set on a successful career in politics. His character serves as a segue into a critique of contemporary Colombian sociopolitics, where corruption, gangs, and urban violence serve as the interstitial fluid between disparate social groups. Miguel's plans, however, are dealt a swift blow as his libido makes him a target for a gang of urban conmen who lure him into a trap with the sexual charms of a female member who sedates him. He manages to escape their van but then falls prey to an attack by a band of juvenile miscreants who leave him naked and disoriented. Another gang comes upon him, and they try to kill him to then sell his cadaver in the international black market for corneas and other organs. They beat Miguel with a pipe—causing the amnesia that leads to the film's title—but he luckily escapes. The plot and the viewer thus are asked to find Miguel, to reconstitute his body and mind as a whole subject. This search will take the once privileged body through the various (invisible) layers of a society and city that has undergone rapid and irrevocable change.

The film begins by connecting the title character with the city—Miguel looks over the balcony of his lush residence one morning and practices a political speech he will deliver later in the day. He recites, "I come to this neighborhood forgotten by the government, forgotten by the administration, forgotten by some politicians to tell them that I am going to work. . . . That's why I'm here. . . . That's why I'm here" ("Vengo a este barrio olvidado por el gobierno, olvidado por la administración, olvidado por algunos políticos a decirles que yo sí voy a trabajar. . . . Por eso estoy aquí. . . . Por eso estoy aquí"). The streets he addresses—treated as a character through the strategic apostrophe—are depicted in the opening images of the film's credits as a car makes its way to his house in the suburbs. These images situate his mansion in the suburbs, in the sprawl and segmentation seen in *El Man*, evocative of "the tendency to suburbanization, with the formation of a diffuse, low density peri-urban area, which prolongs the metropolis in all directions in which this is possible" ("la tendencia a la suburbanización, con la formación de un periurbano difuso, de baja densidad, que prolonga la metrópolis en todas direcciones en que ello es posible"; Mattos 51). The meandering trajectory of the car, read in connection with Miguel's soliloquy, underlines the new urban reality, where unequal and unbalanced development and resemanticization (which is at the core of *El man*) sets the stage for what Jesús Martín-Barbero calls "topographic discrimination" ("discriminación topográfica") (22). The barrio in *El Man* will be for the exclusive use of high-wealth residents, whereas the layfolk who currently live there will be moved to poorer neighborhoods.

In later scenes—where Miguel establishes some sort of stability after the series of attacks—*Buscando* goes to great lengths to demythify the promise of neoliberal growth, showing just how modern skyscrapers coexist and are juxtaposed with rudimentary and economically poor spaces, reflective of Alejandra Jaramillo Morales's claim that in Bogotá "modernity and postmodernity live together" ("conviven modernidad y premodernidad"; 31). These shots are well distributed along *Buscando a Miguel*, and serve to remind the audience of the evolving nature of the urban, no longer as "the spectacle of order [evoked by the image of the center in El Man], of a logical cartography . . . but rather the spectacle of a circus that assembles and dismantles" ("el espectáculo de un orden [evoked by the image of the *centro* in *El Man*], de una cartografía con sentido ... sino más bien el espectáculo de un circo que monta y desmonta"; Cruz Kronfly 208). In several shots without dialogue, we see Miguel peering out of a moving car, not unlike Felipe in the montage I highlight above, guiding our perspective between the images and spaces of poverty and the vertical symbols of economic growth.

The latter is captured in subsequent panning and setting shots that provide a generalized view of the many skyscrapers that dot the city's panorama. One particular image, of a naked and disoriented Miguel after an attack, is striking. We see the character walking along a thoroughfare in the mountainous periphery, his naked body contrasted with a brightly lit skyscraper, laying bare or naked, so to speak, the ethos of the city that the film attempts to capture. The city is no longer defined by the *centro*, or the need to reconstitute it, as is the case of *El man* and the films Suárez identifies, but by this single, undifferentiated urban tower that metonymizes neoliberal urbanity. The image is important in that it is shot from the same Avenida Circunvalar that Felipe traverses in his taxi, linking both films in terms of aesthetics and politics: the dialectic of the subject (Miguel and Felipe) vis-à-vis the changing city is at the core of both films.

In a later scene, immediately after Miguel is rescued and begins to look for his identity and memory, the film provides us with a panning image of the city. Shot from a high point of view, the shot does not necessarily stress the height of one particular building but instead highlights an overall sense of verticality to the city as multiple towers enter the frame. Each grouping of buildings agglomerate apartments, malls, and office space not unlike the development Federico hopes to erect in *El Man*. The image seems to stress verticality as a symbol of modernity, yet paradoxically can be read in tandem with the scenes immediately prior and after. Miguel's search for identity is linked to the panning shot that emphasizes a lack of urban center, as each node is its own microcity, a center within a sprawling constellation of urbanized growth. By panning over the many centers represented by the skyscrapers, the film effectively transposes the lack of a *centro* with the protagonist's amnesia. The conclusion of the film seems to support this reading, as Miguel never fully recovers his past life, just as the city of Bogotá—also a character in the film with a real body and history—is never able to reclaim its lost center. This contrasts with the careful optimism of *El Man*, where urban reshuffling is still a contested act.

A film that is perhaps more similar to the ethos of *El Man* is Sergio Cabrera's *La estrategia del caracol* (1993). The film is centered on the topics of urban renewal and displacement, as a group of neighbors—faced with an eviction notice akin to Federico's tactics—decide to simply upend their building and resettle in the idyllic outskirts of the urban; the film's title thus evokes the snail that takes its home with it. Ending with an iconic long shot, we see all the pieces of the building ready for reassembly, next to a proud and large Colombian flag swaying with Bogotá in the background. The drive towards reconstitution, as seen in the search for Miguel in the previous film, is presented in a more positive light, as the film suggests an eventual "rebuilding" of the (imagined) community outside the chaos of the urban. Jaramillo Morales groups this film with Felipe Aljure's *La gente de la Universal* (1993) (and I would include *El Man*) as films that "present caricaturesque typologies of Bogotá, in which the chaotic vision of the urban space and the image of the odd jobs are evident, of the survival that overwhelms the inhabitants of the capital" ("presentan tipologías caricaturescas de Bogotá, en las que se evidencian la visión caótica del espacio urbano y la imagen del rebusque, de la sobrevivencia que agobia a los capitalinos"; 52).

The verticality of the urban is a secondary concern in *La estrategia*, evoked only in the extreme long, setting shots that situate the narrative in the city. The film, in fact, opens with one such image, as Bogotá is presented as the macrospace in which the plot unfolds. The eviction of the residents of the building located in the historic *centro* (not unlike the nursing home in *El Man*) can be read as iterative of a wider rebuilding that has resulted in the expansive city we are asked to digest in the opening image. The long shot provides an important context to a film that is otherwise localized in the *centro*, and reminds the viewer that the cityspaces framed within the narrative are actually quite secondary or even at the risk of disappearing when juxtaposed to the vertical towers that dot the landscape. The film suggests that this cycle of urban renewal-displacement-settlement is also part of an inevitable continuum: the angle chosen in the long shot clearly poses a line of buildings, suggesting a timeline in which we can locate the demolition. Growth is seen as inevitable, even if the denouement of the plot suggests otherwise as the neighbors are set on rebuilding their home at the outskirts of the city.

In the concluding sections of the film, and as the developer and local officials come to evict the tenants, the neighbors blow up the facade of the building—all that is left is its outer shell, the inside cannibalized and transported to the outskirts. In slow motion, the camera zooms in on a message left for the corrupt city officials behind the crumbling: "Here you have your fucking painted house" ("Ahí tienen su hijueputa casa pintada"). The message, when read with the final images of the community gathering jovially as a narrator proclaims that the task of rebuilding is at hand, can be interpreted as an affront to uninhibited demolition as portrayed at the conclusion of *Buscando a Miguel*. The location of the new settlement, however, invites reflection. The camera tracks a young boy (responsible for detonating the fuses that blow up the facade in the earlier scene) on a bicycle making his way up a hill where the new development is to take place. He joins the band of neighbors conveniently posing around an out-of-place Colombian flag, celebrating as they have seemingly won out over the officials and corrupt real estate developer. As he joins the group and the off-camera narrators take over, the camera zooms out, revealing the location of the new site in the foreground with the towering landscape of Bogotá immediately behind. More specifically, the residence will be rebuilt at the periphery of the periphery, at the very edges of Bogotá's sprawl. The horizontal nature of the urban, a characteristic tangentially suggested by the panning images of *Buscando*, is at the heart of any concluding thesis of *La estrategia*; you can run, but you cannot hide from the inevitability of urbanity, even if the kitschy flag-waving celebrations may suggest otherwise. Like *Buscando* and *La estrategia*, *El Man* conceptualizes and problematizes the redevelopment of the barrio, highlighting the ways in which the superhero genre may conjugate the competing interests of the good (El Man and the residents) and the bad (Federico and the capitalist enterprise).

Becoming the Hero

Now that we have established the source of villainy in the film, and what this captures within a broader matrix of cultural production, I want to draw us to the other side of the dyad, that is, the hero. Specifically, I want to focus on his becoming, the moment that Felipe adopts the persona of El Man to challenge the threat posed by Federico and Camaleón Enterprises. Origin stories are intrinsic to any superhero narrative, and tend to emerge in the hero's first appearance or recurrently across multiple story lines and artifacts (in print, media, film, etc.). They are some of the most well-known and controversial aspects of any character, seemingly in perpetual retelling if the hero enjoys a long shelf life or is rebooted to reflect the interests of studios or the changing of cultural epistemes.

In *Superhero Origins*, Robin Rosenberg provides a schema for the seeds of the superhero narrative. She notes that "origin stories are often tales of transformation—stories in which a pivotal event, or set of events, sets us on a particular path in life" (2).[7] The critic observes that, "A fictional origin story begins by telling us something about a character . . . before the character is transformed. Then an origin story tells us about the pivotal events that initiate the transformation. The significant event usually involves adversity of some kind" (2). This trajectory is at the structural base of *El Man*: in the first scenes we learn of Felipe's trade, character, and economic condition, while the arrival of Federico and his desire to purchase the house is the catalyst for the transformation. The pivotal event itself, however, is the attempted eviction of the seniors from the home. It is in this scene that El Coronel takes Felipe aside and shows him the costume that he had fashioned to one day accompany the latter's mother to a costume party. Felipe at first refuses the outfit, deigning the very idea of becoming a superhero ridiculous and farfetched. El Coronel, however, counters that great men (and not women, of course) have always risen in the face of adversity for the greater good. He cites Gandhi, Jesus, Che Guevara, Martin Luther King, Abraham Lincoln, and Don Quijote as examples of heroes; he even includes El Chapulín in this list, signaling El Man's principal antecessor and inspiration in the genealogy of Latin American superheroes. Importantly, El Chapulín is the *only* superhero he references, thus situating El Man in a distinctly local lineage, which is, however, inflected by its parodic relationship to the North American hero-type. Felipe argues that he doesn't have weapons or superpowers, but El Coronel retorts that he has faith: he gives him a blessed medal that finally convinces Felipe to wear the costume and to rise above for the greater good.

Rosenberg nuances the qualities of the origin story by noting that there are, in broad terms, two types of transformation: "(1) the transformation of the protagonist into a *hero*, if he or she wasn't beforehand; (2) the transformation viz. *special powers*, in which the character develops, discovers, masters, and/or decides to use special powers over the course of the origin story" (4). The former is applicable in Felipe's case, as he effectively lacks powers and only becomes a hero when—in costume— he takes on Rico's thugs. Just as they are about to batter the front door down, fireworks and (nondiegetic) triumphant music accompany El Man as he confronts the bad guys "in the name of the Divine Baby Jesus" ("en nombre del Divino Niño"). He wields two sparklers in exaggerated martial arts movements to seemingly scare off the antagonists, but all he manages is to gather the admiration of the neighbors who look on amazed—the bad guys, however, mock the skinny superhero and continue to batter the door. El Coronel launches fireworks to distract them, while a renewed El Man throws firecrackers to scare them off. The pyrotechnics, however, have little effect on the workers, leading El Man to resort to his one superpower: prayer. His words are answered in the form of a flash thunderstorm and lightning that strikes at the antagonists. They run away in fear and the neighbors and El Man rejoice, having luckily won the first battle over Camaleón.[8]

Essential to the origin moment—the distinct instance of becoming—within the origin story is the process of individuation, that is, when the superhero is publicly named, introduced into the sociopolitical milieu as a *super* actor capable of defending the good against the bad. The origin moment occurs within the origin story, but is distinct in that it is the instance in which an identitarian gesture is made in the narrative, narratologically separating the before from the after, both within the hero's psyche

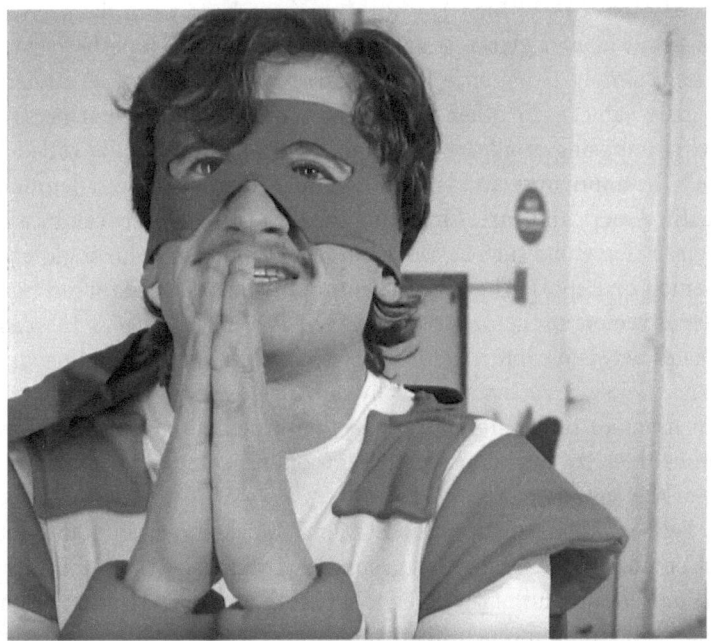

Figure 2.2. Faith as a distinctively local superpower.

and the public's knowledge of the superhero. Origin moments provide viewers with important vectors that serve as a substrate for ideological and ethical analysis, as it situates the superhero within the broader storyworld, thus permitting the metaphorical analysis that is demanded by the genre. The origin moment occurs in *El Man* immediately after the protagonist's first victory. Standing triumphant over his convened admirers, the camera focuses on individual members of the multitude who react to his heroics. Angeluz calls him a "divine daddy" ("papacito divino") that she wants to get married to, whereas another female admirer pronounces in a sultry tone that he "is a superhero" ("es un superhéroe"). In naming him as a superhero, other members of the crowd engage in an exercise of nomenclature; one says that he is "just like Batman" ("igualito a Batman"), while others evoke Aquaman, He-Man, Spiderman, and Superman. Importantly, they compare him to these American characters through the use of the verb *ser* (with the exception of Batman), meaning that he *is* Aquaman et al. and not *like* them. In other words, he is a pirated version of the superhero from the North, a local copy that lacks a singular identity. El Coronel, however, knowing that a hero needs to forge a unique name if he is to be successful, interjects to the crowd's approval and celebration that he "is El Man" ("es El Man"), a new superhero born from the barrio. His name, while at first glance is an appropriation of the superhero nomenclature, is simply a reference to the slang term of "el man" as a reference to a male subject. In other words, the naming of his super-persona is not very imposing at all, analogous to a US superhero being called "The Dude." The anonymity and laity of his super identity is also a leitmotif in the Latin American genre, furthering the idea that anybody can be a hero, as seen in characters such as Menganno and Zenitram (who could equally be Zemog or Zepol). They start chanting his name—recognition being a principal vector in the origin moment of the superhero—as the camera alternates between capturing him in elated glory atop the building and the audience below, focusing specifically on Angeluz sending him kisses. The origin moment thus culminates with the presentation of Angeluz as his amorous interest, an important (though often neglected) complementary facet of the superhero.

Felipe's transformation into El Man is quick and early in the feature. It lacks mystery or extensive background, as Trompetero keeps the narrative in the present instead of diverting to a past that may serve as an originary trauma or defining moment that would suggest that Felipe was somehow destined to become El Man. Instead, it is through a series of fortunate accidents and the materializing of a threat in the form of Federico that serves to coalesce the factors around the origin moment of El Man. The film is thus more preoccupied with the actions of the superhero proper and not so much the personal/social conditions that may have led to his becoming; what is of import in *El Man* is the protagonist's fight against Rico and the agents of capitalist reurbanization, and not the economic and political conditions that lead to the very idea of Camaleón purchasing and rezoning the barrio. The film, therefore, stands in contrast to other films such as *Mirageman* that place a greater emphasis on the past and how this may conjugate the hero in the present.

The Superhero and Challenging Masculinities

All this is not to say, however, that the film is not preoccupied with the issues facing the socially mimetic characters and structures of the storyworld, as, after all, it is the predatory nature of Camaleón Enterprises that triggers Felipe's transformation into El Man. Once he is established as a superhero with a costume, questionable superpowers, and a love interest, Trompetero turns our attention to the defining characteristic of the superhero—the presence of a tangible and well-developed villain.

Writing on the origins of the superhero genre, Peter Coogan argues that there are five essential types of supervillains: "the monster, the enemy commander, the mad scientist, the criminal mastermind, and the inverted-superhero supervillain" (*Superhero* 61).[9] Coogan adds that, "just as a hero represents the virtues and values of a society or culture, a villain represents an inversion of those values" (61). Supervillains, however, are not simple metonyms of the ethically cruel or suspect, but rather play an important narratological role in the genre in that they have "the ability to enact that inversion, to bring the normal activities of a society to a halt and force a hero to arise to defend those virtues" (61). This is plainly evident in the becoming sequence of *El Man*, as it is Federico—the supervillain—who catalyzes the crisis in the neighborhood and primes the conditions for Felipe to become El Man.

In which archetypal mold does Federico fit? It bears mentioning that these five categories "are non-exclusive, that is, a supervillain like Spider-Man's foe the Lizard is both a monster and a mad scientist" (Coogan 61).[10] Through simple observation, it is evident that he is neither a monster, a mad scientist, nor an inverted-superhero. He is also not a criminal mastermind, as his end game is not criminality for its own sake outside the law, but rather capital accumulation through the operations of a legal, capitalist enterprise. Federico is in effect an enemy commander as he "has the resources of a state behind him and is in a position of legal authority within that society" (63). He operates from within the (corrupt) machinations of the state and its actors, enlisting local politicians and the police when it comes to evicting tenants, and the bank (as institution) when it comes to raising property taxes by 300 percent to price the current owners out of the neighborhood. While the enemy commander may "be the king, tyrant, dictator, or other absolute ruler," Federico follows the second acceptation of the term; that is, he is "the true power behind the throne" (63), his financial might overshadowing the electoral process and any other claims to rights by the citizenry. The neoliberal enemy commander thus operates outside the parameters of the democracy, as a member of a hegemonic super class that endures the politicoeconomic fluctuations of the nation.

While Federico metonymizes late-capitalist accumulation, urbanization, and disenfranchisement on a macro level—all of which are processes that provoke the ontological transformation of Felipe—he also codes for an antagonical intimate position vis-à-vis the superhero. Some supervillains closely resemble their adversaries in physical traits and powers; such is the case of Trompo and the Zanates in *Capitán Centroamérica*. In other cases, the supervillain is constructed and portrayed in clearly distinct terms. Such is the case in the Batman-Penguin dyad, where a stout, short, and unmuscular bad guy stands in stark contrast to the toned physique of Bruce Wayne. The converse is true in *El Man*, as the superhero's skinny, short frame and unremarkable clothing choices are contrasted with the tall, commanding build and power suits of the supervillain. In essence, Felipe (as taxi driver *and* as El Man) is phenotypically antonymic to Federico the supervillain.

This typing of the two characters is important, as it evokes Jeffrey Brown's ideas on the superhero parody, which he argues is a "relatively overlooked" aspect of the film genre (132). Importantly, Brown identifies how superhero parodies initiate a conversation on how the genre participates in the popular creation of gender stereotypes. Superhero scholarship, after all, has largely focused on issues of the portrayal and transmission of political and gender ideologies.[11] The male-dominated nature of these films naturally results in them working through issues of masculinity (and to a much lesser extent, femininities and queerities). The genre's linkage to gender is inescapable, as its narratological base explicitly evokes not only the becoming of the superhero, but also the public performance of his gender position. Brown summarizes this in noting that the "obsessional focus in the films on the moment that the regular man becomes the superhero is a ritualized presentation of masculinization. The shift from 'less-than-ordinary' to 'extraordinary' masculinity is literally and symbolically written onto the hero's body" (134). El Man's performance of gender is inevitable and unavoidable in the moment he puts on the mask and the yellow spandex that accentuates his lack of musculature and height.

The problematics of masculinity are at the core of the superhero genre, and are particularly pronounced in the parodic subgenre. Brown continues in this line of thinking:

> Given the superhero film genre's overwhelming concern with models of hegemonic masculinity, it comes as no surprise that the central premise of contemporary superhero parodies is the substitution of a typically heroic male lead with a figure of failed masculinity. Where the mainstream superhero film has the wimpy male transform into a paragon of heroic masculinity, the parodies deny the physical transformation. The less-than-ideal male becomes the less-than-ideal superhero. This change in the superhero's level of masculinity allows the parodies to offer up a critique of the traditional hegemonic masculinity at the core of the genre. But, for the most part, the critique of masculinity is only superficial and even the parodies ultimately reinforce our cultural conceptions of heroism and masculinity. (139)

There is much to unpack in this analysis. First, Brown is evoking Raewyn Connell's seminal theories on hegemonic masculinity. In quick strokes, Connell erects a "gender structuring of practice" (*Masculinities* 73), wherein a matrix of masculinities contours social interactions. Masculine expression is here structured in an organizational chart revolving around four distinct types: hegemonic, complicit, subordinate, and marginalized masculinities. Hegemonic masculinity describes "how particular groups of men inhabit positions of power and wealth, and how they legitimate and reproduce the social relationships that generate their dominance" (Carrigan et al. 179). It is an apical gender expression that controls subjectivities, bodies, and performance; it controls what is deemed acceptable and what is expelled into the realm of taboo. Connell's complicit masculinities, in turn, are "constructed in ways that realize the patriarchal dividend, without the tensions or risks of being the frontline of troops of patriarchy" (*Masculinities* 79); complicit masculinities may passively enjoy the injustice of patriarchy and "often involve extensive compromises with women rather than naked domination" (79). Subordinate masculinities, in turn, are inherently important in the construction of a hegemonic position (while complicit masculinities come after the establishing of a dominant position). Perhaps the most visible trope of subordinate masculinity is the gay male who is rejected and oppressed by a heteronormative structure installed and perpetuated by heterosexual men. Connell argues that "this is much more than a cultural stigmatization of homosexuality or gay identity" and that "gay men are subordinated to straight men by an array of quite material practices" (78). This position is occupied by an effeminate hairdresser who lives in the neighborhood (played by popular television actor Julio César Herrera, the real-life spouse of Aida Bossa, who plays Angeluz).[12] Marginalized masculinities are performed and embodied by subjects who are somehow disqualified from the hegemonic position; the marginal element is usually race, which moves them into a separate (though not entirely disconnected) tableau.

Let us plot these ideas over *El Man* and the dyad of the superhero-supervillain. Felipe embodies neither a marginalized nor subordinate masculinity, but is instead representative of complicit masculinity. He participates in the homosocial (of the barrio and the group of taxi drivers), but is excluded from a position of hegemony given his physical stature, economic position, and lack of success with women: he is skinny and unexceptional; lives with his mother; and his only love interest, Angeluz, ignores his advances and instead falls head over heels for El Man. The triangle between Felipe, Angeluz, and El Man is a repeated trope in the superhero genre, where the object of affection ignores the regular Joe while falling for the superhero. Again, the Latin American superhero is an amalgam of influences, showing here how the parodic archetype (of El Chapulín) comes into contact with hegemonic conventions (such as the love triangle).

As a superhero, Felipe's gender position morphs into something else, an expression that escapes tangible and mimetic structures for an enhanced, transnational system. This is evident in the becoming moment when the assembled neighbors name the hero and clearly name such archetypes of hegemony as Superman and Batman. El Man's masculinity operates on (at least) two planes. On the local level, he supersedes the hierarchy established by the hegemon, as he is a *super*hero, more than human, and thus overshadows even the most perfect masculine specimen. Transnationally, however, his yellow spandex and measly moustache pale in comparison to the assemblage of North American types the *vecinos* name, thus situating the hero and the film within the realms of parody.

This brings me to the other side of the hero-villain dyad, as Federico's gender position is more complex than it first seems. He is well-built, tall, and neatly coiffed, visibly establishing himself over Felipe and the other members of the homosocial in the neighborhood. His strong financial position and the fact that he only hires the most beautiful women to work at the Camaleón offices (and presumably sleeps with them) underline his dominant stature vis-à-vis complicit and subordinate masculinities (such as Felipe and the effeminate hairdresser respectively). Like Felipe, however, his gender position also operates on a transnational level in that his character metonymizes global neoliberal practices (which is especially clear in him wearing a business suit in every scene of the film).

The interpellation of gender and globalization is a wide field, but what interests me here is the relationship between the sociostructual systems of masculinity (that are largely intrinsic) and the intervention of global flows of gender construction and performance. Connell and Julian Wood argue that "hegemonic forms of masculinity in modernity are historically derived from the growth of industrial capitalism and the growth of imperialism," and that "locally hegemonic patterns of masculinity were typically integrated with the local patterns of capitalism" (348). They argue that "capitalism changes," and that "one of its central trends has been the replacement of family enterprises by corporations, which, in turn, have grown on an ever-larger scale" (348). This shift is at the very core of *El Man*, as it is the growth of the corporation that leads to the potential displacement of the neighbors and their businesses, evocative of the idea that today "the most powerful institutions, excepting only major states, are transnational corporations operating in global markets" (Connell and Wood 347).

Corporations (like any other social institution) inculcate a specific culture that includes codes and practices of gender that are circulated across political frontiers, participating in what Connell has (controversially) termed a "world gender order" ("Masculinities and Globalization" 9).[13] With the proliferation of particular institutions—in this case corporations—"the patterns of masculinity embedded in them may become global standards" (11).[14] In this sense, the brand of masculinity cultivated within corporate culture has enjoyed a global diffusion and hegemony, as it is unambiguously linked to the success of corporations in evicting the state as the principal denominator of geopolitical power. This transnational business masculinity supersedes local hegemons (though these are allowed to operate), establishing a global hierarchy of macropositions. This is evident in that "almost every political leader in the world now wears the uniform of the Western business executive" (11) as a de facto costume in their public performance of power.

Transnational business masculinity—the gender position portrayed by Federico—is an evolution of masculinities of conquest and settlement, empire, and postcolonialism (Connell, "Masculinities and Globalization" 12–15). Wearing business suits and flouting branded products recognized by a global elite, its subjects are "marked by increasing egocentrism, very conditional loyalties . . . and a declining sense of responsibility for others" (16). This is evident in Federico's behavior throughout the film: he is narcissistic and arrogant in the workplace and with his employees; and he is disdainful of the neighbors who have always called the barrio their home. Wood and Connell add that "there is little of the old content of bourgeois masculinity—domestic patriarchy, snobbery, social authority, patriotism, religion, and so on" (361). While Federico is a snob (as seen by his supposed allergy to fatty foods, these being his kryptonite), he does eschew patriotism and religion, which are two defining characteristics of the superhero. Transnational business masculinity also "does not require bodily force" (Connell, "Masculinities and Globalization" 16), as the strong Federico has his henchmen do the dirty work of evicting residents and confronting El Man. This masculinity, however, "differs from traditional bourgeois masculinity by its increasingly libertarian sexuality" (16). This is evident in a scene after the first eviction when El Man confronts Federico with fried chorizo in his office, demanding that he cancel the property tax hike on the small businesses and homes in the neighborhood. The superhero makes the supervillain disrobe, and we see that Federico is wearing pink zebra-print thong underwear. While this clothing choice would normally move the character into the subordinate realm (due to the associations typically made with both the color and cut of the clothing piece), it is simply a kinky detail here in his performance of transnational business masculinity as a position that overrides local norms and practices.

But this is not to say that his business suit and financial might preclude him from attacks: when security arrives, El Man covers himself as though he were a woman and screams rape while running from the office. An enraged Federico follows him out, but is mocked by his female employees. Though we cannot discern their snide comments, we can easily infer what they are commenting about—one of his male aides repeatedly yells, "He doesn't have a small one!" ("¡Él no lo tiene chiquito!"). In other words, the pink thong is not the source of laughter (though it would be if worn by a local masculine subject such as Felipe) but rather the issue of whether his penis is large or small that is a topic of debate. Penis size is a local signifier of masculinity within the storyworld (and even, arguably, a universal quality) and thus escapes the smoothening logic of a transnational gender order that is suggested by the pink thong. The body does matter, after all.

The film engages in this type of juvenile sexist humor—within the register of parody—in other places (most notably in scenes with the hairdresser), and thus perpetuates systems of hegemonic masculinity (both local and transnational) instead of unequivocally challenging them through the aesthetics and gender expression of the superhero. *El Man* thus reinforces Brown's observation that "parodies also function to ultimately reinforce the dominant messages of the mainstream superhero films and to validate the very model of masculinity that it superficially condemns" (132). In this regard, superhero parodies such as *El Man* that put forth a parodic superhero "function in a more complex manner to support hegemonic masculinity as a cultural norm than do mainstream superhero films" (132). The question to tackle here is which iteration of hegemonic masculinity is supported; that is, does the film uphold a local or transnational position as the organizing axis around which the gendered storyworld is constructed?

Subversive Ideologies

Writing in the now canonical "The Myth of Superman," Umberto Eco performs a detailed reading of the character and his enemies to arrive at the conclusion that the superhero is a "perfect example of civic consciousness, completely split from political consciousness," as "*the only visible form that evil assumes is an attempt on private property*" (22; emphasis in the original). Synthesizing Eco's analysis, Robert Peaslee notes that

> the prevailing view of Superman (and superheroes generally) as mythical saviors was, by way of myopia, in error;

> instead . . . analysts should be attuned to the particularly American qualities of Superman, who eschews fighting injustice on the macro or structural level and prefers instead to wage smaller battles of immediate and palpable significance. The effect of this decision . . . is an implicit acceptance and defense . . . of the tenets of capitalism and bureaucracy, such as property ownership, legality, and due process. In sum, Superman is ideology. (37)

While this may be true for the Man of Steel, his North American peers, and other global contemporaries, the same logic does not apply in the case of *El Man*, as what is contested by means of the superhero-supervillain dyad is the very nature of capitalist accumulation, that is, the extradiegetic status quo.

The challenge of Federico's urban intentions is the first sign of this political gesture, but it is not the strongest indicator of the superhero's anti-capitalist ethos, which occurs about halfway into the film after the occupation of the senior home by Camaleón Enterprises and the neighbors taking in the displaced seniors. We learn that the taxi cooperative that Felipe drives for has been bought by Camaleón and that its employees, including Angeluz, now work for the villain. An enraged Felipe refuses to be another cog in the capitalist machine and resigns from his job, while Angeluz prays that El Man will reappear to get their co-op back. Unemployed, Felipe makes his rounds to the neighborhood businesses looking for work. In each meeting, he learns that none of them are hiring as their income is severely constrained by the new taxes; in effect, Camaleón Enterprises is suffocating economic activity with the endgame of taking over the businesses and then rebuilding the barrio as a mixture of malls and apartments.

A distraught Felipe retakes the cape and confronts Federico (in the pink thong scene) but his demands fall on deaf ears. Disillusioned and facing economic and housing precarity, he loiters in the public spaces of the neighborhood bemoaning its collapse. An Afro-Colombian lady carrying shopping bags full of groceries interrupts his lamenting and asks to hire the taxi. He informs her that he cannot legally drive her as he no longer belongs to the cooperative and is therefore unlicensed. It is at this juncture that the film engages an anti-capitalist gesture that characters such as Superman never undertake: she tells him that "we don't need money to subsist" ("no necesitamos dinero para subsistir"), and that the answer to their impasse is "trueque" or a barter system. Felipe provides her with a ride back home and she gives him fruit in exchange, thus sidestepping the legal constraints of not having a taxi license. Seeing how this simple exchange circumvents Federico's (capitalist) tactics, a hopeful Felipe brings this proposal to Angeluz and El Coronel. They, however, do not see this system as a viable alternative as they are incapable of conceptualizing an economic system empty of currency and monetary exchange. The capitalist status quo is ingrained in them to such an extent that an alternative, emancipatory ideology and praxis is dismissed as an impossibility.

Felipe, however, knows that undermining Camaleón and convincing the neighbors of the possibilities of *truque* are not tasks for a simple mortal, and thus puts on the yellow spandex once again. Dressed as El Man, he informs Angeluz of his intentions of borrowing the taxi for a few days to put into practice a system that will safeguard the economic interests of the neighborhood and the cooperative, to which she gives him an approving passionate kiss on the lips. He commandeers Felipe's taxi and, in an accelerated montage, goes about creating a public marketplace in a plaza for the neighborhood businesses. Herein lies El Man's ideological intervention, as a superhero championing the anti-capitalist mantle that is narratologically ratified by the heteronormative kiss. Angeluz's labial seal is an important element in this plot point, as it signals to the viewer that the superhero's actions are ethically good and meriting our approval. The love interest within the superhero genre is not simply a romantic element or foil to the hero, but also importantly a vector of ideology, politics, and ethics—it is *her* job to indicate to the audience (by means of a kiss or other heterosexual advance) what is deserving of our endorsement, which in this case is the anti-capitalist venture of the barter market.[15]

The marketplace enjoys resounding success and the neighborhood is seemingly reinvigorated as its inhabitants and businesses can go about daily life without the need for currency. *El Man*'s anti-capitalist space is understandably utopic, as it simplistically portrays the neighbors as content in exchanging chickens for bread, or mechanic repair services for fruits, but importantly does not solve the tax hike or the threat of Camaleón purchasing the houses. This observation aside, the success of the market sets in motion the events leading to the climactic duel between the superhero and the villain. The camera cuts from the public market to the offices of the corporation where we see an employee stomping towards a manager. She exclaims that she is fed up with the working conditions and demands of Federico and hands in her resignation notice. She walks off to the cubicle of her now ex-colleagues and asks them if they have brought the items for barter—she exchanges a knapsack for embroidered placemats and leaves the office affirming that she is "free!" ("¡libre!"). The inference to be made here is that the economic ideology of the barrio is seeping out into the transnational space, posing for its workers an attractive alternative that rejects Federico's insistence on maximum profits.

The camera cuts to a close up of Federico that zooms out just as he exclaims, "Barter? Who can explain to me what potatoes have to do with arepas?" ("¿Trueque? ¿Quién me puede explicar qué tienen que ver las papas con las arepas?"). An aide explains that the market is disrupting their "operating system" ("sistema operativo"; i.e., capitalism) and that their employees are beginning to resign, as they prefer the alternative economy. An angry Federico takes up the challenge and decides to go to the marketplace himself in lieu of only sending his henchmen. This is the very first and only instance of him physically setting foot in the barrio to threaten its inhabitants, as in previous scenes he visits to buy the buildings. Herein we witness the narrative conditions for the final battle between Federico and El Man, between the villain and the superhero, and between capitalism and anti-capitalism.

The image cuts to a clown announcing the wonders of the barter system and the camera follows several neighbors going about different trades for their daily needs. Ominous music, however, interrupts this vignette of economic utopia as it accompanies the arrival of an entourage of cars transporting Federico and his cronies. The villain walks through the crowd criticizing the market as an archaic system unfitting of a modern city. The contrast between Federico and the others bears mentioning here, as a low-angle camera emphasizes his domineering height and physique, as well as his neat business suit and bright red dress shirt in contrast to the clothes worn by the neighbors. He instructs his men to end this detour away from capitalist logic by buying up all the goods. Felipe confronts him, and another low-angle shot emphasizes the size difference between the two as we clearly see him looking up at the imposing villain. He tells them to leave if they have nothing to barter with, to which Federico responds, "Everything in this life has its price" ("Todo en esta vida tiene su precio"). He adds that his issue is not Felipe and the lower-class residents of the barrio (as signaled by his disgust of the *pelanga* sausage grilled by a street vendor). They can do whatever they please, as long as it does not infringe on his designs of renovating the neighborhood for new residents, as "the middle class does want to grow" ("la clase media sí tiene espuma afán").

When another merchant rejects his money (and ridicules his red shirt), he decides to leave "lest squalor be contagious" ("no sea que la miseria sea contagiosa"). Importantly, Federico leaves believing that he will still get his way, even if the merchants refuse to sell him all their goods, as he has the political and financial system gamed to squeeze out the small business owner.

The next scene takes place in his lush mansion, as a maid brings him a dish made of *chunchullo*, *bofe*, and *longaniza* not unlike the food that provokes his allergies in the market scene. She apologizes for the plate, saying that the meats are the only foods she has been able to source since the advent of the *trueque* market. It is not that other items such as vegetables and more exquisite meats are unavailable, but rather that they are only attainable through a currencyless exchange. He scolds her by saying that he does not eat meat, only "fresh fruit, vegetables, and whole grain rice" ("frutas frescas, verduras, arroz integral")—all "light" foods. Having the fatty sausage and other innards before him is what ultimately sets off and angers Federico to rashly take action against the market. In a villainous voice and pose, he declares that he will immediately "put an end to that ruckus" ("acabar con esa guachafita"), that is, the barter market.

This scene reverts the viewer to the character's gender expression, as we must remember that transnational business masculinity is deeply concerned with the body, but not solely as a site of male virility or musculature (which is the general norm in local iterations of hegemony), but rather as the embodiment of the ethos of self-responsibility and individualism that marks the neoliberal episteme. Expanding on this line of thinking, María del Carmen Caña Jiménez argues that "with the implementation of neoliberal economic policies the subject becomes solely responsible for their health, their welfare, and work for much-desired personal success. The citizen, therefore, ceases to be the object of state responsibility" ("con la implementación de las políticas económicas neoliberales el sujeto pasa a convertirse en el único responsable de velar por su salud, asegurar su bienestar y trabajar por el tan ansiado éxito personal. El ciudadano deja de ser, pues, objeto de la responsabilidad estatal"; 188).[16] The onus placed on the individual to manage his or her own health is not only a reality of everyday life, but also a signifier of the class struggles of late capitalism; as Kate Cairns and Josée Johnston argue, "The logic of health as personal responsibility reaffirms the boundary work of white middle-class populations able to adopt 'healthy lifestyle' practices, working to distance themselves from unhealthy Others . . . and often serving to justify their own privilege" (156). Francisco Ortega adds that adopting a healthy lifestyle and controlling one's dietary intake has become a "characteristic criteria for class distinction of the middle class" ("criterio de distinción de clase característico del habitus de las clases medias"; 195)—the same "clase media" that Federico wants to repopulate the barrio with.

This focus on quantitative and qualitative metrics for managing the body is commonly known as healthism, or an "ideology of health and the cult of the body" ("ideología de la salud y del culto al cuerpo"; Caña Jiménez 192), and is clearly evoked when Federico rejects the *embutido*, asking instead for fruit and vegetables, as he has to maintain his physique. He draws the line on the barter economy now when it begins to affect his own health and nutrition—challenging his position as masculine hegemon—and not previously when he simply assumed that the capitalist model would win out (as it has proven to in post–Cold War geopolitics).[17]

In the subsequent scene, Federico and his entourage arrive at the neighborhood by night when the market is closed. They destroy merchandise and set the booths on fire to "put an end to this nonsense" ("acabar con esta bobada"). The neighbors react in shock, while El Coronel and Felipe look on from a balcony and hatch a plan to stop Camaleón. El Coronel sets off sparklers to distract them while Felipe becomes El Man. Slow-motion visuals and exultant music accompany his appearance, signaling to the audience that the actions of the supervillain will not go unchallenged. Trompetero again uses low-angle shots as he did with Federico walking through the market, but this time they emphasize El Man's position over the melee below (he stands atop an unseen stack of boxes or other such structure); that is, he is now spatially above Federico and his henchmen, while before Felipe was clearly below. The sleight of the camera parallels the adoption of the costume in that it visually renders for the audience and the diegetic characters that the protagonist is now a superhero.

El Man's dramatic entrance and its accompanying sense of hope (for the neighbors and audience) are, however, quickly neutralized when he comes down to street level and engages Federico and his thugs in combat. His uncoordinated kicks and punches—very much unlike the skillful maneuvers of Mirageman—are ineffective, and he resorts to his one true superpower. He desperately invokes "baby Jesus" ("el niño Jesús") to come to his aid, and, in a flourish of the fantastic, CGI silhouettes in the shape of angels lift him above the bad guys. What bears highlighting in this manifestation of his "super" power, however, is that only the audience is privy to the angels. In the first image, we see the silhouettes surround and lift him, but then Trompetero quickly cuts to the villains, the neighbors, and then back to El Man. In the final image, we see him floating without the support of the heavenly bodies, thus implying—through the spectacularity and points of view of the montage—that his levitation is unassisted and "super" and not a religious miracle.

The appearance of his power triggers fear in the supervillain and his cronies as they come to realize that El Man is not "a common and ordinary superhero" ("un superhéroe común y corriente"). Empowered and towering above the bad guys, he gives them a penance of prayer to Jesus and launches more fireworks causing them to scamper off—all that is left of Camaleón to face the superhero is Federico. Cornered and alone, he first tries to come to a financial agreement with the neighbors, but then takes Angeluz hostage at gunpoint when he realizes that they are unwilling to cooperate. A heroic El Man offers himself instead of her, and Federico jumps at the chance of defeating the hero who left him in a pink thong among his employees.

With El Man bound in rope, Federico is not interested in killing the hero; instead, he wants to land the ultimate blow; that is, he wants to unmask the superhero for all to see. The unmasking trope is an important narratological plot point in the genre, and one that is perhaps more prevalent in the Latin American genre than in the North American blockbuster. It is a recurring moment across the films analyzed in *Capitán Latinoamérica*, suggesting that what makes the superhero "super" is really the persona (created by the mask) per se more than any real superhuman power. Unmasking the hero is an antithetical gesture vis-à-vis the origin moment, as it lays bare to the *public* the true identity of the superhero, who in most cases is a character not associated with the position of hegemonic masculinity. I theorize the importance of the mask in greater detail in the following chapter, but I leave the reader here with the importance of the unmasking scene in these films as an ethical vector that provokes an affective reaction from the viewer, as they realize that the possibilities for the good are on thin ice in the face of the villain who is moments from victory.

Like most villains in these moments of control over the superhero, Federico takes too long to do anything, allowing El Coronel to free El Man. He lunges at the villain who in a slow motion shot fires his revolver, seemingly killing El Man. Trompetero cuts between an overhead shot of El Man, the public reaction, and Federico affirming that there will be "no more barter" ("no más trueque"), that the neighbors are to turn in their houses and businesses, and that all the young women (like Angeluz) are to now work for him under Camaleón. Caught up in all this is El Man who realizes that the bullet only impacted the Jesus medallion given to him by El Coronel. His prayers are answered again, it seems, as he miraculously rises and fights off the supervillain. But this is not a tête-à-tête between the two, but rather a communal effort as the entire neighborhood turns on Federico and chases him off.

The scene predictably concludes with Angeluz in his arms and them sharing a kiss, the romantic component again serving as an ethical stamp of approval that effectively brings closure to the narrative arc. The kiss, furthermore, signals to the diegetic characters and to the audience that El Man's super, local masculinity trumps Federico's transnational gender expression, challenging the possibilities and tenets of a global gender order. Importantly, the film makes no claims as to the future of the barrio, suggesting that while the battle is won today, the war against late capitalist urban designs is still in progress.

Chapter 3

Allegories of Trauma and Transition in *Mirageman*

The Latin American superhero film is a reactive genre, erupting in a moment of political and ethical compromise wherein its intervention is a hermeneutic gesture vis-à-vis wider social, political, and economic concerns. Ernesto Díaz Espinoza's *Mirageman* (2007), a Chilean superhero flick starring martial arts expert Marko Zaror, was filmed and screened at a moment of cultural and mnemonic reckoning, wherein the antics and acrobatics of the protagonical character can be understood following Steven Shaviro's thesis of a productive cinema, that is, a cinema that does "not *represent* social processes, so much as [it] participate[s] actively in these processes, and help[s] constitute them" (2).[1] Within the contextual terrain of contemporary Chile, Díaz Espinoza's film poses—among scenes of comic relief, action-packed fights, and subtle romance—a thoughtful and coherent meditation on the cultural politics of memory and postdictatorial efforts of reconciliation.[2] The film opened in national theatres in March 2008, claiming the number three spot behind two North American productions (*10,000 BC* and *Dr. Seuss' Horton Hears a Who*). In fact, it was the only Chilean film in the top 25 that week, posting a stronger opening than another debutant, Paramount Pictures' *The Spiderwick Chronicles*.

Díaz Espinoza is known for his genre films that include *Kiltro* (2006), *Mandrill* (2009), *Tráigame la cabeza de la Mujer Metralleta* (2012), *Santiago Violenta* (2014), *Redeemer* (2014) and *Fuerzas especiales 2: Cabos sueltos* (2015). The titles of these films demonstrate the director's affinity for genre, with a strong local inflection that sets the stage for the many action scenes that characterize his films. In this regard, it is unsurprising that he has partnered with his childhood-friend Zaror in a total of four films that largely rely on the latter's physique and fighting abilities (and not his somewhat lacking acting chops). Díaz Espinoza began making films at a time when Chilean cinema was entering the present boom; as Antonella Estévez affirms, the first decade of the twenty-first century was the most productive decade, in quantitative terms, for Chilean cinema. More than 330 feature-length films were made and screened between 2000 and 2009 (16). In discussing recent Chilean cinema, Jacqueline Mouesca and Carlos Orellana observe that "the quality of several of the films shown speaks of a more solid cinema, a mature cinema capable of comparing itself with the best cinema produced in Latin America" ("la calidad de varios de los films exhibidos hablan de un cine más sólido, un cine adulto capaz de cotejarse con pergaminos equiparables con lo mejor que se produce en Latinoamérica"; 207).[3] With domestic and international success, a film industry that was relatively quiet during the twentieth century is now gaining traction as a veritable force in the Spanish-speaking world.

Writing on this boom, Ascancio Cavallo and Gonzalo Maza include Díaz Espinoza in their proposal of a "novísimo cine chileno" to describe the generation of twenty-first-century directors who are shaping the field. These filmmakers "are children of their history and are intimately connected to the New Chilean Cinema of the '60s" ("son hijos de su historia y están conectados íntimamente con el Nuevo Cine Chileno de los sesenta"; 14). They are, however, also knowledgeable of current trends and aesthetics of the global portfolios of Jean-Pierre and Luc Dardenne, Béla Tarr, Jim Jarmusch, Aki Kaurismäki, and Apichatpong Weerasethakul (14), and have received professional training in local university programs, which, to an extent, explains the self-reflexive nature of many of their films. *Novísimo* directors, importantly, shun strictly commercial success in favor of "their own language and anxieties" ("un lenguaje y preocupaciones propias"; 15).[4] In their compilation, Cavallo and Maza thus situate Díaz Espinoza alongside contemporaries such as Matías Bize, Fernando Lavanderos, Alicia Scherson, Alberto Fuguet, Pablo Larraín, and Elisa Eliash.

Commenting on his presence in *El novísimo cine chileno*, Jonathan Risner correctly notes that Díaz Espinoza's inclusion "under the rubric of *novísimo cine chileno* represents a paradoxical selection," given the director's preference for action films that draw on the genres of "exploitation and superhero films and buddy-cop comedies" (609n10) that appeal to a wide audience. Like Risner, I disassociate Díaz Espinoza's work from the list of directors cited above, which more accurately adhere to Carolina Urrutia

Neno's notion of a centrifugal Chilean cinema grounded in "the poetics of the time-image, its disinterest in a cause-effect logic, and, a contrary interest . . . in the relation between memory that begins with the construction of shots that are autonomous and uncertain in their motivation" (18).⁵ Instead, we may more accurately put Díaz Espinoza's oeuvre within a gesture that is "centripetal" cinema, a commercial cinema that follows "hegemonic narratives formulated by the US film industry" (Urrutia Neno 13). *Mirageman*, like all of Díaz Espinoza's films, is a centripetal venture that, in its adherence to genre, "relates to its spectator in a different way" (Risner 600). This "different way," is made possible largely by the director's devotion to the conventions and qualities of genre, which in the case of *Mirageman*, is the superhero flick that has dominated world box offices in the twenty-first century.

Whether centripetal or centrifugal, it goes without saying that Díaz Espinoza belongs to a generation of filmmakers whose films "ratify the re-encounter between the national filmgoer and their cinema" ("ratifica[n] ese reencuentro del espectador nacional con su cinematografía"; Mouesca and Orellana 207), especially given the commercial success of *Kiltro* and *Mirageman*. More than just a popular, centripetal genre film (that would normally marginalize it within the national cinema), *Mirageman* has gone on to garner several national and international accolades, including a nomination for the Premio Pedro Sienna (2009) alongside José Luis Torres Leiva's *El cielo, la tierra y la lluvia*, Pablo Larraín's *Tony Manero*, and the eventual winner, Andrés Wood's *La buena vida*. The film also won audience awards at the Riofan Festival Fantástico (Brazil, 2008), Fantastic Fest (USA, 2007), Festival Internacional de Cine de Valdivia (Chile, 2007), and Festival Internacional de Cine de Lebu (Chile, 2008). The character has also appeared in television, web programs, and print media, demonstrating the proliferation of Zaror's superhero within the popular imaginary. An entire episode of Nicolás López and Miguel Asensio's short-lived sketch comedy vignettes, "Transantiaguinos," is dedicated to the character. Appearing on Canal 13 in 2008, the show was meant to be a comedic take on everyday life in Santiago. In this particular episode, the show's actors discuss the lack of a national superhero. One of them ponders that "We are alone. . . . Nobody protects us. . . . The gringos have Superman, Spiderman, Donald Duck. . . . Even the Chinese have superheroes. We, on the other hand, have nobody" ("Estamos solos. . . . Nadie nos protege. . . . Los gringos tienen a Superman, al hombre araña, al Pato Donald. . . . Incluso los chinos tienen a superhéroes. En cambio nosotros no tenemos a nadie"). Another character quickly retorts that

"We have Mirageman" ("Tenemos a Mirageman"), a truly Chilean hero, to the incredulity of the first actor. The other actors try to convince him that Zaror's character does exist, and is there to rescue the common Chilean from crime, a detailed proved to be true when the character appears later in the skit.

Mirageman begins with the undifferentiated sounds of the city foregrounding opening credits, previsually placing the narrative within the cityspace that opens the visual register of the film. This cityspace is local, as viewers quickly recognize the black and yellow taxicabs that populate the busy streets of Santiago.[6] Aside from providing a narrative setting, that is, a distinct real *place* of buildings, streets, and neighborhoods wherein the hero narrative may take shape and evolve, the opening sounds and shot collocate the narrative within a particular sociocultural location and zeitgeist that the superhero must negotiate.[7] The linking of place to the hero is hinted at as the audio track progressively moves away from urban noise to the sounds of body parts coming into contact with training gear, as the film moves from the outside of the city to the inside of a basement, intimately linking both in symbiotic stasis.

From a narrative standpoint, *Mirageman* follows a familiar arc wherein a past trauma, combined with a present need for justice, sets up the conversion of the layperson into a superhuman character. Maco Gutiérrez works by night as a bouncer at the *Passapoga* nightclub, a real club that opened its doors in 2002.[8] He spends his days as a recluse in the basement apartment, training in different styles of martial arts. We are introduced to the character in the very first scene of the film, when a close shot frames several images and documents that lay out the genesis of the plot. The viewer is presented with a series of photos of two boys, and drawings depicting two young male figures (presumably the same two boys) dealing with a criminal attack. These photos—not of an idyllic childhood that may be fetishized by any stretch—are not glossy digital prints, but taken by an older camera and clearly dated. The first sketch shows two boys running into a house with a gargantuan, diabolic, humanoid monster overhead. In a close shot, the camera lingers over a dateless newspaper clipping that explains the montage of photos and comic-style drawings: "Family devastated in armed robbery. Parents killed, older son brutally beaten and younger son raped by the assailants" ("Familia devastada en robo a mano armada. Padres mueren asesinados, hijo mayor brutalmente golpeado e hijo menor violado por los asaltantes"). We learn more details of the originary trauma from this article: they lived in the

Ñuñoa commune in Santiago. Located in the northeastern sector of the capital, Ñuñoa today is known for its high quality of life and desirability among the upper-middle class and young urban professionals. During the dictatorship of Augusto Pinochet from 1973 to 1990, however, the National Stadium located in the heart of the *comuna* was infamously known as a torture center and death camp. This minute detail in the article will be of special importance when we analyze the underlying critique of the film as it relates to the diegetic and extradiegetic present. The image then cuts to an extreme close up of the latter part of the headline, highlighting the rape of the younger brother who we had seen in the earlier photos. Subsequently, the viewer is presented, by means of a sliding camera, with Maco sparring at the *makiwara* (a padded post used as a training tool in karate), his blows lending a rhythmic offset to the somber music backgrounding this introductory montage.

Like many films in the genre (and in any other genre, really), the opening sequence provides us with much of the thematic foundation for the plot. In the case of *Mirageman*, we observe how personal trauma at the hand of crime—as in the case of Bruce Wayne or Peter Parker—sets up the conditions for the assumption of a heroic identity. The personal crux behind what will be Maco's transformation is not so much the actual murder of his parents, as the headline may lead us to believe, but the fact that his younger sibling was raped in the act. The brother, Tito, is marked by this rape, and is now confined to a psychiatric ward where he spends his days in a catatonic state. Maco, in turn, trains at a furious pace, perhaps less in an attempt to avenge the beating received and the death of his parents, and more as a result of being unable to protect his family. At the core of this ontoformative trauma is the issue of sexual violence and torture and, importantly, how they then impact the gendered becoming of the two brothers. Maco's physical hypermasculinity is the result of his martial arts and weight training, which may be interpreted as a sort of acting out as a result of the trauma, whereas Tito lingers in a psychological and physiological limbo, a forever-child crystalized at the moment of rape. Importantly, the introductory traumatic moment is not death and torture, but rather its aftermath, as Maco's life (and decision to become a superhero) is centered around his brother.

Díaz Espinoza's film wastes no time in setting in motion the transformation of the perturbed older brother into the crime fighter that will later adopt the title character's name. In the subsequent scene, a camera tracks Maco as he jogs through his neighborhood at night. The off-camera shriek of a female in despair sparks the protagonist's attention, and he proceeds to interrupt a home invasion—one that may not have been altogether different from the one that ended his parents' lives. In fact, we may interpret this early scene as a closing of a narrative arc typical of the genre: the previously attacked and emasculated character is, after hours of martial arts training (or happening upon and then perfecting a superpower), allowed to symbolically confront the perpetrators of his origin narrative.[9] The genre trope is a situation of ethical confluence where characters standing in for "good" and "bad" grapple in a moment of reckoning in which one is vanquished and the other comes through to an "other side" of the conflict, renewed and evolved in his or her powers and motives. This plot point, however, occurs at the very beginning of *Mirageman*, and not later in the climax of the narrative (as tends to be the case in the genre), thus suggesting that there is something else that displaces this trope from being the central ethical and poietic dialectic around which we are to understand the figure of the hero.

Superhero narratives tend to follow circular patterns and repetitions, permitting thus a congealing of disparate narratives, heroes, and contexts into a clearly recognizable genre. This genre trope—inherent to and repeated in a wide variety of international superhero films that focus on the origin or becoming story of a character—however, is only addressed at a symbolic level, as it is not the same criminals here but iterative character types who are now attempting to rob and rape a woman that we later find out is Carol Valdivieso, a star television reporter.[10] Valdivieso then brings news of this masked hero to the masses, including Tito who miraculously shows cognitive and behavioral improvements at the thought of a masked hero fighting off would be attackers.

Seeing how his actions from the previous night resuscitate his brother, and that his becoming a hero-like figure can effect real change, Maco decides to embrace the persona of the masked enforcer. In subsequent scenes and montages, Maco goes through the routine of trying on and designing different prototypes of a costume, finally settling on a blue mask and what could be described as street clothing, that is, athletic pants and a jacket. The film eschews the capes and leotards first popularized in the genre—and later parodied in *El Chapulín*, *El Man*, and *Chinche Man*—for an urban style more evocative of Walter Kovacs, the complex character behind Rorschach from the critically acclaimed *Watchmen* line. *Mirageman* also breaks from the caped crusader model of the genre when Maco asks the public to contact him via email with missions and requests for help. He envisions himself as a sort of layperson's hero, a resource to be called when the police or other entities of the law are unable to help, somewhat like El Santo, who sat behind his office desk waiting for a poor child or woman to approach him. As one would expect, his many adventures in and around Santiago, especially in the Paseo Ahumada, garner interest from the mass media, and he quickly becomes fodder for a series of magazines and television shows.

It is in one of the emails that he is alerted of the presence a ring of pedophiles in Santiago, and the case of a missing girl. This case becomes the narratological axis around which the film revolves, as Maco resolves to liberate the child from her captors. In the climactic scene of the film, he frees her, only to be shot by one of the criminals, and fall into a pond. The media quickly christen him as a public hero, a martyr who paid the ultimate price to ensure the safety of the young girl (and all other girls, one would think). Ultimately, he dies protecting the child-figure he was unable to save in the origin-moment of his brother's rape.

The film concludes with a reborn Tito outside, practicing martial arts moves, and Mirageman looking down on him, thus providing an aura of "superhumanness" to the character that otherwise lacks any true powers. The concluding scene of *Mirageman* poses an open ending, thus following a narrative convention seen in 21st-century superhero films that hesitate to tie-up all the narrative threads in case a sequel proves lucrative.

Memory

While eschewing any direct references to the recent history of Chile, *Mirageman* does allude to—in several scenes, characters, and narrative twists—the cultural politics of memory and reconciliation in the country. On September 11, 1973, the US-backed armed forces assaulted *La Moneda* in a coup d'état to overthrow the democratically elected government of Salvador Allende. Led by General Augusto Pinochet, the coup ended democratic rule of the country and installed a brutal military dictatorship that only ended after a plebiscite in 1990. The military junta that took the place of Allende's government quickly set up a structure of governance that put democratic institutions and constitutional law into a prolonged chokehold. Censorship and curfews were regimented, and political activism was swiftly and brutally persecuted.

Pinochet wasted no time in consolidating power. The junta quickly gave way to him assuming complete control as president of the country in 1974, a position strengthened by a plebiscite on constitutional reform in 1980. This reform included a provision that scheduled a new plebiscite eight years later that would prove pivotal in the country's history. With mounting international pressure, 1988 saw the enactment of a decisive referendum, where the "No" vote garnered 56% of the vote. A year later, in what would be considered the first democratic elections of the transition towards democratic rule, Patricio Aylwin, representing the Concertación de Partidos por la Democracia (a coalition of the opposition), won the popular vote. Like all democratic transitions away from dictatorships, the process was marred by political stalwarts and legislative caveats that safeguarded the interests of the incumbent *pinochetista* regime.[11] One such clause was the installment of Pinochet as the commander in chief of the army (until 1988), and his subsequent appointment as lifetime senator. Also hindering the transition was the enactment of an amnesty law that protected the military from judicial processes.[12]

Amnesty provided protection for the military forces that were responsible for the massive assault on human life and rights during the entire tenure of the dictatorship.[13] Immediately after the coup, thousands were taken to the National Stadium and systematically executed. More than simply killing its adversaries, Pinochet's government initiated a paradigm of state terrorism that decimated any and all opposition: "Pinochet's Chile pioneered a new technique of repression in the Latin American context: systematic 'disappearance' of people. After the point of abduction, people vanished in a cloud of secrecy, denial, and misinformation by the state" (Stern xxiv). According to the Rettig Report (a document composed by the Comisión Nacional de Verdad y Reconciliación formed by Aylwin in 1990), almost 3,000 people were disappeared and killed.[14] Following the report, Aylwin proposed what would be called the Doctrina Aylwin, a policy that affirmed that the Amnesty Law of 1978 "did not relieve the courts of a legal duty first to investigate and establish the facts and the individual criminal responsibilities of a case, *before* they could apply an amnesty" (Stern 88; emphasis in the original). The implication of this were crucial in the cultural politics of memory in post-Pinochet Chile.

Also important in the aftermath of Rettig was the publication of the Valech Report in 2004 (mandated by the government of Ricardo Lagos, the third Concertación president), which addressed the violations that had slipped through the cracks of the Rettig's pages: namely, the systematic practice of torture and imprisonment that was meted out during the years of the dictatorship. In over 30,000 testimonies, the Valech Report confirmed what many already knew: that "in Chile, the use of torture was more widespread than the practice of forced disappearance" (Ros 107). The report was also groundbreaking in that it focused on the abuses suffered by women and the prevalence of sexual and sexualized torture of women and men. The Valech Report came about largely due to the fact that many who had had their rights trampled on during the dictatorship and who were still living with the trauma of abuse had not been publicly acknowledged during the transition and in the Rettig Report.

The move to democracy became a balancing act of moving forward-looking back, a paradoxical tension that largely defined the cultural politics of memory at the turn of the century. Amnesty granted to the military made looking back an ethically complex and legally treacherous affair, where criminals, even once identified, were allowed to live their lives scot-free, even if the Concertación pushed for reconciliation and consensus (Lazzara 16; Ros 119). The Valech Report serves as a contextual reference for understanding the cultural parameters of mnemonics in contemporary Chile, as "Chileans began to see the past-within-the-present with new eyes, able to take in legacies once pushed to the edge of a narrower visual field" (Stern 297): in essence, the "stretching of the memory question to include what had once been marginalized coincided with a larger reshuffling of that which mattered in politics and culture" (Stern 347).

All this is not to say, however, that memory work is linear or logical in contemporary Chile. Even with the Valech Report, there has been a struggle to engineer a society-wide process of mourning and closure. As Antonella Estévez confirms:

> The impossibility of mourning in the face of crimes that have affected so many Chileans in a personal way and the whole nation in a social and historical way has its consequences. . . . Without mourning there is no possibility of healing, but in this case the impossibility is even more brutal since, despite not being able to face this fact directly, there is an awareness that the current situation in Chile is built on the bodies of other Chileans.
>
> (La imposibilidad de realizar un duelo frente a crímenes que han afectado a tantos chilenos de manera personal y a toda la nación de manera social e histórica tiene sus consecuencias. . . . Sin duelo no hay posibilidad de sanación, pero en este caso la imposibilidad es todavía más brutal ya que, a pesar

> de no poder enfrentarse a este hecho de manera directa, sí hay conciencia de que la situación del Chile Actual se construye sobre los cadáveres de otros chilenos; 19)

The narrative cinema of the early years of the transition was initially slow to take up the task of memory work in cultural production.[15] In fact—and with a few exceptions—"there are very few references to the immediate past and, especially, the transition in the Chilean cinema of the '90s" ("en el cine chileno de los 90 escasean las referencias a la historia inmediata y, en especial, de la transición"; Cavallo, Douzet, and Rodríguez 24). Some films like Ricardo Larraín's *La frontera* (1991), however, created an allegory of the transition instead of a direct, visual and narrative representation of the dictatorship and its aftermath. The film chronicles the banishment of Ramiro Orellana, a high school teacher, to the periphery, the costal south away from the politicoeconomic center of Santiago, for having protested the kidnapping of a colleague. In this bleak terrain, he finds himself surrounded by other castaways of the dictatorship. The film ends on a somber note, as a tidal wave washes over the village, and Ramiro is left to return to Santiago. Given the tenuous political, judicial, and cultural terrain of the immediate years of democracy, Larraín's film only "suggests that a new national hero must arise from the turbulent political waters. These so-called heroes will be . . . the public voice of those who cannot speak. In this sense, Ramiro adopts the memory framework associated with the moral awakening of conscience that opposes the amnesiac discourse of mindful forgetting" (B. Franco 410).[16] Films like *La frontera* broached the issue of the dictatorship and its aftermath through narrative strategies that required a conscientious reader and reading in a hermeneutic exercise that was readily available for those prepared and willing to confront memory work in the moving image. Many films of the transition adopted common tropes, including the trope of orphanhood and the abundance of secret spaces that are the settings for some sort of internal trauma (Cavallo, Douzet, and Rodríguez 30).[17]

The intensifying focus on public memory culture of the new century, however, brought about a parallel shift in narrative cinematic production (though of course, not in a causal relationship, but rather as an associated process evocative of Shaviro's productive cinema).[18] Andrés Wood's *Machuca* (2004) is a watershed moment in understanding the politics of recent Chilean film, as its story of injustice and rights abuse during the dictatorship was eaten up by the masses. The film "caught the cultural moment—and strengthened it. It connected to a sentiment of desire, a certain yearning to fill the void that cut across memory camp lines" (Stern

311). The production and screening of other films such as *El baño* (2005), *Mi mejor enemigo* (2005), and Pablo Larraín's informal trilogy of *Tony Manero* (2008), *Post Mortem* (2010), and *No* (2012)—combined with the screening of television serials that actively addressed the past—ensured a privileged place for the moving image in contemporary Chilean memory politics (Barraza Toledo 160–61).

It is in this production-transmission-circulation substrate that I want to read *Mirageman*, and not as simply a one-off superhero film by a genre director, as I argue that Díaz Espinoza's interpretation of the genre is strongly inflected by a local element that cannot and should not be lost in the melee of roundhouse kicks and punch combinations. Superhero cinema in the twenty-first century is, after all, a highly politico-contextual genre, and *Mirageman* is just another example of how a masked hero may channel, negotiate, and digest broader sociocultural anxieties.

In fact, the very first scene of the film conjures up Ascanio Cavallo, Pablo Douzet, and Cecilia Rodríguez's identification of orphanhood and secret spaces in the cinema of the transition. In the reclusive basement—a place where Maco, through his training, mulls over an internal trauma—the camera moves over a series of images in a prefatory montage that sets up the premise of the plot and its characters. The newspaper clipping that is featured in a close shot explains Maco's training and Tito's seclusion due to the home invasion that left them as orphans.[19] While seemingly innocuous at face value, a close reading of its text opens the door for interpreting the film as something more than a simple calque of the superhero genre, but instead as a meditation on the mnemonic culture of the democracy. The text reads as follows:

> The director general of police Hernán Mendonca showed special concern in this case since it has been repeated several times in recent months. This does not mean that it was the same group of delinquents, rather it is the violent entry into homes that worries him since apparently the objective is not only to steal: "They are acts of absolute evil, they do not care what they steal, they also want to damage. The neighbors are in a state of panic. . . ."

> (El general director de carabineros Hernán Mendonca mostró especial preocupación en este caso ya que se ha repetido en varias oportunidades en los últimos meses. Esto no significa que fuera el mismo grupo de delincuentes, es el ingreso

violento a hogares lo que le preocupa ya que al parecer el objetivo no es solamente robar: "Son actos de maldad absoluta, como que no les importara lo que roban, también quieren dañar. Los vecinos están en estado de pánico. . . .")

Keeping in mind that the film attempts a chronological and topological verisimilitude (as observed in the use of the nightclub, situating the plot after 2003), the chief of police should either be Manuel Ugarte Soto (1997–2001) or Alberto Cienfuegos Becerra (2001–05).[20] The fictive Hernán Mendonca, however, is a thinly veiled allusion to César Mendoza Durán, chief of police during the Pinochet years. Mendoza Durán was part of the armed conspiracy against Allende, and took over the reins of the police from the deposed José María Sepúlveda. Importantly, Mendoza Durán realigned the Carabineros from a civil unit to one under the umbrella of the Ministry of Defense (1974). This realignment corresponded with an increased collaboration between Carabineros and the feared DINA (Dirección de Inteligencia Nacional) and subsequent CNI (Central Nacional de Información), the intelligence wings of the regime that enforced censorship, executions, and disappearances. Mendoza Durán also created an intelligence office in Carabineros, the DICOMCAR (Dirección de Comunicaciones de Carabineros) that was responsible for the murder of three members of the Communist Party in 1985—the Caso Degollados—which led to public outcry and his eventual resignation.[21]

By alluding to Mendoza Durán (and not Ugarte Soto or Cienfuegos Becerra), the newspaper clipping situates the originary trauma during the years of the dictatorship. This detail, however, is seemingly contradicted when Maco first visits Tito and we are told by his doctor that he has been there for three years, catatonic since the attack. If the Passapoga club only opened in 2003, and Maco started working as an adult (that is, after the attack), then the very latest the attack could have taken place is in the year 2000, clearly much after the dictatorship when Mendoza Durán was the chief of police. Yet the events described in the article very much resemble the tactics of the DINA and the police during the heyday of the government's repression of civilians: "the violent entry into homes"; "They are acts of absolute evil, they do not care what they steal, they also want to damage." What Mendonca/Mendoza describes is the very act of state terrorism, where the actual crime is to instill fear in the citizenry through "acts of absolute evil" that "ha[ve] been repeated several times in recent months," leaving the "the neighbors . . . in a state of panic."

The article is not describing an isolated home invasion but rather a systematic practice of human rights abuses. In other words, the originary trauma—introduced in the very first scene of *Miragemen*—posits two readings. At face value, it is a generic murder and rape (taking place during the democracy) that fuels the transformation of the protagonist into the title superhero; an allegorical reading, however, poses that the terrorist tactics of the regime and the paradigm of fear it imparted on the population is the root cause of Maco and Tito's trauma, and therefore the engine behind the transformation into Mirageman.[22]

The latter interpretation would thus suggest that the hero figure is really born from a societal trauma, his donning of the mask and the persona a conscious act of working through a widespread, communal suffering that remains pervasive in the twenty-first century. This would reflect Ana Ros's affirmation that "the Valech Report confronted Chileans with an unbearable reality: a vast segment of the population lived with the psychological and physical wounds of torture, abuse, and humiliation. Chile has more torture survivors in proportion to its total population than any of the countries of the Southern Cone" (114). The film, then, follows the themes and narrative turns of the superhero genre—allowing the viewer to lose themselves in the well-known and expected jokes, actions, and dialogues—but also poses a reflection on the condition of memory, trauma, and human rights discourse in contemporary Chile. The film stages an intervention right where the Valech Report leaves off, adopting as axiomatic the omnipresent experience of torture and sexual violence, and proposing a working through by means of the superhero character and genre.[23]

In the first action sequence where Maco stumbles upon the home invasion of Carol Valdivieso's house (and delivers the first of many roundhouse kicks), the image quickly cuts to the monster villain from the sketches in the introductory montage. The bald, menacing humanoid figure now comes alive, as the static sketch becomes animated. The image then cuts to Maco looking over the first goon, and then to another animated sketch of his parents in the foreground and two criminals behind them. This sketch is particularly moving, as we see the parents lying on the ground, propped up against the wall, with the two criminals brandishing knives.[24]

What interests me in this drawing, however, are the bloodstains on the wall behind the parental characters. The fact that the splatter is behind them suggests that the forensic evidence is congruous with a bullet exiting on the dorsal side of the victim, and not the frontal splatter that

Figure 3.1. Trauma resurfaces in a jarring memory from the past.

one would expect from a knife attack. The specifics of the sketch thus suggest that the parents were executed in their own home by gunfire (and not what is drawn), further evoking the practices of the Chilean secret service and police during the harshest years of political oppression. This sketch is a memory-artifact, a visual narrative of a traumatic event that, in representation, repeats the action of violence in the psyche of the affected. The sketch is Tito and Maco's memory of that fateful night, coming to life in animation that is looped in repetition, evocative of a psychological acting out of trauma. It is, furthermore, subjective and phenomenological, as the accuracy of the event it aims to represent is called into question by the incongruent forensics of the blood splatter and the knives held by the criminals, suggesting that the originary trauma is metaphorical and not literal; that is, the death of their parents is not to be interpreted as an actual event but rather as symbolic of something else.

The brief montage of the sketches immediately precedes Maco's decision to don the first attacker's ski mask, as though his decision to cover his face—to follow the first rudimentary trope of the superhero genre—is contingent on the traumatic past. Again, on a diegetic level, this is reference to the murder and assault; on an interpretive, allegorical level, it is in reference to the actions of state terrorism during the dictatorship. When he enters the house, Carol is bound and about to be raped. The

ALLEGORIES OF TRAUMA AND TRANSITION

Figure 3.2. Forensic clues in the moment of action.

mise-en-scène is provocative: she is tied and gagged, bent over a dining table with her aggressor behind her. In front sits an older lady, perhaps her mother, also bound and gagged. The tableau presented to Maco and the viewer consisting of a victim about to be assaulted while another sits bound, waiting for her turn to be raped, is one that may have taken place during the illegal incarcerations and abuses. Carol's bright red undergarments contrast with the dark lighting and colors of the scene, drawing our attention to the specter of sexual violence and torture that was brought to the national imaginary in the Valech Report. Maco swiftly disarms the criminal, but when he goes to free her, she whimpers an audible "¡no!," afraid that he too may rape her. Her fear is remedied when Maco quickly pulls her dress down and puts her to ease as he goes on to disarm the rest of the crooks. It bears mentioning that akin to the criminals who killed his parents, this group is not only looking to rob but to also perform "acts of absolute evil, they do not care what they steal, they also want to damage." If those who killed his parents evoke the crimes published in the Rettig Report, then the actions of the criminals here are analogous to the thousands of testimonies collected for the Valech Report.

By building strong mnemonic and narrative links between the present and the past, the film engages an audience in-the-know to reconsider the concept of temporality and to read beyond the tropic tools and registers of the superhero genre. It encourages the viewer to consider *Mirageman* as an introspection on postdictatorship Chile through the careful and implicit allusions to the Pinochet years and the trauma experienced on a collective level. In this regard, the film takes up Nelly Richard's comment that "the work of memory may be reimagined. It may be reconceived not as a passive memory of an objectified recollection, but as a memory-subject capable of formulating constructive and productive ties between past and present" (19). *Mirageman* and Mirageman as memory-subject thus function beyond the frontiers of genre and erupt onto a broader politicocultural terrain that is conditioned by the events of the past fifty years.

Such a reading may be framed within Macarena Gómez-Barris's idea of the *afterlife* of post-Pinochet Chile. She notes that, "although I also invoke the term *aftermath*, mostly to describe political and economic legacies, I find the term *afterlife* to be closer to the material struggles and realities endured by populations living through political violence. Therefore, I define the *afterlife* of political violence as the continuing and persistent symbolic and material effects of the original event of violence on people's daily lives, their social and psychic identities, and their ongoing wrestling with the past in the present" (6). *Mirageman* can therefore be considered an exploration of the afterlife of contemporary Chile as told through the narrative mode and register of the superhero genre, a decidedly original interpretation of the harsh realities and the persistence of political violence and state terrorism.

The narrative and mnemonic suture of the past and present is underscored in Maco's first visit to Tito's ward. We see the younger brother despondent and speechless, his only expression the many drawings of the fateful night. These sketches (like those in Maco's basement) are static and repetitive representations of the traumatic event, and contrast with the animated drawings that were included in the poietic montage that introduced us to a masked Maco. The character's recourse to drawing—and not speaking or writing about his trauma—evokes Idelber Avelar's assertion that "the dilemma of the tortured subject is always, then, a dilemma of representability" ("el dilema del sujeto torturado es siempre, entonces, un dilema de representabilidad," "La práctica" 184).[25] Reviewing ideas by thinkers such as Elaine Scarry who have theorized the somatic, epistemological, and semantic exchanges borne from torture, Avelar argues that

> the traumatized subject finds itself, then, caught in a crossroads: there is no elaboration and overcoming of the trauma

without the articulation of a narrative in which the traumatic experience is inserted significantly, inserted in meaning. Yet this same insertion cannot but be perceived by the subject as a true betrayal of the uniqueness and intractability of the experience. . . .

(El sujeto traumatizado se encuentra, entonces, atrapado en una encrucijada: no hay elaboración y superación del trauma sin la articulación de una narrativa en la que la experiencia traumática se inserte significativamente, se inserte en tanto significación. Pero esta misma inserción no puede sino ser percibida por el sujeto como una verdadera traición de la singularidad e intratabilidad de la experiencia . . . ; 184)

In drawing these sketches, Tito addresses the dilemma of representation by evading language and using instead the visual poetics of the comic to bring to the fore the event of torture. The sketch occupies a liminal position in the mnemonic trajectory of the character toward recuperation: it acknowledges the past event, bringing it out of the recesses of the psyche, but does not in any way engage it within a therapeutic or psychoanalytic framework. The sketches, like the events of that night, continue to haunt Tito as he remains paralyzed in the medical ward.

A dejected Maco leaves the room with a doctor in tow, who comments, "I've thought it through. I think the only alternative we have, Maco, is that you let me give him the remedy that I mentioned" ("Lo he pensado mucho. Pienso que la única alternativa que tenemos, Maco, es que me dejes darle el remedio que te digo"), to which Maco responds with a nonverbal negative gesture of the head.[26] This remedy is never explained and lingers over Tito's fragile psychiatric state as a sort of last-ditch effort to resuscitate him from his metaphorical coma. The fact that Maco knows what the remedy is and that the audience doesn't suggests that the viewer should make their own tangential presuppositions as to what the cure is; in other words, we are asked to be active interlocutors in Tito's illness and recovery. By leaving the door open as to what the remedy is, the film suggests that the remedy may not only be for Tito but, instead, for an allegorical body that has also suffered trauma—the social body.

Following this conversation, the image cuts to a shot of a television screen and a newscaster reporting on "another case of a disappeared child. This is already the third case this month . . ." ("un nuevo caso de niña desaparecida. Ya son tres menores este mes . . ."). She then suggests that the disappearances may be linked to a pedophile ring which is "terrifying parents" ("tiene aterrados a sus padres"). The screen cuts to an interview of the father who pleads for information about his missing daughter, to then cut to a medium shot of Maco stretching in the upper left corner of the screen and the television set placed in the bottom right. The newscaster pivots to a story on the assault on Carol Valdivieso, who we find out is also a reporter for the station. Making eye contact with the camera, Carol presents the hero who saved her to the country: "This is not a man of steel. He does not climb walls like a spider. He is not a multimillionaire as to have a batmobile. He also cannot fly. He is a man of flesh and blood, like you or like me, a man with guts, with will, that when seeing people in danger, he risks his life to save us" ("Este no es un hombre de acero. No trepa murallas como una araña. No es multimilionario como para tener un batmobile. Tampoco puede volar. Es un hombre de carne y hueso, como usted o como yo, un hombre con agallas, con voluntad, que al ver a gente en peligro, arriesga su vida para salvarnos"). She goes on to describe the attack, providing Maco with an inspiration for the persona: "He appeared and disappeared like a mirage" ("aparecio y desaparecio como un espejismo"). Finally, she directly addresses him: "Hero: where are you? . . . People like you give this society hope" ("Héroe: ¿dónde estás? . . . Personas como tú dan esperanza a esta sociedad").

The above scene is critical in understanding the trajectory of the superhero figure, as it provides the two narrative points around which his development will revolve. First, the relationship with Carol, which will come to dominate the mass and paparazzi media, and will allow Mirageman to come into contact with a wider swath of society. Her praising him on national television has a collateral effect: Tito sees the broadcast and undergoes a miraculous transformation, a detail I will expand upon further in the next section. Second, the abduction report becomes the principal crime that the character engages in the film. "Mirageman against the Pedophile Ring" ("Mirageman contra la red de pedofilia") is supposedly the twenty-eighth mission that the character pursues, but is only one of a few that is shown on screen. It will, however, be the primary narrative point around which Mirageman will focus his strengths in the latter half of the film.

Of particular importance are the words used by the journalist to describe the story: "another case of a disappeared child. This is already the third case this month . . ." ("un nuevo caso de niña desaparecida. Ya son tres menores este mes . . ."). The repetition of the kidnappings reverts us to the newspaper article in the opening montage, therefore suggesting that the disappearance of the child is systematic and systemic, evocative of the *disappearances* during the dictatorship. Like the home invasions that conjure images of a state of terrorism, the kidnappings "terrify the parents." The kidnappings in the present of the narrative effectively become what Alexander Wilde calls "irruptions of memory," or "public events that break in upon Chile's national consciousness, unbidden and often suddenly, to evoke associations with symbols, figures, causes, ways of life which to an unusual degree, are associated with a political past that is still present in the lived experience of a major part of the population" (475).[27] Irruptions are a sort of communal reemergence of a wound, not unlike Cathy Caruth's theorization of trauma, memory, and the persistence of wounds in the individual psyche. The kidnappings are irruptions in that they are public events (as channeled by the mass media) that precipitously evoke the human rights abuses of the past.

In this line of thinking, we may also understand the home invasion as an irruption, in that it is too (made) public and conjures up images of the routine DINA visits of the 1970s and 1980s. Both irruptions come in the context of Maco's transformation to Mirageman. In costume, he begins addressing the different concerns forwarded by the populace via email, setting out to rid Santiago of crime and criminals. His is a public odyssey, as his missions are guided by direct requests from citizens in need, and not by some official intermediary (like the police) or superhuman power (like hearing or a sixth sense). Díaz Espinoza uses handheld and improvised long shots to give these crime-fighting scenes a gritty air of cinéma vérité; by doing so, the film leaves, albeit momentarily, the realm of fiction for that of the real and public, suturing the hero and crime to the cultural and spatial reality of the first years of the twenty-first century. Setting the narrative in Santiago—with its easily identified streets and landmarks—situates the film within a particular cultural and mnemonic moment, thereby building hermeneutic links between the actions of the superhero and the social.

Though it would be easy to simply dismiss *Mirageman* as a Chilean caper, an adaptation of a North American hero and genre to a local film ecosystem, I prefer to follow Juan Murillo's analysis of the film: "It is impossible to speak of *Mirageman* only as *Mirageman*, since the film itself talks about other things, even if it pretends to do it involuntarily, as if those things were not there, or as if they were told by others" ("no es posible hablar de *Mirageman* sólo como *Mirageman*, si la propia película habla de otras cosas, aunque pretenda hacerlo involuntariamente, como si esas cosas no estuvieran allí, o como si las dijeran otros"). These other things are the irruptions in the narrative and their correlative events that are extratextual. By reading the principal criminal knots in the plot as irruptions, we build analytic threads between the plot and the extratextual public context in which the Valech Report and other efforts to address the past circulate. It is in this public context that the film addresses another key aspect of Wilde's idea of the irruption: the existence and conflict of public debate. Wilde notes that

> during "irruptions," such as that triggered by Pinochet's arrest, Chile becomes an arena of deeply divided public discourse, shot through with contending and mutually exclusive collective representations of the past. These charged events are woven into the very fabric of its politics today—symbolic issues, beyond the institutional arrangements well analysed by political scientists, which continue to constrain it in an arrested state. (475)

Wilde's definition leads us to reconsider the kidnapping and home invasion as irruptions. Though they evoke the memory and experience of disappearances, torture, and murder, they do not encourage a "deeply divided public discourse"—everybody is in agreement that pedophilia is morally and criminally reprehensible, as are home invasions and rape. By creating an affective and narrative link between the *desaparecidos* and children, the film solders together the innocence of the child with the rights of the many who disagreed with the Pinochet regime. In effect, this link annuls any possible justification for state terrorism in Chile, an issue till this day where certain segments of an older generation who lived the dictatorship somehow justifies its brutality in the interest of national "peace" and economic growth. The Rettig Report, and especially the Valech document, however, have made short work of any such justifications. In effect, the moral compass now hinged upon the fact that the "reality, massiveness, and indefensibility of human rights violations turned more irrefutable" (Stern 297). The principal antagonist in *Mirageman* therefore not only evokes the atrocities of the past, but also renders an ethical treatise over it, not allowing for the existence of any moral debate that usually erupts after a memory irruption.

That, however, doesn't mean that the film operates on a simple ethical axis where the good and bad are clearly delineated. In fact, the only element that comes under public scrutiny and deliberation is the very presence of the superhero. Immediately following an extended scene in which Mirageman takes on a gang of street thugs who lure him to a fight with an innocuous email asking for help, the film employs a series of interviews carried out by the press with the "common Chilean" ("chileno común"; Murillo). There is no journalist present in these shots to serve as an intermediary with the viewer. Instead, all we see is a microphone held in a bottom corner, lending these vignettes the quality of nonfiction, further blurring the boundaries between the genre and the real. What can be assumed to be interviews broadcasted during the nightly news are assembled in several montages throughout the film to call into question the actions of the protagonist in fighting crime. Some see him in a negative light: as a vigilante outside the law who answers to no one and no authority; or as a performer trying to trick the media into giving him his own reality television show. Others, however, appraise his crime fighting in a positive tone, as much-needed work, given the futility of the police in curbing criminal activity.

What is of importance in these montages is not so much what the layperson opines about the superhero—as these objections and accolades are recycled from other films in the genre—but the fact that the debate occurs in a perpendicular relationship to the irruptions (kidnappings and home invasions). Instead of debating these memory-acts (a largely impossible task since they are unanimously unacceptable), what is debated is the presence of a hero who somehow manages to alleviate or bring closure to the ethically bad. In other words, what is up for debate is the institutional response (as a social actor) to memory-acts or processes; under consideration are not the details and testimonies of the Valech Report, as an example, but rather the actual impetus to collect and publish said report and the collateral political and ethical fissures that it may open. The tension between self-interested amnesia and collective remembering, between sectioning-off the dictatorship and moving towards a future, forms the substrate of these montages. Importantly, these sequences are more informative than didactic, a showing rather than an instructing of the ethical implications of memory work.

When read in relation to the crimes and the eruption of Mirageman in the public consciousness, the montages lay out a political platform in the film that places it firmly in the context of contemporary debates of memory and rights. The film, then, is not a simple Chilean adaptation of already-in-place genre conventions, but a genre film that tackles serious sociocultural questions and schisms.

Discussing the lack of a clear political message in *Mirageman*, Murillo comments:

> And how does the film avoid getting into that undesirable place that demands a point of view? Not only by declaring itself as a strictly genre film, which would automatically immunize it from certain uncomfortable questions. Because if it were just that, I would also be rehearsing tai chi steps like Ariel Mateluna. The problem, in my opinion, is that its director avoids incriminating himself, giving the floor to the "common Chilean," the layperson they interview in the corner of Lyon with Providencia. Rather, it is as if it were the opinion of the ordinary Chilean. Then, of course, the film breathes a sigh of relief: we do not say it, the people say it. . . .
>
> (¿Y cómo hace la película para evitar meterse en ese indeseable lugar que exige un punto de vista? No solamente declarándose como una película estrictamente de género, lo que la inmunizaría automáticamente de ciertas preguntas incómodas. Porque si fuera solo eso, yo también estaría ensayando pasos taichi como Ariel Mateluna. Lo grave, en mi opinión, es que su director evita incriminarse, cediendo la palabra al "chileno común," aquel que encuestan en la esquina de Lyon con Providencia. Más bien, hace como si esa fuera la opinión del chileno corriente. Entonces, claro, la película respira aliviada: no lo decimos nosotros, lo dice la gente . . . ; Murillo)

Murillo of course tempers this critique by later declaring that "it is impossible to speak of *Mirageman* only as *Mirageman*" ("no es posible hablar de *Mirageman* sólo como *Mirageman*"), posing that there is *more* to the film than the humor and butt-kicking of Zaror. I completely agree, and argue that the use of the layperson is precisely how the film traces a politics that sutures the protagonist and his antagonists squarely in the center of a pervading public debate. This tactic is not one of evasiveness or indirect allusion, but rather an exercise in mimesis wherein the superhero (and his genre) serves as an organizing principle for the allegory of the present.

The linkage between the hero and the institution is at the core of the principal crime case of the film: "Misión 28: Mirageman contra la red de pedofilia."[28] Maco receives in his inbox a message from Juan Moli, an investigator on the case. The camera homes in on Maco's email (elvigilante@zami.com), where we see messages from the international media (Mark Sullivan asking for an interview with CNN), Pseudo-Robin (a Mirageman aficionado who is obsessed with becoming Maco's sidekick), and other emails insulting him ("Your costume stinks, you look like a Power Ranger you fucking clown" ["Tu traje apesta, parecí power ranger payaso culiao!"]). He clicks on Moli's message, and the somber audio transitions to a worried Moli providing the voice-over for the email we see on the screen:

Mirageman,

I have a mission that you cannot refuse.

Investigations have confirmed that children disappeared in the last two months are victims of the Pedophilia Network. I know where the leader of the gang is hiding and it is likely that the missing girl is there. But the Investigations Department does not have enough evidence to lead the way.

Mirageman, you're the only hope to end this macabre abuse. . . .

(Mirageman,

Tengo una misión que no puedes rechazar.

Investigaciones confirmó que los niños desaparecidos en los últimos dos meses son víctimas de la Red de Pedofilia. Sé dónde se esconde el líder de la banda y es probable que ahí esté la niña desaparecida. Pero el Departamento de Investigaciones no tiene pruebas suficientes para allanar el lugar.

Mirageman, eres la única esperanza de acabar con este macabro abuso. . . .)

Moli goes on the say that he will leave a bag in an alley at the intersection of Teatinos and Compañía with all the information needed to apprehend the kidnappers and save the girl. The image cuts to Maco walking Teatinos by night as the voice-over continues. He quickly dons the mask in an alley before running over and retrieving the bag; the responsibility of the law is transferred from the police (who have their hands tied by legal constraints) to the superhero.

Important in this short scene is that the superhero as social actor is carefully linked to the powerlessness of the institution in being able to render justice. This is highlighted by the location in which the exchange takes place. Teatinos is a main artery in the administrative center of Santiago. Located along its ten blocks are a series of government buildings (the Treasury, Internal Revenue, Ministries of Justice and Foreign Affairs, etc.), the Palacio de La Moneda, the Plaza de la Constitución, and the Plaza de la Ciudadanía. La Moneda is the seat of the president, and was the site of the most dramatic events of the coup when the air force, under the directives of the military conspirators, bombed the building. On the morning of September 11, the conspirators quickly seized control of the entire country save the center of Santiago. With Allende refusing to resign, the air force came in and bombed the building, but not before Allende broadcasted his now well-known farewell speech at 9:10 a.m. With troops closing in, the democratically elected president took his own life with an assault rifle. Importantly, the images of the La Moneda bombing and the audio from the farewell speech have come to dictate the collective consciousness of the illegitimacy of the coup.

Also on Teatinos is the Plaza de la Constitución, the topological center of the country's political identity, given the number of statues that adorn it. Among these sculptures is a monument to Allende erected, after almost a decade of planning and debate, by the Lagos government in 2000. Wearing his iconic black-framed glasses and wearing a cape of the Chilean flag, the memorial reads, "'I have faith in Chile and its destiny.' 11 September 1973" ("'Tengo fe en Chile y su destino.' 11 de septiembre de 1973"). The monument is also a monument to the deep divisions in Chilean society today. It took years of political handwringing and bickering to even decide on having a statue. Once this was approved, the actual composition and placement of the statue was up for more controversy. To cap things off, the inauguration ceremony was marred by protests from all sides of the political spectrum.[29]

At first glance, the composition of the statue strikes the viewer. Suited up and striding forward, this is a depiction of a hero who refused to capitulate to the military. The flag around his torso, almost like a cape, evokes another kind of hero, a superhero who—through words and memory—has taken on the enemies of the Republic. Describing the legacy of the monument, Katherine Hite notes that "the monument now plays a role in the passing of Chile's memory from one generation to the next. On an outing to La Moneda, the father of a six-year-old girl told me he found himself explaining Allende's fate to his daughter 'as if it were some kind of action thriller. I moved around firing shots and gesturing and making noises, pah, pah, pah'" (Hite). While I am not suggesting that monument fashioned by Chilean sculptor Arturo Hevia is Allende as a superhero, I am posing the idea that the statue does play on popular images of the *super*hero to thereby deify the place of the president within the cultural politics and memory movements of the present.[30] By situating the exchange of information between Moli and Maco in Teatinos, the film conjures up memories, tensions, and images of 1973 and the dictatorship. It also implicitly addresses the paradoxical political paradigm of the transition, and the judicial and executive impasse of the Concertación governments in meting out justice for the human rights abuses, a process that is still very much in flux despite the publication of the Rettig and Valech Reports. By handing off responsibility to Mirageman, the film addresses Moli's (as stand-in for the institutions of law) inability to save the children from the bad guys.

Returning to the film, Maco takes the dossier back to his basement and pores over its contents. In addition to a hand-drawn blueprint of where the band of kidnappers are located is a bulletproof vest (an important detail later in the film), which Maco tries on to make sure it fits under the jacket he wears as part of the Mirageman costume. The map not only indicates the route he should take but the location of armed guards in the building. One may ask where Moli got such detailed information? We may interpret this oversight in the plot either as a genuine mistake by Díaz Espinoza or as an indication of the police being involved in the gang, as insiders within the crime organization, either undercover or as actual criminals. In the subsequent scene, Maco makes his way to the building and dons the mask, crouched below a tree. He then surreptitiously enters the building, which looks like an abandoned school in a poor neighborhood.

The setting for Misión 28 is significant in that it repeats a spatial trope seen in the transition cinema of the 1990s, that is, the abundance of secret spaces that set the stage for the representation of some sort of visceral violence and trauma (Cavallo, Douzet, and Rodríguez 30). In analyzing a wide corpus of postdictatorship films, such as *La luna en el espejo* (Caiozzi, 1990), *La niña en la palomera* (Rates, 1990), and *Punto rojo* (Daiber, 1996), Cavallo, Douzet, and Rodríguez expand on this observation:

In the Chilean cinema of the '90s, there is a recurrence of terrifying places in the midst of apparent normality. These are spaces where the worst perversions take place and the greatest sufferings are suffered, all of which, due to ignorance or indifference, go unnoticed by the people who are nearby. They are like small doors to the infernos of the human condition. Their special meaning comes from the fact that they are installed within an accepted normality.

(El cine chileno de los 90 prodiga lugares pavorosos en medio de la normalidad aparente. Se trata de espacios donde se realizan las peores perversiones y se padecen los mayores sufrimientos, todos los cuales, por ignorancia o indiferencia, pasan inadvertidos para la gente que está en las cercanías. Son como pequeñas puertas de acceso a los infiernos de la condición humana. Pero su significado especial procede de que están instalados dentro de una normalidad aceptada y corriente; 72)

By first showing Maco on the outside transforming into Mirageman on a normal street, and then entering the building as a superhero, the film encourages an evaluation of the narrative space. It is not simply the abandoned warehouse or lair where the villain keeps the victim in the superhero genre, but is instead one of these "terrifying places" that are "are installed within an accepted normality." The space evokes one of the many torture chambers of the DINA that were in operation in normal areas of the city and not in isolated prisons or military camps. It is akin to, though in larger proportion, the domestic space at the start of the film that is the setting for the home invasion. The criminals who enter and attempt to rape Carol Valdivieso use the space as the secret police would have done in the early years of the dictatorship. The home becomes a place of trauma for the layperson, easily lost and anonymized among the day-to-day of the everyday. In effect, the abuse of rights was part of daily life, and not something carried out in an inherently evil place, topographically sectioned off from the general population.

Once inside the building, Maco is ambushed by a guard and brought to a room with the rest of the gang members. As they kick and beat him to a pulp, the image breaks and cuts to the animated images of Tito's sketches. Like in the early home invasion scene, the film poses a narrative and traumatic link between the present and the past, the criminals of today and those who left the two brothers as orphans. In this montage of live-action and animation, the image cuts to a medium shot of a window within the room. The camera zooms in on the window from where a young girl peers out. She is well dressed, her hair neatly combed, which would be somewhat incongruous to the conditions in which she has been kidnapped. Her out-of-place looks may also suggest that though kidnapped, she hasn't yet been raped or harmed by the gang, but is being kept in a holding cell, perhaps to be sold to the highest bidder. The image cuts to a zooming close-up of Mirageman laying sideways on the floor as he receives a beating. His black goggle-eyes look back at the girl, establishing an eyeline match between the two. The zooming of the camera momentarily distracts the viewer from this technique, but subsequent images in the montage underline the visual link between the two subjects in the scene. The close-up of Mirageman then cuts to a portrait shot of Tito looking back at him, then back to Mirageman, and then back to the young girl who now cowers behind the window frame, looking on with one eye.

In essence, Díaz Espinoza creates a tripartite image stitched together by the gaze in the eyeline matches between the three characters. The triangle defies the laws of space and temporality and establishes the critical nexus around which Misión 28 takes place. The young, nameless girl is not simply a stand-in for (saving) Tito; instead, she, like him, is a victim of a criminality that originates in and replicates—via the cutting to the early sketches—an atemporal and collective past. They are two sides of the same coin, the victim at the moment of potential abuse and the victim who must live with an unresolved trauma. By setting them in a geometric relationship with Mirageman, the film provokes a meditation on the temporality of trauma in Chile: Is it located in a carefully partitioned past, where its victims are relegated to the pages of a report, exile, or death; or is it that the victim of trauma remains alive and suffering today, whether as firsthand survivor or as the recipient of a postmemory?[31] What role does Mirageman as the focal point of this visual exercise play in all this?

The scene then cuts to the entrance of who is presumably the boss of the gang. He is dressed in a suit, and his round face subtly resembles the main antagonist in Tito's sketches. Another member pulls Mirageman's mask off to reveal a bloodied Maco. He looks at the boss, and the image predictably cuts to animated sketch of the villain. The previously silent animation now speaks the words spoken by the boss in the scene: "To the river" ("Al río"). The connection made between the past and present and between the different criminal acts is now explicit.

Two of the gang members take Maco to the banks of a river, which we may assume is the Mapocho that divides the city in two. Here they prepare him to be disappeared by tying him to a block of concrete before throwing him in its waters. At first glance, the site of this scene is not unusual, as it is where one would expect a mafioso to get rid of a body. Read contextually, however, the disappearing of Maco in the river evokes the many bodies that were seen floating downriver in the immediate days after the coup.[32] For an audience knowledgeable of the details of the abuses of the secret services, this quick and seemingly innocuous scene draws powerful tangents to the years of the dictatorship and a justice that has yet to come, as there has been no official inquiry into the many firsthand reports of bodies in the Mapocho.[33]

Just as Maco is about to be disappeared, one of the goons turns on the other and executes him. He instructs Mirageman to disappear before pointing the gun at his own arm and shooting. We learn later in the film that this criminal is in fact Juan Moli, who had infiltrated the gang and was thus able to provide Mirageman with a hand drawn map of the building. He shoots himself to maintain his cover while allowing the protagonist to escape. A distraught and broken Maco appears in the next scene, crying in his basement after failing to save the young girl. The image cuts to a series of images of the front page of several magazines and newspapers with headlines that indicate that Mirageman has disappeared from the streets of Santiago.[34] Another headline states that the kidnapped girl is indeed in the hands of the pedophile ring.[35] The image cuts to a shot of a television screen where the newscaster confirms that Mirageman has not appeared in the past two weeks. The newscaster goes on to speculate that he has hung up his costume due to the deluge of criticisms received from the media and public for his "mediocre labor" in fighting crime. The camera cuts to a studied shot of a downcast Maco sitting in his basement, and then to another image of an even more despondent Tito sitting on the floor of his ward. The character in the latter rocks back and forth in a physical representation of the mental trauma he is undergoing, perhaps as a result of the disappearance of Mirageman from the nightly news. The medium shot of Tito pulls outwards and we see Maco sitting with him in the room. In the next shot, we see Maco outside with the doctor who informs him that Tito was progressing in his therapy while Mirageman appeared in the news, giving him hope in overcoming his inner demons.[36]

With his disappearance, Tito has regressed considerably, going back to the stage of traumatic acting out instead of possible resolution.

The subsequent narrative knots in the film deviate from the principal storyline of the pedophile ring: we see the emergence of Pseudo-Robin, who puts on the mask to take on the common criminal, albeit with little success given his lack of martial arts training. We also see a sort of culmination to the Carol-Mirageman affair as she stages a fake kidnapping and broadcasts a plea for help. Accompanied by Pseudo-Robin, Mirageman reappears in the streets of Santiago in "Misión 29: Mirageman and Pseudo-Robin to the rescue of Carol Valdivieso" ("Misión 29: Mirageman y Pseudo-Robin al rescate de Carol Valdivieso"). In the longest sequence of the film, and through an aesthetics that likens the narrative to a linear video game mission, the camera follows Zaror as he puts on a butt-kicking display. He goes through a bevy of criminals before entering the building where Carol is being held. Cut into this sequence are several close-ups of security cameras watching his every step. After overpowering a few more assailants, he unties and rescues Carol, who is dressed for a night out on the town, and not like a distressed victim. Mirageman accompanies her to her house, where she seduces him, looks at a security camera mounted on the ceiling, and quickly removes his mask. When he realizes that Carol does this in plain view of the camera, a betrayed Maco flees. In the nightly news, he realizes that the entire mission was a spectacle orchestrated by Valdivieso and the television station to unmask him, in a reality show for the masses.

Maco becomes visibly agitated and takes out his frustrations on the television. The lack of dialogue by Zaror leaves the audience clueless as to why the story would cause him to breakdown in tears. We get an answer, however, in the next scene when we see Maco consoling Tito in the clinic: he too watched the broadcast and realized that his brother is the superhero, opening up a never-healing wound in his psyche as a series of sketches flash through the screen. If before Mirageman was able to give Tito hope, now his identity as Maco simply rekindles the originary trauma that is responsible for his unresponsive mental state. In the subsequent scene, Maco stands on a roof overlooking the city. He gazes down with his arms wide stretched contemplating suicide, but is interrupted by Moli, who lets him (and the viewer) know that he was the gang member who allowed him to escape in the riverside scene. Moli reassures him by stating that he has "tampered with evidence" ("manipulado información") so that nobody would know the identity of the superhero.[37] He promises Maco to help with more information to finally apprehend the kidnappers, giving the protagonist a raison d'être to put on the mask. He praises him for all he is done, as, "for the first time, I saw people lose their fear . . . to have hope" ("por primera vez vi a la gente perder el miedo . . . tener esperanza"). He encourages Maco to once again become Mirageman and to rescue the girl.[38]

The final confrontation with the pedophile gang ("Misión 30: Mirageman against the Pedophile Ring, Attempt #2" ["Misión 30: Mirageman contra la red de pedofilia, intento #2"]) covers the last segment of the film. With little or no ambient music, the camera follows Mirageman into their lair. Unlike earlier scenes that were set to a funky retro soundtrack, there is no kitsch here. There is also no lighting to highlight Mirageman and his physique in the action sequences, as what we see are dark shapes engaging each other. The change in tone and mood reminds the viewer of the seriousness of what is at stake. Another difference between this mission and the other scenes is the technique used by the protagonist to overcome his assailants. While earlier scenes relied on Zaror's martial arts expertise to make short work of the bad guys, Mirageman now uses increasing brutal force to overcome the kidnappers. The first goon, for example, is met with a thrown knife that stabs him in the center of his chest; the next thug has his head brutally smashed after shooting Mirageman who, thankfully for the audience, is wearing the bulletproof vest given to him by Moli before the first attack on the ring. Another villain is shot twice after struggling with the protagonist. This detail is significant in that the shooting is not simply the result of the struggle for the gun, as a single bullet would have quickly disabled the bad guy. By firing again, the sequence shows us to what extent Mirageman's psyche has been transformed, how his moral compass has been reoriented as a result of the broader ethics of what is at stake with the child kidnappings. The gritty and graphic nature of the fight sequence underlines the importance of his work not simply as a popular crime fighter, but as a bastion of a ethical and political reckoning with the perpetrators of violence.

The scene draws to closure when Miragemen enters the center of the gang's stronghold, in the same space where he was earlier beaten to a pulp. A musical track now overlays the visual register, but it is in a tone that reflects the significance of the scene in the development of climactic tension. The leader of the gang ambushes him, firing away with two pistols that have the hero cowering for cover. Interjected into the climax are animated sketches that reaffirm the association to be made between this criminal and earlier actions. Also spliced in is an image of Tito cowering (like Mirageman) in his ward, thus completing the multilateral (and multitemporal) readings that are to be construed from this one scene. The villain runs out of bullets and takes Mirageman to be dead. He, after all, doesn't know that our hero has been working with the police and has been given a bulletproof vest. He approaches the seemingly dead body in victory and is about to pull out a gun when Mirageman releases a blade hidden in his sleeve and cuts off the villain's head. The decapitation is the culminating action in the brutality of this final mission. We may even read the action metaphorically, if the villain is to be understood as a stand-in for the originary trauma in the past; his death and decapitation is a politicosymbolic gesture as a way out of the mnemonic impasse of the present.[39]

The hero's recourse to violence is at first glance quite surprising, given the superhero genre's general aversion to killing villains; Batman, for example, has a specific code to not kill his adversaries. This is not always the case, however, for the Latin American superhero, as justice cannot be always trusted to the law. The institutions and channels of civic judisprudence, after all, have failed in the case of Mirageman (and Chile, in a broader sense) in bringing justice to the many victims of the pedophile ring (and the dictatorship). It is up to the superhero alone to render justice by using brutal violence to symbolically neutralize the source-agent of trauma. A similar narrative strategy occurs in *Capitán Centroamérica*, and is perhaps even more pronounced given the impotence and corruption of the law to face down extant criminality in the region.

A wounded Mirageman rescues the girl while being shot at by the last remaining gang member. He asks her to run for help and almost gets away, but is shot in the neck (the one area not covered by the vest) and falls into a pond. Moli quickly intervenes and kills the villain, suggesting that he was following Mirageman during the entire mission, therefore being involved in the case though not officially participating. The newscaster who previously questioned his actions and motivations in previous scenes now appears on screen in a somber mood, announcing that "Mirageman, our national hero" ("Mirageman, nuestro héroe nacional"), has passed away. Carol then appears and gives the viewers the rundown on what transpired the night before. She stands in front of the pond and explains that the superhero's body has yet to be found, as the image cuts to several long shots of the water.[40] An emotional Carol declares that his saving of the young girl is the "most heroic act seen in our country during the past few decades" ("acto más heroico de las últimas décadas de nuestro país"), linking the diegesis with extradiegetic events. The scene ends with a montage of newspaper headlines praising him, showing a throng of people marching in his memory and others refusing to believe that he has died.

As is typical in the genre, the music draws the viewer into an emotive closure—Tito's nurse and doctor peer out of a window and see the young teenager practicing martial arts moves. The emergence of the superhero and his vanquishing of the bad guys—experienced, of course, in tandem with allegorical overtones—have done just enough to move Tito from the closed quarters of the ward (where he acted out), to the outside where he enters the psychic realm of working through. The camera pans from right to left as Tito rehearses different maneuvers. He abruptly stops and looks up to see Mirageman observing him. A long shot of the hero on a rooftop cuts to a medium image, and then back to a close shot of Tito who musters a smile. The music hits a crescendo as the final shot of the film reveals that Mirageman is no longer there, but is perhaps now back in his basement waiting for the next email from Moli.

Masks

Mirageman is an important film in this small and inconclusive genre of Latin American superhero films, because it carves out its own niche vis-à-vis established genre conventions without necessarily falling into the narrative mode of parody and tandem satire of local politics. While an analysis along thematic lines that have tended to guide Southern Cone studies, such as trauma, memory, and *los desaparecidos* demonstrates how engaged the film is with the predominating sociopolitical issues of the turn of the century, the film may also be examined for its nonallegorical strategies. It is on this semiotioc and cognitive layer—an area not as engaged with the politicosocial substrate of the diegesis—that I want to examine, as I believe the film, by including and replicating well-known elements of the genre, permits a point of entry into analyzing these same components for their value beyond simple narrative devices and visual accoutrements. This critical gesture allows for an understanding of how the superhero genre may operate in contexts quite different from the Anglo production and distribution ecosystem; that is, I am interested in examining certain elements of the film that explicitly align and identify it with the superhero genre for a local and international audience that has already been saturated in the last two decades with the Marvel and DC cinematic universes. To engage these genre elements, I am posing a phenomenological analysis that evades linguistic acumen; in essence, I argue that certain elements in the film are easily identified and associated with the superhero genre (even for a public that watches the film with subtitles) due to the reactions they provoke in the viewer. In other words, finite visual elements associated with and then circulated through superhero films provoke affective intensities that establish certain characters as viable heroes aligned with the thematic and narrative conventions of the genre.[41]

Examining phenomenology (and the potential for affect) is a relatively new modus operandi in superhero studies, but I suggest it outlines important matrices for the transnationality of the genre, given the potential for affect to operate across linguistic and cultural barriers.[42] The superhero film is, after all, built on the generation of particular emotions around the characters, their story arcs, and their working through various ethical situations. The audience experiences hope when Superman comes back to life after a rendezvous with kryptonite; we await with anticipation when Commissioner Gordon illuminates the sky of Gotham with the sign of the Batman; we move to anticipatory excitement when we see Iron Man's electromagnetic heart glow. Note here that the generation of emotion is tied to specific elements vis-à-vis the definition of the superhero; that is, the moving image elicits emotive responses through the direct (and at times indirect) representation of particular forms. It is not these forms in themselves that provoke an emotive response in the viewer, but the coalescing of an affective economy around them that then fuses into emotion, and then moving that emotion into a generalized, multi-body experience of the superhero.

Let us outline some definitions. Parting from a Deleuzian school of thought, Brian Massumi argues that *emotion*, unlike affect, "is contextual. Affect is situational, eventfully ingressive to context. Serially so: affect is transsituational. As processual as it is precessual, affect inhabits the passage. . . . Impersonal affect is the connecting thread of experience. . . . The world-glue of event of an autonomy of event-connection continuing across its own serialized capture in context" (217). Unpacking this distinction, Eric Shouse triangulates the two terms with *feeling*: "Feeling is a sensation that has been checked against previous experiences " (3). He adds that emotion is "the projection/display of a feeling" (4). In opposition to the previous two ideas, affect is "a non-conscious experience of intensity . . . a moment of unformed and unstructured potential" (5).

In relation to emotions and feelings, "affect is the most abstract because [it] cannot be fully realised in language, because affect is always prior to and/or outside of consciousness" (5). If emotion is our outward display of feeling—hope, anticipation, excitement—then affect is its precursor; that is, affect, as manifested in intensities, sensations, and impulses (re)configure and impact the somatic experience of engaging the moving image. In other words, the emotions provoked by the examples above are first gestured towards, built up, and then intensified through the production and transmission of affect. With these definitions in mind, I am suggesting that in the superhero genre, there are particular forms that house affective intensities.[43] This was clear with the mask of El Santo, or the large cross that appeared in earlier wrestler-superhero films to ward off evil; even the cozy tones and shapes of El Chapulín's costume evoke a particular reaction in the viewer.

Nevertheless, I am not moving to the theoretical extreme that Eugenie Brinkema poses in *The Forms of the Affects*, which, while arguing for a turn to formalism over phenomenology in affect theory, also states that "affect . . . has fully shed the subject" (25). Brinkema "regards any individual affect as a self-folding exteriority that manifests in, as, and with textual form" (25). While I agree that a formalist approach does invigorate affective critique—as opposed to a purely subject-based exploration of "feelings" generated by the moving image—I contend that form can only be productively examined for affect, that is, as signifier of particular affects, when its relationship to a spectatorial body is taken into consideration. That is, it is not the dynamic movements of affect between a particular signifier and subject that is in play, but a collective circulation.

Discussing the circulation of affect and emotion, Sara Ahmed notes that "affect does not reside in an object or sign, but is an effect of the circulation between objects and signs (the accumulation of affective value). Signs increase in affective value as an effect of the movement between signs: the more signs circulate, the more affective they become" (*Cultural Politics* 45). Ahmed argues that certain signs become "stickier" as they circulate, provoking intensities of affect that then generate assessable value to the signifier, in what Ahmed terms "affective economies." This, of course, stands in contraposition to Brinkema's self-professed radical formalism that abjures the subject, and therefore any potential circulation. I find value in Brinkema's gesture (albeit not in its complete denouncement of the subject) by relating her insistence on form with Ahmed's own meditation: "We could hence ask how the circulation of signs of affect shapes the materialization of collective bodies, for example the 'body of the nation'" ("Affective Economies" 121). If affective transmissions can shape collective bodies, does this same centripetal force also not work in the opposite direction? In other words, the form itself is shaped (and not only becomes stickier) through its circulation and transmission, thus becoming ready for identification and analysis. I agree with Brinkema, that affects thus can have forms, but disagree in that this consideration may occur outside of an intercognitive mechanism of cyclical production and reception. In the superhero genre in particular, the affective economy around certain signs, symbols, and even narrative arcs makes these characters recognizable and captivating to an audience overflowing with affective transmissions.[44] Their deployment within the moving image engenders affective transmission, which, cyclically, reinvigorates and feeds their condition as forms of a particular affect.

It is in this act that the superhero becomes a consecrated figure, one that "has certain tropes—familiar and repeated moments, iconic images and actions, figures of speech, patterns of characterization—that have resonance; that is, they embody or symbolize some aspect of the character, and have gained this resonance through repeated use by storytellers" (Coogan, *Superhero* 6-7). Superheroes become "recognizable," their evocation charged with feeling and emotion in the crowd through simple symbolic nuances and forms, engendering intensities. At the conclusion of Christopher Nolan's *Batman Begins*, Gordon hands Batman a Joker playing card, a clue as to who the villain in the sequel would be. Neither character directly references the protagonist's arch nemesis, but an audience in the know is immediately primed in anticipation for the prospect of seeing the "Clown Prince of Crime."[45] This feeling and emotion is made possible by the signifier of the playing card that has become sticky with affect across its use in different media (and memorable performances by the likes of Jack Nicholson). In the case of this particular concluding scene, a learned viewer affectively engages with the form of the playing card in a way that an unknowledgeable viewer simply cannot. The feelings evoked in the latter harbor anticipation and excitement, whereas the latter may only feel curiosity as to what this playing card could mean. To coalesce into excitement, however, requires a formal affective transmission, one that reaches peak intensities towards feeling and emotion.

Let us return to the potential for the creation of an affective economy of signifiers in *Mirageman*. The film follows Coogan's principal characteristics of the genre, and includes many of the well-known devices seen in recent Hollywood features. I want to focus on one element in particular—the protagonist's mask—first in its presence in the mise-en-scène, and then its circulation along the course of the film as it gains affective value. The mask in *Mirageman* is the only outward signifier that shows that Maco has adopted his heroic persona. It is the only aesthetic and semantic element that distinguishes the protagonist from his alter ego as he fights crime in the streets of Santiago. It is the only part of his vestment that is brightly colored and easily recognizable, as his jacket, pants, and even gloves are in somber neutrals.

In studying this particular trait of superheroes, Miroslav Kohut argues that "the reasons for superheroes wearing masks are twofold: external, derived from the environment in which the character operates; and internal, rooted in the psychology and motivation of each particular character" (28). Addressing the former, Maco's donning of the mask may be explained by his desire to maintain his anonymity, an ironic gesture as he is, in effect, quite invisible to those around him. He maintains no close relationships, lives in a basement, and holds a job as a nighttime bouncer at a strip club. He is the invisible muscle in his workplace, as what are put on display in the mise-en-scène of the Passapoga are the gyrating bodies of the dancers. Yet maybe it is this very nameless existence that he intentionally upholds that provokes him to don the mask, as in doing so he is permitted to maintain anonymity.

The psychological reasons for the mask are, however, more complex. In the opening action sequence where he comes upon the home invasion, Maco quickly disables an attacker and decides to put on the criminal's ski mask. His decision is punctuated by the splicing in of images of the drawings of the childhood attack that first appeared in the opening montage. Now, however, the images are animated and brought to life, given an agency in the psychological machinations of the character. Maco quickly puts on the ski mask and assumes an unsophisticated identity that lacks the trimmings of more established heroes. To note here is the stitching together of the sartorial action and the traumatic memory, a strategy at the core of several superhero narratives and of special importance here as I outline in the previous section. Herein (and early on) is a poietic gesture in the film, as the montage of images introduces the mask (and the masked protagonist) into an already-in-place affective economy, generating lines of contact and transmissions with the sticky signifier of the mask (as it appears throughout the genre). This may explain Maco's actions in further anonymizing his already anonymous self as he enters the house to save the damsel in distress, as the character recognizes (perhaps through viewing other superhero films or reading comics) the value of the mask in establishing a hero-figure as an antagonist to the villain.

The mask, in fact, becomes the only identifying element of the character in the nightly news and the public's collective consciousness, as Valdivieso informs her audience that a masked hero saved her from a violent crime. In introducing this segment, the television anchor calls the news "an incident worthy of a comic book or Hollywood movie" ("un incidente digno de revista de cómic o película de Hollywood"), subliminally acknowledging the affective economy in which *Mirageman* engages. Valdivieso informs the audience that there is indeed nothing "super" about this hero: the only thing that sets him apart from any other citizen in Santiago is the mask. The mask, as Lisa Gotto argues, "is not clandestine but attracts attention" (48). In regards to the semiotics of the film vis-à-vis the long Chilean transition, the mask takes on a metaphorical role, "a means of covering as well as of uncovering. While the masked is seen to be masked, the secret is revealed to be no secret at all. Thus, the mask indicates a presence of absence. It reveals what it hides, and it hides what it reveals" (Gotto 48).

Evidence of the import of the mask in delineating himself as a local (super)hero is seen in the scenes immediately after the newscast. Maco is called to Tito's psychiatric ward, as there is news on the condition of his traumatized brother. In the following image, the camera is placed behind the protagonist and the doctor as they stand at the threshold of the ward, a back view that privileges the action inside (both for the diegetic characters and for the audience). We see a standing Tito seemingly energized by the news of a hero martial artist, now performing simulated karate moves in his hospital room. He is not the despondent and speechless shell of a character, but an animated subject kinesthetically addressing an inner psychic knot. The doctor informs us that "everything started last night . . . with the news of the superhero that saved the journalist" ("todo empezó anoche . . . con la noticia del superhéroe que salvó a la periodista"). He continues that the transformation in the patient is "incredible" ("increíble"), as the camera centers in a close shot on Maco, the background music reaching an inspirational crescendo as Maco (and the viewer) recognize the superhero's potential for the production of massive affective intensities, which may result in very real and tangible changes such as the reshaping of Tito as a metonym of trauma. This shot lays the groundwork for Maco's own transformation from a simple hero who rescued a woman during a home invasion to a true superhero cognizant of the affective economies and genre tropes that come in association with adopting a new persona.

Of import in this transformational scene (of both the narrative and the protagonist) is the fact that Tito has fashioned for himself a rudimentary mask made out of toilet paper. The camera placed behind Maco and the doctor as a masked Tito moves about the room emphasizes the hermeneutic potential for this action, as we are given the privilege of evaluating (albeit from a critical distance) Maco's perspective on his brother's transformation. Adding to this dynamic is the fact that Tito is situated inside the room, the doorframe separating the exterior observers from his internal change. We thus are met with a framed image within a frame, where two planes of spectatorship are oriented towards the masked teenager. If this image provokes a self-reflection on the part of Maco, it also engenders a moment of reflection in the viewer, begging a consideration of the mask (as form) in the shaping of an affective economy around the signifier of the hero. It is the simple, toilet paper mask around Tito's face—and not the ski mask donned in the earlier scene by Maco—that generates an affective intensity around the form of the mask and the notion of the superhero, as we see firsthand how its form both psychologically and physically impacts the younger brother. The mask provokes affective intensities, feelings, and then an emotion of hope and survival in the teenager. There is a somatic reaction in the diegetic character-spectator that provokes a collateral somatic movement in the viewer. This is underlined by a shift in the dynamics of viewing in the scene when the image cuts to a close up of Maco as the camera is reoriented to be placed inside the room. We read in his face an emotive change as he goes from looking downwards in a pensive, brooding mood to directing his vision upwards towards his masked brother.

This small detail serves two purposes. First, it establishes the transformative portion of the narrative, that is, when the character realizes that he must fashion an identity built around the (superhero) mask. Second, the change in feeling and emotion in the protagonist provokes a parallel deliberation in the spectator, as we are instructed on the affective potential of the mask as signifier and form. The mask is thus imbued with affective and symbolic capital as it begins to circulate through and across the film, between characters and the diegesis, and between the image and the spectator. Moving across intensities, the mask generates a feeling and emotion that is built on the foundation of other similar characters in the genre that appear in print and film.

The insistence on the mask as signifier of the hero, combined with Tito's transformation, follows Ahmed's contention that "affect does not reside positively in the sign or commodity, but is produced only as an effect of its circulation" ("Affective Economies" 120). The ski mask in the early scene only gains and produces affect when circulated through news and then replicated in the ward scene. The mask thus becomes the crux of the transformation narrative as Maco embarks on assuming the identity of Mirageman. He makes a shopping list before heading to a local mall: "Accessories: mask, gloves, belt, flexible pants, lightweight shoes . . ." ("Implementos: máscara, guantes, cinturón, pantalones flexibles, zapatillas livianas . . ."). It is unsurprising that the very first element of his costume is the mask. In what is perhaps the least serious montage of the film, Maco goes through a set of different prototypes that he himself sketches, all of which are based on easily recognizable characters from the Marvel and DC universes such as Wolverine, Batman, and Deadpool. Though lacking any dialogue and narratological importance, this quick scene does, however, link the sartorial aesthetics of the Chilean hero to an already-in-place circulation of superhero forms. Such a gesture quickly and efficiently allows for the generation of affect within an economy, and the potential for the blue mask to also become a sticky form that is recognizable and emotive for audiences. After many a failed sketch, Maco finally settles on an outfit outlined by Tito, where what is prominently featured is the mask.[46] Tito's prototype for the hero lacks a branding symbol (like a red heart, bat, capital "S," or a thunder sign), cape, or special tools—the only identifiable characteristic of the drawing is the monochromatic mask. The drawing also gives the protagonist a name for his masked crime fighter: Mirageman.

The mask identifies the hero in the urban milieu, but also plays an affective role by generating intensities (such as in a moment of crime-fighting action) that may materialize in feelings and emotions in the diegetic characters and the audience. The mask becomes both sign and emotion, giving the general populace hope and transforming Tito from being a traumatized victim to a subject who gains agency. It is telling that in the final scene of the film, a reinvigorated Tito looks up to see Mirageman, and not his brother, on the rooftop. The monochromatic blue of the mask is striking against the drab buildings and sky, and provokes a smile of acknowledgement in Tito, signaling the potential for the mask—and the hero—to effect transformational change.

Mirageman is an important case study in how a non-Hollywood superhero may be conceived, materialized, and then put into circulation in the Latin American cinematic ecosystem. It is unsurprising that its principal actor, Zaror, has now caught the attention of global superhero fans—he appears as the character Shaft in Marvel's *The Defenders*, a 2017 series in Marvel's Netflix universe that includes *Daredevil*, *Jessica Jones*, *Luke Cage*, and *Iron Fist*.

Unlike films of the parodic mood that rely on renegotiating the affective and symbolic capital of already-in-place forms (as is the case with *El Man* and *Chinche Man*), the film lays out a roadmap for creating an autochthonous character with his own identity, mission, and psychological complexity. In doing so, the film—highlighting the importance of form in any superhero movie—exemplifies the linkages to be found between affect and form, and that both are inextricably linked in the production, reception, and circulation of the moving image. In doing so, Díaz Espinoza successfully reimagines the schema for memory work and narrative in contemporary Chile. By moving into the realm of allegory—within, of course, an easily identifiable and enjoyable genre such as the superhero movie—the director engages the viewer in the surprisingly complex task of unearthing the past and exploring its consequences in the present. The optimistic concluding scene, furthermore, suggests that working through trauma, even by means of the superhero genre, is not only possible but also highly viable. The film evokes Michael Lazzara's meditation on the poetics and politics of memory during the Chilean transition:

> To be certain, the question today, more than three decades after the coup, no longer has to do with *whether* atrocities did or did not occur, but rather with *how* they are being interpreted, understood, and told. . . . The issue is at once political and ethical. It implies, on one hand, *naming* torture and disappearance. . . . On the other hand, it implies choosing "appropriate" narrative forms for the telling of "limit experiences." . . . (12; emphasis in the original)

Though not as narratologically intricate or thematically "serious" as the texts Lazzara examines, *Mirageman* enters into the fray of *how* these traumas may be "interpreted, understood, and told." The film engages humor and genre conventions to broaden the scope of memory work and narrative, taking what has been a rather conservative genre (in terms of ethics and politics) to a popular audience that can (wish to) read between the lines.

Chapter 4

The Superhero and a Death Foretold

Chinche Man in San Pedro Sula

On the afternoon of January 17, 2017, Igor Padilla was ambushed in front of the Fabryka toy store in the Suyapa neighborhood of San Pedro Sula, in the Cortés Department of northern Honduras.[1] At least twenty-five rounds from a semi-automatic AR-15 were found at the scene.[2] Witnesses reported that the four assailants dressed as police officers quickly sped off after riddling the victim with bullets. Padilla, aged thirty-eight, a popular journalist and comic artist in the sketch comedy show *Los Verduleros* for the Hable Como Hable (HCH) television station, was filming an advertisement for one of his many programs.[3] Hours after the murder, police rounded up a total of seventeen suspects, including Cristian Ariel Cálix Hernández, also known as "Little Sam," a Mara Barrio 18 leader who had been imprisoned in the federal El Pozo jail in December 2015 on charges of drug and arms trafficking. Investigative reporting by journalists from *El Heraldo* uncovered that Little Sam was freed on November 24, 2016 after having paid a bond of 20 million lempiras, a detail local authorities had kept from the press and general public.

Two days after Padilla's murder, units from the Fuerza Nacional Antiextorsión (FNA) and Policía Militar del Orden Público (PMOP) apprehended Martha Yolanda Ortez, also known as "La Gordita," in the Ramón Villeda Morales airport outside San Pedro Sula. She confessed to calling Padilla and luring him to the spot of the execution at the behest of members of Mara 18, including Little Sam. She was released hours later due to a lack of evidence. The inquiry into the members of the Mara

18 gang associated with the crime was shrouded in secrecy. Journalists were unable to uncover any details of the investigation, so much so that the Office of the United Nations High Commissioner for Human Rights in Honduras issued a public statement asking that the authorities clarify the details of the murder and the investigation. Three men were formally charged with Padilla's murder: Aaron Alejandro Aguilar Alemán (also known as "El Sufrido"), David René Benítez Sarmiento (also known as "Hellboy"), and José Hernández Rivas (also known as "El Inquieto"). The other twelve who were arrested in the original investigation were charged with the illegal use of arms and criminal association. The case went to court in June 2019, with all parties found culpable.

Months later, on July 9, 2017, Padilla's cameraman, Edwin Rivera Paz, was executed in the San Diego neighborhood of Acayucan, in the Mexican state of Veracruz. He was chased down by two men on a motorcycle, and shot in broad daylight near his apartment. Rivera Paz had fled Honduras shortly after the murder of Padilla, and was seeking refugee status in Mexico. Again, as of December 2018, no arrests have been made and the case remains open.

Padilla and Rivera Paz's murders fall in line with a long series of journalist killings in Mexico and Central America at the hand of organized crime. The motivations behind both murders remain unclear, though they may be linked to the project Padilla was working on at the time of his death—the filming of a movie titled *El Reportero*, about a journalist who is recruited by a criminal gang. The film was scheduled to be released in 2017, though the fate of the project is now unclear given Padilla's demise.

The murder of Igor Padilla made local and national news, but failed to register on the international news circuit, due in part to the large number of homicides and gang violence prevalent in Honduras and in neighboring Central American countries. Padilla and Rivera Paz, after all, are simply two more murders among the many that now characterize the contemporaneity of life in the region. What interests me about these cases in particular, however, is their relationship to the superhero genre, as Padilla was—quite ironically—the creator and writer of the first Honduran/Central American superhero film to ever be made, *Chinche Man* (dir. Thomas Chí, 2015). Depicted as a crime-fighting hero for the masses, Chinche Man took on the likes of those who, in real life, gunned down his creator in cold blood.

The character originated in a sketch screened during a *Los Verduleros* program. The show airs live on Saturday evenings and rebroadcasts on

Sunday, and is a satire of everyday life in San Pedro Sula, poking fun at local issues, public figures, and news stories. Chinche Man debuted as a sort of parodic character, a languid and shirtless youngster who donned a *luchador* mask to become a hero.[4] This early prototype of the character has no superpowers aside from the aura of the mask, and embarks on defending the layperson from acts of injustice. Padilla cleverly took advantage of the open production and emission platform of YouTube to popularize individual skits from *Los Verduleros*, including Chinche Man. The character made his first appearance on television in 2011, and was uploaded to Padilla's YouTube channel on December 22, 2014. Padilla's channel has over 46,000 subscribers. The Chinche Man video has amassed over 337,000 views, including more than 2,300 "I like this" and only 207 "I dislike this" clicks.

The popularity of the sketch—both in domestic and international circles (given the comments on the YouTube video from viewers across the Americas)—led Padilla to write, produce, and direct a feature-length film.[5] *Chinche Man* debuted in national movie theaters on May 27, 2015, albeit with a heftier production budget, professional actors, and an actual costume for the hero. The film in its entirety was uploaded to Padilla's YouTube channel nine days after his death and has already amassed over 309,000 views. The plot is unassuming and follows a familiar narrative arc in the origin-type superhero film. Pedro Zaldívar is young and down on his luck. He is harassed by Don Manuel, a local mafioso that happens to be his landlord, who continually extorts the protagonist for money, going as far as trying to steal his girlfriend Clarita. After a series of misfortunes, Pedro finally lands a job working in a tailor shop, but is quickly fired when Don Manuel threatens his boss. With the walls closing in on his employment opportunities, Pedro becomes a cleaner in an electronics repair store. When the store is robbed, he goes to jail accused of a crime he did not commit. Despondent and overwhelmed in an overcrowded cell, Pedro observes how the other inmates, who are locked up for crimes such as drug dealing and dog fighting, are terrified of a simple *chinche*, or kissing bug (known for its transmission of Chagas disease). Seeing how the insect inspires fear even in the most hardened of offenders, Pedro decides to become Chinche Man and to fight back against the likes of Don Manuel. With the help of a genius inventor (Chico)—who, a la Lucius Fox or Q, helps him craft a costume that has secret weapons, such as electrocuting gloves that discharge mega-watt punches—and a martial arts sensei (Don Hipólito), Chinche Man confronts Don Manuel and his criminal organization. The film has a predictable ending: the hero saves the girl and the bad guy goes to jail, while our hero, looking over the city he is now charged with protecting, receives a call about a new mission. The film ends with a closing caption of "Continuará," leaving the door open for more crime-fighting adventures and a possible sequel (which is really the defining characteristic of twenty-first-century superhero movies).[6]

Reviewing the film for *Remezcla*, Vanessa Erazo writes that "with its dubstep soundtrack and its super campy aesthetic, *Chinche Man* proves that you don't need to have superpowers in order to fight crime." While this is true, especially given that North American superhero films are an exercise in computer-assisted powers, the lack of true superpowers really aligns the protagonist with several Latin American superheroes, including Mirageman, and its origin character from the skit, that is, the wrestler-superhero archetype. In other words, the lack of powers gestures towards a lineage of superheroes that fight crime in spite of their normalcy. I also believe that the film needs to be properly situated within a national (or even regional) moment and filmic industry. *Chinche Man*, like other twenty-first-century Latin American superhero movies, is deeply embedded within a sociopolitical milieu and must be read in dialogic association within a broader cultural horizon.

The diegesis of the film is the present moment, a contemporaneity molded by decades of conflict, demographic change, and economic transformation. To understand the "crime" that Erazo identifies requires a deep digging of its roots, that is, a gesture beyond the superficiality of linking crime to the ontology of the urban (such as that in the film), or even to the actions of Don Manuel the landlord. Writing on Central American cinema in broad terms, and specifically on Honduran film, Euclides Valdés Flores argues that "the political events of 2009 generated a new theme, as seen in films such as *¿Quién dijo miedo?* [2010] . . . *El Xendra* [2012]" ("los hechos políticos de 2009 generaron una nueva temática, reflejada en películas como *¿Quién dijo miedo?* [2010] . . . *El Xendra* [2012]") and *Chinche Man*. Valdés Flores is referring to the US-supported coup d'état by the military against then-president José Zelaya, a liberal elected into office with a slim margin of victory, who in 2009 instigated a process of constitutional reform that was not viewed kindly by the traditional pillars of political and economic power in the country. These reforms, after all, were suggested to modernize the country's fiscal and administrative structures. The deposing of Zelaya cast Honduras in a negative light in international circles, as the global community viewed the military intervention as an abuse of democratic and institutional process. Zelaya was succeeded by an acting president, Roberto Micheletti, who was then replaced in a controversial and suspect election by the candidate from the conservative Partido Nacional, Porfirio Lobo, in early 2010. Lobo served his four-year term and was then replaced by another candidate from his own party, the now infamous Juan Orlando Hernández.

The events of 2009, however, did not occur in a vacuum or in a salient cause-and-effect relationship, but were rather symptomatic of a history of political instability, military intervention, and government corruption of institutions and processes of rule. Zelaya's removal is only the most recent in a long line of similar moves dating to the early twentieth century; though Honduras escaped the civil bloodshed and genocide experienced by the diverse populations of its immediate neighbors, the fragile politicoeconomic landscape—a legacy of the banana republics—bred deep social fissures and unrest. This, combined with US interventionist politics pre-1990 (and to extent in the twenty-first century with the Plan Colombia) and the setting up of drug routes and cartels in the country in the 1980s onwards, has paved the way for a rising wave of criminality and violence.

Also implicated in this shift is the redefinition of the national economy along the broader neoliberal turn in Latin America. Though the Central American Free Trade Agreement (CAFTA) was signed in 2004, the country embarked on neoliberal reform in the early 1990s, specifically with the Ley de Modernización Agrícola of 1992, which set in motion a series of policies that increased the presence of foreign companies and manufacturing in the country. While proponents of the neoliberal dogma argued that it would improve macroeconomic indicators, the reality was quite the opposite. As María del Carmen Caña Jiménez observes, the shift "is not resulting in the betterment of quality of life and the elimination of poverty but rather in the increase in juvenile delinquency and corruption within the police and the judiciary" ("no está resultando en la mejora de la calidad de vida y eliminación de la pobreza . . . sino, más bien, en el incremento de la delincuencia juvenil y la corrupción dentro del cuerpo de la policía y los sistemas judiciales"; "El asco" 219)—effects that are clearly portrayed in the plot of *Chinche Man*.

These programs of economic restructuring favored neoliberal policies that weakened the national economy and widened socioeconomic schisms at the behest and favor of multinational and globalist interests. The macroeconomic strategies undertaken by the government resulted in microeconomic tactics that transformed the country (and its regional peers) into what Rafael Cuevas Molina calls "repúblicas maquileras" (2) or sweatshop republics.[7] The opening and privatization of markets, the reorganization of everyday life, and the resultant wave of criminality provokes a "cultural stress" ("estrés cultural"; 7), in what Cuevas Molina calls

> a veritable *change of era*. This would imply a new identity profile, one of whose defining features would be the break with the past, which would be expressed in a devaluation of history and a loss of traditions. The process would be accompanied and reinforced by many cultural referents located in spaces that are outside the aegis of the nation-state.
>
> (un verdadero *cambio de época*. Este implicaría un perfil identitario inédito, uno de cuyos rasgos definitorios sería la ruptura con el pasado, que se expresaría en una desvalorización de la historia y una pérdida de tradiciones. El proceso estaría acompañado y reforzado por muchos referentes culturales ubicados en espacios que se encuentran fuera de la égida del Estado-nación; 17)

In summary, then, the present in *Chinche Man* is a time marked by economic and social precarity, and profound political instability anchored in a history of contentious policies and institutions. Cuevas Molina, furthermore, links the neoliberal shift to broader globalization, in a tandem that goes hand-in-hand in terms of cultural production. Taking this into account, I want to suggest that the San Pedro Sula in which the film takes place is not the city per se, but a city-image, or as Jean-Clet Martin argues:

> Neither the profile of a city, variable to infinity, nor the construction of a panoramic territory refers to a state of things. Rather, . . . an errant line that runs through space as a scaffolding of relations, a maze of depths, relative to the more or less typical place that one occupies—which implies that every landscape is a virtual construction in relation to a memory able to stock piles of images in all their encroachments upon one another. . . . So there contracts a découpage of images, cut out upon the blue background of the sky, which is nothing like an objectively realized solid. (66)

As a city-image, the urban expanse in which the film takes place metonymizes the *cambio de época* in which Central America is subsumed in the early twenty-first century. The film, importantly, never names the city (though its streets and businesses are evident for the casual viewer to be San Pedro Sula), allowing it to be expressed as an iteration of a virtual image of Central American space. We can thus read *Chinche Man* along two axes: as a meditation on post-2009, neoliberal Honduras; and as an examination of crime and criminality in a broader isthmic space.

Such a gesture permits an extrapolation of the film onto a wider, and less kitschy and genre-specific horizon. It permits us to ask, How has Central American cultural production reacted to this *cambio de época*? In terms of primarily a literary context, critics have coined ideas such as an aesthetics of cynicism (Cortez 2) and an aesthetics of disgust (Caña Jiménez, "El asco" 218) to describe postwar production, while Alexandra Ortiz Wallner posits the notion of a "frictional and hybrid literature ("literatura friccional e híbrida"; 18).[8] What may be called festival circuit cinema emblemizes these tropes and aesthetics in a parallel fashion, as noted by the academic and critical interest in works by directors such as Julio Hernández Cordón, Esteban Ramírez, Paz Fábrega, Arturo Menéndez, and Jayro Bustamante. These films, however, have not enjoyed commercial success—whether in theatres or on Internet streaming platforms—as comedy has been the genre that has succeeded in local Honduran theatres, as seen by the popularity of films such as *Amor y frijoles* (2009), *¿Quién paga la cuenta?* (2013), and *Una loca navidad catracha* (2014) and its natural sequel only a year later, *Un loco verano catracho* (2015) (Valdés Flores). This comes as no surprise, given the readiness of neoliberal economies to adapt and embrace popular genres of North American cinema, such as comedy and romantic comedy, that allow viewers to vicariously live and embody the shifts in lived experience perpetuated by the economic system (Sánchez Prado 7).[9] In fact, this adoption of Anglo genres and a distinct structure of feeling conforms with Cuevas Molina's observation that "globalization itself has an important cultural component, which is expressed strongly in the adoption of cultural patterns that are exposed through the media" ("la globalización misma tiene un importante componente cultural, que se expresa de forma fuerte en la adopción de patrones culturales que son expuestos a través de los medios de comunicación"; 7).[10] We may thus view the production and popularity of *Chinche Man* as another exponent of this thesis, as a local expression of a global cultural pattern that dominates international box offices in the post-2001 world.

The film's popularity resides in it being a local version of a successful film type that has broken barriers and sales records. It is even more telling that the film is born from the local/global dialectic of neoliberal change, given the lack of a superhero in Honduran and Central American print culture.[11] Unlike peer heroes that appear in *Capitán Latinoamérica* who have a national history of the superhero in earlier multimedia, *Chinche Man* emerges as an unanchored phenomenon that is, instead, situated along a global trend of the moving image.

Let us now turn away from the context and move onto the film itself. The protagonist's hero persona is built along the familiar dyad of nonhuman/human in its naming and aesthetics. There are countless examples of this convention, including the familiar Spiderman, Ant-Man, El Gato Negro, Black Panther, and Batman. These characters hybridize the animal and the human in a combination that overcomes the limits of the latter in asserting a hero persona. The nonhuman defines the character's potential and abilities as a super entity, often for awesome effect, yet also to insert parody within the ontology of the hero. In the latter category we encounter The Tick, and the Latin American superhero par excellence, El Chapulín Colorado.[12] Created by famed Mexican humorist Roberto Gómez Bolaños (known for *Chespirito*, *El Chavo del Ocho*, and *El Chapulín*, among other shows), the character emphasized parody as the originary narrative and aesthetic mode for engaging the superhero in Latin American moving images and print culture.[13] He is parodic of the conventions and tropes of the genre, demonstrating an intertextual dialogue with comics, films, and other media representations of the superhero. Parody may be understood along the definition posed by João Luiz Vieira and Robert Stam as a "reflexive mode of discourse which renders explicit the processes of intertextuality through distortion, exaggeration or elaboration of a pre-existing text or body of texts" (21).[14] It is furthermore, as Linda Hutcheon understands it, "one of the major forms of modern self-reflexivity; it is a form of inter-art discourse" (*A Theory* 2); thus serving as an especially propitious mode for depicting the superhero, who traverses media platforms and narrative modes.

Chinche Man maintains this mode, but moves beyond the comedy of El Chapulín in favor of a more gritty, nuanced, and self-reflexive composition. The character is not a parody of another text (which is the case of *Capitán Centroamérica*), but rather a parody "in relation to . . . [the] general iconic conventions" (Hutcheon 12) of the genre. Parody here is "a form of imitation, but imitation characterized by ironic inversion. . . . [It is] repetition with critical distance, which marks difference rather than similarity" (6). I will go into greater detail on the politics of parody in the Central American superhero in the analysis of *Capitán Centroamérica*, but for now want to underline that, though Padilla's hero is born from a parodic naming, his characteristics and actions within the narrative suggest a more serious take on the possibilities of the hero vis-à-vis the Central American present. This is signaled in the origin scene of the jail cell I note above, where what inspires him to adopt the persona is the (albeit humorous) fear that hardened criminals harbor towards the insect. He becomes Chinche Man as a result of this fear, seeing how these metonymic stand-ins for broader social ills recoil at the presence of a miniscule bug.

The tenor of the film is evident from the opening credits: high octane music—which aligns the film with the action genre—is accompanied by a montage of images of the hero in action, both in and out of costume. The images are spliced from different points in the narrative, including images of Pedro: dressed as the superhero in battle; in a *karategi* training; riding his motorbike in costume; apprehending a criminal on a street, in the act of doling out a megawatt punch; and laying injured as Chinche Man after being attacked by a gang. The images, however, are not simple screen captures from the film, but images stylized as comic book sketches; that is, they are photographic images that have been reproduced through a digital sketch filter. The camera in these credits pans across the sketches, showing each to be a segment in a multipanel sequence in a comic strip, not unlike the *fotomontaje* technique of the Santo comic books.[15] The aesthetics of the credits merit examination, since *Chinche Man* is not an adaptation from print media, but rather an extension of a television sketch character.[16]

The aesthetics of the opening credits collocate the film within a visual category that Dru Jeffries identifies as "comic book film style," or "the results of an intermedial relationship between comics and film, whereby the latter medium appropriates and transforms certain of the formal attributes unique to the former as a means of stylization" (2).[17] Jeffries argues that "comic book film style can be described as a set of self-reflexive gestures in which the different representational abilities of comics and film are put on simultaneous display in a cinematic work" (3). He elaborates upon Jay David Bolter and Richard Grusin's idea of remediation, or the "dialectical process through which one medium takes the form of another medium as its content or style, effectively resulting in the representation of one medium within another" (Jeffries 3). Jeffries adds that

> remediating comic book form into cinematic style inserts an additional layer of mediation between the diegetic world and its cinematic representation. In other words, the storyworld is filtered through both comics and cinema before it reaches the viewer's perception, resulting in self-consciously stylized or "hypermediated" representations, as opposed to a logic of transparency or "immediacy." . . . It is something that is *imposed upon* the diegesis, not something that emerges from it. (3; emphasis in the original)

The opening images thus associate the film with a print hero, as materiality and genealogy that outruns the limited presence of the superhero in Central America, suturing *Chinche Man* instead to a transnational phenomenon that is global and rooted in the conventions and characters of the genre. Why stylize the opening credits along the aesthetics and materiality of the print form? Perhaps as a synonymous gesture of the opening Marvel Studios title in every film from their cinematic universe, which explicitly places the films in a direct reference to their almost eighty years of print culture. In line with this, by alluding to print—a "higher" art than the superhero film—Padilla instills an aura of seriousness to his hero, albeit a hero named after an insect. Yet also perhaps by posing a text prior to the narrative proper, that is, a (fictional) source material that is adapted into the images that follow, Padilla inculcates a notion of genealogy to the film, thus imbuing it with a historicity that politicizes representation.[18] In fact, though possibly in a more implicit fashion, we may connect the credits montage to the voice-over in *Kalimán*, as it encourages audience participation with and orientation towards the on-screen character.

The imposition of the comic, that is, the request made of the viewer to filter the diegesis not only through the contemporaneity of the narrative but through the textuality of the comic, lays out a filmic cartography for the spectator to traverse. As Jeffries understands it, "Comic book film style is nondiegetic, but it influences and conditions our access to the diegetic world on display in the film" (3). It directs us to Tom Conley's idea "that in its first shots a film establishes a geography with which every spectator is asked to contend" (2). This geography can be real and metaphorical: the opening credits place the hero within the streets of San Pedro Sula, yet also ask the viewer to filter its images through a multimedia platform that is imposed onto the diegesis. In other words, the geography we must traverse in *Chinche Man* is not solely spatial, but also hermeneutic in that it requires an engagement beyond the narrative plot and with diverse epistemics.

The film opens with an interaction between two characters that has little to do with the rest of the plot. A man shoots out running from a house in a quiet neighborhood and is quickly followed by his angry wife swinging a machete, played by an actor in drag. She takes him down a few meters away, and tells him (to his surprise) that she was only bringing the weapon since he had forgotten it before going to work in the fields. He responds in relief, "Ay, you scared me! I thought you realized that I've courted my stepdaughter!" ("¡Ay vieja, qué susto me sacaste! Pensé que te habías dado cuenta que he enamorado a mi hijastra!"). A now-enraged wife takes the machete to him and we hear her cut into him off-camera. A wipe transition brings us to the next vignette, where the same wife is now washing dishes in her kitchen. Her young son (played by a much older actor) enters and interrupts her chores. She chides him and complains about her husband, leading us to assume that the machete attack in the previous scene was less serious than the blade-cutting-through-flesh sound implied. The young boy, wearing a superman cap, asks for an Android cellphone, since he is the only one in his class without a phone. The mother responds that she knows he only wants the phone to send and receive naked pictures, but that she will get him one since he is the apple of her eye.

In the third vignette, the camera follows her as she walks into a shopping mall, one of the many that now dot the neoliberal landscape of Central America. The woman asks the attendants if they could delete a set of nude male photos on her phone, which she claims not to have downloaded. Her son apparently showed his father the images, who then beat her for being unfaithful. The dialogue in this scene is loosely connected to the previous two, but lacks narrative continuity in that her coming to the cellphone store—following the request in the second scene—should be to purchase a phone for her son. She then spies a group of men playing cards in the back of the store. When she approaches them, she learns that one of them is a famous magician. She asks him to "tirarme las cartas" (literally, "throw me the cards") or to read her fortune. The magician follows her request and throws the deck of cards in her face.

In the fourth scene, the woman exits the mall and loudly laments that her car has been towed. A man approaches her to help, and after a short discussion, the woman realizes that she does not have a car. The short, comic scene concludes with the two characters walking separately off camera, followed by a title slide stating "Sketch. Los Verduleros." The camera then cuts to a frontal shot of Padilla and a colleague sitting on a couch and talking directly to the audience. The image contains the lines and icons of a viewfinder within the frame, that is, the two characters appear within the coordinates of an image within an image, where the viewer is situated behind the eyepiece. Padilla appears in a cameo role as himself, thanking various advertisers for sponsoring this particular episode of Los Verduleros, thus inserting the television show (the previous vignettes) within the diegesis. This short sequence is another example of remediation in the film, as the media of television is introduced and remediated into the cinematographic. The image then cuts to a cameraman sitting in front of the sofa, before cutting again to a viewfinder image. This short transition between images dislocates and relocates the viewer in relation to the eyepiece—remediation here is self-reflexive and not gratuitous. The sequence helps us understand the previous comical scenes as sketches within the show we are now involved in filming, and not as random episodes. By moving our points of cognition, the film encourages an active viewership wherein the positionality of the viewer engenders an involved and active reading.

The shot of Padilla on the sofa then transitions to a fast-paced montage of videos of different actors and sketches from Los Verduleros. Each image appears in a frame-within-a-frame that moves in multiple directions, as though in a multimedia storyboard or comic book panel. The montage cuts to Padilla and his companion on the couch after filming; that is, the scene is no longer mediated through television but is instead part of the diegesis. Padilla hands his microphone off to a set technician before engaging his companion in a discussion about something he just got wind of, a hero who is giving the police and other branches of law enforcement competition in fighting crime. He is, of course, talking about none other than Chinche Man, who "goes about solving the problems of unprotected people" ("anda solucionando los problemas a la gente desprotegida"). Padilla then begins to explain the history of Chinche Man, as the image dissolves into a setting image of Pedro walking the streets of San Pedro Sula.

The plot of *Chinche Man* is thus framed through the narrative device of the flashback, as it is mediated through Padilla's reporting of the background of the crime fighter. By remediating television and deploying Padilla as a truth-teller in his role as a journalist, the film situates the viewer within a tangible and immediate chronotope. This gesture runs in opposition to the opening credits and comic book film style that represent a "self-consciously stylized or 'hypermediated'" representation, which opposed "a logic of transparency or 'immediacy'" (Jeffries 3). While the filming of the television program and personality within the film may be read as another example of hypermediation, I want to suggest that it, counterintuitively, instead "attempts to achieve immediacy by ignoring or denying the presence of the medium and the act of mediation" (Bolter and Grusin 11), where the medium is not the television program within the diegesis, but cinema. In other words, the employment of television (sketches, program, and character) within the film attempts to delink the moving image from the medium of the feature film, as though what is to come is really a nonfiction report by journalist Igor Padilla to his weekly public. In mediating television onto the film, Padilla and Chí posit an ethics of viewership that delinks the film from the fantastic of the superhero, in favor of a positionality within the epistemics of the nondiegetic space.

By engaging in this movement, the introductory sequences of *Chinche Man* call our attention to the here and now, the immediate time and space of Honduras that appears in the news and everyday life: the Honduras, and more specifically, the city-image of San Pedro Sula that sees Padilla gunned down. The popularity of the character (initially as sketch and then in film) reflects Angela Ndalianis's assertion that "one aspect of this extraordinary commercial success [of superhero films] has been the connection to major contemporary events. . . . As we might expect, superhero narratives seem to be inextricably linked to the realities of social and political life" (1). In fact, the first scene of the film proper, that is, not the preliminary sketches, take the viewer to the streets of the city. We see Pedro (the same actor who plays the magician in the earlier sketch) crossing a busy intersection as Padilla's voice fades out: "He was looking for work everywhere . . ." ("Andaba pidiendo chamba en todos lados . . ."): Pedro here is actively looking for work. He walks past several storefronts before entering "El Mundo de las Sandalias," a real store located in the east of the city. When told that there are no vacancies, a dejected Pedro returns to his rented house in the outskirts, where the principal antagonist, Don Manuel, first makes an appearance. Accompanied by two henchmen, he angrily demands rent monies from the protagonist, who is unable to pay. After a brief argument (and many threats from the landlord), they reach a compromise in that Pedro will pay what is owed in twenty-four hours. A distraught Pedro proceeds to wander the streets again looking for work. He fortuitously stumbles upon a hardware store (Ferretería Jesús M.

Bendeck, another real business in the city) that desperately needs a porter to load a truck with cement bags. The well-built protagonist is tasked with loading the truck in under two hours, something deemed unlikely by the owner of the store, "unless Pedro is a superhero or something of the sort" ("a menos que [Pedro sea] un superhéroe o algo así"). Pedro completes the job in record time and is paid for his hard work, but is robbed at knifepoint by common crooks when he leaves the business. They hand him a thorough beating for good measure to humiliate and prevent him from fighting back—the hero, after all, must hit rock bottom first before transforming into a superhero.

In the next scene, ominous music sets the stage for Don Manuel's return. The image cuts to an indoor setting where an injured Pedro is nursed by a female neighbor (Clarita), while another character, a flamboyant male who we are to suppose is gay (played by the same actor in drag from the early sketches), criticizes Don Manuel's vicious tactics.[19] We then see Don Manuel's thugs remove the protagonist's property from the home, including his furniture and clothing, as a shaken Pedro confronts them. He effusively asks for clemency, stating that he had the money but was robbed, but is only met with punches that further humiliate him in front of his neighbors and friends. Chí employs a slow-motion camera to capture a thug first pouring gasoline on the items and then setting them on fire. A medium shot captures this action in a dramatic composition: the mattress burns in the foreground as a beseeching and bloody Pedro is held back by a goon; another thug stands parallel to the left, looking on with the bottle of gasoline in hand; two groups of neighbors stand behind the frontal characters, their gestures expressing sadness and horror at the unfairness of the punishment. The audio track is composed of Pedro uselessly imploring them to show mercy, the sound of material burning, and the maniacal and exaggerated laughter of an off-camera Don Manuel delighting in the absolute destitution and misery of the protagonist. The image fades to black before the audio fades to silence, as the viewer is left to digest the sounds of evil laughter and the crackling of Pedro's life.

This early scene and the presented tableau in slow motion is important in establishing the ethical framework from which *Chinche Man* arises. Superheroes, after all, emerge from discrete and finite moments of conflict, where a triggering event or action sets in motion a poietic and political process of reaction. The aesthetics of the scene—namely, the medium composition shot, the use of slow-motion imagery, and the caricature-like laughter of the villain—delineate the sequence as an anti-apotheotic moment

Figure 4.1. Axiographic schema in the opening minutes of the superhero genre.

for the protagonist, who now must *react* to right a wrong. The reaction is a diametrically opposed trajectory, where the character is apotheosized as a superhero that renders poetic justice to the villain. Writing on the ethos of the superhero vis-à-vis Roland Barthes's ideas of the myth, Peter Coogan argues that

> the ideological import of the superhero is to inflict a sense of powerlessness and resignation on readers. This resignation is expressed in an acceptance of things as they are, which is, according to Roland Barthes, the conservative function of myth. . . . (143)

> A key ideological myth of the superhero comic is that the normal and everyday enshrines positive values that must be defended through heroic action—and defended over and over again almost without respite against an endless battery of menaces determined to remake the world. . . . The normal is valuable and is constantly under attack, which means that almost by definition the superhero is battling on behalf of the status quo. (236–37)

Coogan builds off ideas first posed by Richard Reynolds, who argues that "villains are concerned with change and the heroes with the maintenance of the status quo" (51). While this may be true of the North American superhero (and even El Santo and Kalimán), in both explicit and implicit readings, the opposite rings true for the Central American (and, really, contemporary Latin American) filmic superhero.[20] His reaction is against a status quo of injustice and impunity, where the poor are denied social mobility by the forces of criminality. The hero's aim is to reform this dystopic present (as represented in the composition shot) into a more utopic, just, and arguably fictional society.[21]

Importantly, Pedro doesn't embark on the transformation into the hero after this scene, but rather after another trigger. In the subsequent act, the neighbors hatch a plan to seek justice. One suggests going to the *fiscalía* to ask the police to get involved; another neighbor argues that they should go with this information to a television station to "publicly denounce" ("denunciar públicamente") the nefarious and predatory behavior of Don Manuel. The group goes to the police station to lodge a complaint, where they are met with an officer who takes down the details of the case. He stoically informs them that an investigation will follow "following the law" ("conforme a la ley"). The neighbors then track down a reporter who records their complaint on live television. The reporter ends the broadcast by telling her audience that the station will follow the case as it progresses.

Chí uses a fade to black to transition between this montage and the following scene where we see Pedro sitting by the base of a tree at night. He rips up grass to show his frustration, and his thoughts appear in a voice-over: "What can I do with my life? . . . There has to be a way to stop [Don Manuel]. . . . Maybe if he didn't know who I am. . . . So that when I confront him, he doesn't see me. . . . And what if I dress in a different way? . . . Like a superhero. . . . In costume to defend people. I'm going to be a hero!" ("¿Qué puedo hacer de mi vida? . . . Debe de haber una manera de poder frenarle [a Don Manuel]. . . . Quizás si tan solo él no supiera quién soy. . . . Si para enfrentármele él no me viera. . . . ¿Y si me visto de una manera diferente? . . . Como un superhéroe . . . disfrazado para defender a la gente. ¡Voy a ser un héroe!").

The transition effect between the two scenes is important in tracing the becoming of the hero; it is not the composition image of the burning mattress in the earlier sequence that triggers his decision, but rather the events in the preceding montage where the neighbors go to the police and the news media. The fade to black is a transition that indicates a change in time or space in the narrative: the shot of Pedro deciding to become a superhero can thus be interpreted as occurring during an indefinite sometime after the report to the police. This period of time is not immediate, but rather delayed, given the lingering on the black frame in the transition. In other words, the fade-to-black technique implicitly indicates that some time has passed and that neither the police nor the news media have been able to do much in censuring Don Manuel for his criminal tactics. Pedro's decision and transformation—the origin moment of the title superhero—is predicated on the inefficiency of the law and social institutions, a reflection of the impunity of crime and the ineptitude of the police to mitigate violence in contemporary Honduras.

The relationship between the superhero, the law, and crime actors is an integral triumvirate of the genre. Matthew J. Costello and Kent Worcester observe:

> The superhero genre also enjoys a special connection to questions of law, justice, and public order. Superheroes typically fight crime, which means that their stories are required on some level to depict and sometimes deconstruct the boundary between the law and lawlessness. While superhero stories sometimes embrace the idea that the state is an instrument of legitimate authority, they often express the ambivalence and even hostility that many citizens feel toward their own government. Superheroes regularly interfere with the normal prerogatives of states, implying that legal processes are insufficient, and perhaps even that inner-directed morality is superior to other-directed legality. (86)

Chinche Man does not fight crime with the police—as is the case of Las Luchadoras decades before—but in spite of the police, taking up the causes of justice that permeate everyday life. After all, and blurring the lines between fiction and nonfiction, the police have proven to be quite useless, as judged by the investigation into Padilla's murder.

After deciding to become a hero, Pedro engages the logical next step, which is to decide what kind of persona he will adopt. The image cuts to him securing a job as a cleaner in a tailor shop, a wink perhaps to the proliferation of *maquilas* across the region. The film then moves into a montage with alternating images from two distinct narrative lines: a continuation of Pedro under the tree embarking on a design for his costume; and a collage of shots of Pedro learning to stitch and cleaning the shop. Inspirational orchestral music overlays this visual montage, as what is important is not the actions of the character or any dialogue per se, but the compendium of images and actions that coalesce into a recognizable hero within a cinematic moment that is the becoming trope. The becoming trope is an integral element of the comic book movie, and one that translates across linguistic and national borders. The becoming sequence in *Chinche Man*, however, is incomplete, as Pedro has yet to decide on the ontologically "super" element for his hero: his costume design is highlighted by a conspicuous interrogation mark on what would be the chest of the uniform.

The poietic development of the hero triggers a parallel development of the villain. In the next scene, we discover that Don Manuel is not a simple landlord asking for rent, but a crime boss who extorts clients, such as the owner of a scrapyard who already complied with his payment plan. He gives the man an ultimatum: pay by five o'clock that afternoon or deal with the consequences. The film then cuts to Pedro reporting for work one morning, only to be told that he has been laid off. His boss congratulates him for being an excellent worker and apprentice, but that "external factors" ("cosas externas"), and not sloppy work or client complaints, are behind him making the decision to let Pedro go. This external factor, we can easily intuit, is Don Manuel, a supposition confirmed by the owner after the protagonist badgers him for answers. An unemployed and increasingly frustrated Pedro now finds a job in an electronics repair store. Again, the film is set in real business locations, suturing (for a local viewer) the narrative to the spatial and sociocultural coordinates of San Pedro Sula. He also starts dating his neighbor, Clarita, who will appear in transition montages later in the film as his romantic interest: a necessary and generally secondary role afforded to women in the genre.

It is here that the becoming trope further develops, as Pedro meets Chico, a technician, who accidentally stumbles upon the former's sketches for a costume. An intrigued Chico notes that "this looks like a superhero" ("esto parece un superhéroe"), and asks who it is. Chico is a "super, mega fan" of comic books and promises to help Pedro develop the hero. As in the opening credits, the film gestures towards the print medium, situating itself in relation to, though not an adaptation of, comic book superheroes. Chico peruses the sketches, and says that he can design some weapons for the costume. Pedro asks if these weapons could be real weapons, to which Chico responds: "No way! That would be fucking awesome!" ("¡No jodas! Eso sería super mega macizo"), realizing that the sketch is indeed to be a blueprint for a real hero of flesh and blood and not a 2D comic.

Time passes by in a montage of Chico going about his work, indicating that the police and the press still have yet to intervene in the case. This then segues into a scene of Chico demonstrating the first weapon for the hero costume, a 35,000-watt megapunch device. Pedro's optimism, however, is short lived, when in the subsequent scene he comes upon the shop in shambles after a robbery. The owner arrives and immediately accuses him of pillaging the store; as in the mattress image earlier, we are to identify with Pedro due to the unfair treatment he receives. His plight is the predicament of the most defenseless among us. This, his pathetic begging for mercy, and the rough and dramatic manner in which the police (who finally reappear) arrest him, effectively situate the protagonist in an ethically favorable position and one for which the audience readily feels empathy. The scene is followed by Don Manuel physically and verbally harassing Clarita. She rejects his advances, and he responds, "I have all the power. . . . I have everything under control" ("Tengo todo el poder . . . tengo todo controlado"). As he rides off, she receives a phone call that Pedro has just been taken away by the police. Again, we may intuit that he is behind the robbery and Pedro's incarceration, as in having "everything under control," he takes advantage of the protagonist's misfortune to make the moves on his love interest.

Pedro's becoming is complete when the other inmates in the jail cell show a larger-than-life fear of a *chinche*. He is released after the shop owner realizes that he was not responsible for the crime and retracts the charges. A renewed Pedro now finds a job in a bodega working for Don Hipólito, the son of a man who worked with Pedro's father. Hipólito holds the father in great esteem for being an honest man, and hires Pedro on the spot. He also informs the audience that Pedro's father was shot and killed in a bus robbery. The fate of his mother is unknown, though her absence in the dialogue and plot suggests that she too has succumbed to violent criminality (or perhaps migrated to the North like Capitán Centroamérica's mother). Hipólito's unveiling of Pedro's family origin is important in that it aligns the character with another convention of the superhero genre: as Kara Kvaran reminds us, "almost all modern superheroes are orphans. They lose their parents in sudden, awful acts of violence, which cause them future angst and spur epic heroics" (219). This detail is the proverbial icing on the cake in Chinche Man's becoming trope, and the suturing of Padilla's film to a genre despite its lack of originary printed text.

Another montage of Pedro getting to work and learning the ins and outs of the bodega business follows, a repetition of similar images when he first started working at the tailor and repair shops. With cheery instrumental music providing ambience for the snippets of him cleaning and stocking, the montage demonstrates the value placed on a strong work ethic—Pedro is poor and living in precariety not because he is lazy or criminal, but rather because of circumstance. The montage, furthermore, builds empathic bridges between the character and audience, who identify and align themselves with the hardworking citizen. Finally, the repetition of the work montage throughout the film highlights the indefinite temporality of the narrative, as it is implied that weeks, and even months, have passed since the original request for justice. The protagonist's improving labor fortunes coincide with an improving love life, as he goes on an extravagant date with Clarita, ending in an apartment hotel with swimming pool. One may wonder where he gets the money to finance this evening, but that thought is on the backburner as the loud dance music of the audio track and the two characters cavorting like lovebirds distracts the viewer from taking a critical loop to the narrative: everything is wonderful as the crooks that characterized much of the narrative to this point seemingly disappear.

Superhero movies play on the oscillation between the positive and negative, pleasure and pain, to enthrall their audience in a rollercoaster of emotions and ethical identifications—even at the expense of narrative and character depth. Just as Pedro begins to live the happy life, he (predictably) stumbles upon a robbery taking place in the bodega. He quickly puts on the costume (which had, for some reason, been kept in a backpack in the store) and confronts the two thieves. They make short work of our hero, as he is discovered the next morning by Hipólito covered in bruises: we must remember that there is nothing inherently super about Chinche Man beyond his desire to fight crime. He explains to Hipólito how he became Chinche Man and his motivations for seeking a more just society, who calmly (and quite sensibly) replies, "You have seen too many action movies, kid" ("Vos ha visto demasiadas películas de acción muchacho").

Though initially skeptical of the possibilities of a superhero in San Pedro Sula, Hipólito opens up to the protagonist and confesses that he was once a martial arts fighter and teacher, but gave up his training when his wife was killed in a robbery—he too is a victim of everyday crime, stating, "I think violence follows me" ("Creo que la violencia me sigue"). He thus acquiesces to train Pedro in different fighting skills as a way to redeem himself and to ensure that Chinche Man makes a difference in ending violence. The film cuts to a montage of Pedro and Hipólito going through different drills and exercises, suggesting a passing of more time, a time in which Don Manuel continues to harass and extort money from local business. When his henchmen threaten the owner of the electronics business, Pedro chances upon them. He puts on the uniform as the thugs pull a gun on the boss. After considerable training, Chinche Man quickly and efficiently neutralizes the baddies, warning them, "Tell Don Manuel that his days of mischief are over" ("Decile a Don Manuel que sus días de hacer fechorías han terminado").

An emboldened hero needs the proper tools to combat crime—in the next scene, Pedro visits Chico in his new workshop, where the latter reveals that he has been developing several weapons, including a specialized motorbike. Every superhero worth his or her salt (especially superheroes without kinesthetic powers) needs a technologically enhanced vehicle to get around the urban jungle. The bike, however, is not yet ready for use as Chico is weaponizing it, presumably for the film's sequel. Pedro returns to his apartment in high moods at the prospect of having more tools to add to his costume, but is ambushed when he sees Don Manuel's gang kidnap Clarita. He quickly returns to the workshop and is allowed to take the bike to get her back. Our hero is finally a complete superhero—as the conventions of the genre would have it—as he rides down a main avenue in full dress as the film's title song from the original soundtrack, "Chinche Man," comes on. Sung by Keny Bianchy and Tony Mejía, the track is an anthem, describing and praising his crime-fighting abilities. It preps the audience for the culminating event between good and evil, as the superhero engages the thugs in Don Manuel's warehouse. Chí adds torrential rain and slow-motion effects to the combat scene for added dramatic effect. The results of training with Hipólito are evidenced in Pedro ruthlessly neutralizing everything and everyone that is thrown at him. He rescues Clarita and is about to take her to safety when Don Manuel attacks him with a sledgehammer. In a medium shot, both characters part from opposite sides of the frame as the music hits a climax. They are about to make contact when the image abruptly cuts to black, leaving the viewer on tenterhooks. *Chinche Man* lacks the budget for a high-action confrontation between good and bad, using instead the breakaway technique to leave the action sequence to the imagination of the audience.

The black image cuts back to a shot of the newscaster who appeared previously reporting on the events of the night. She looks directly at the camera and is accompanied by a police chief who informs the audience that a dangerous criminal, Don Manuel, has been apprehended. He thanks an anonymous helper that goes by Chinche Man for putting the mafioso behind bars in a maximum security prison so that he doesn't escape. The irony is not lost on the viewer, as the media and police only reappear once the dirty work is done, taking credit for an arrest they had played no role in.

In retrospect, it is also ironic that they decide to send Don Manuel to a maximum-security prison not unlike the one that housed Little Sam immediately before Padilla's murder. Like the fictive case, Little Sam's prison sentence was supposed to keep him away from terrorizing the citizens of San Pedro Sula, leaving us to wonder just for how long Don Manuel will be off the streets. In hindsight, the ending of the film serves as a sort of chronicle of a death foretold for Padilla, a reporter who did not shy away from challenging the least savory elements of his city.

The film ends with the superhero at a lookout over San Pedro Sula as the image cuts to a point-of-view shot of the protagonist surveying the vast urban landscape before him, then to a medium shot behind the character; his body coming between the viewer and the city, thereby stitching the hero (as trope and embodiment of the cultural anxieties of contemporary Honduras) with the city-image. The moment is interrupted by a phone call from an undisclosed caller who informs Chinche Man that the prices of gasoline and toll have gone up. He resolutely puts the phone away and decides to fight the price gouging, an implied effect of the neoliberal economy. The Central American superhero is there to fight microcrimes (such as those perpetrated by Don Manuel) and systematic macrocrimes that are committed by national and transnational players. He launches his right fist above his head and jumps, expecting to fly like Superman. We know, however, that the powers of the Anglo hero do not translate to the Global South, as outlined by the Enchufetv sketch. The parodic nature of the film rears its head here, as the character points out, "Eh, but I can't fly" ("Eh, si no puedo volar") and goes on his way, as the ending black caption "To be continued" ("Continuará") appears.

Chinche Man is at face value a tale of a down-and-out common man who becomes a superhero to surmount the obstacles placed in front of him. That being said, there are several points of contact between *Chinche Man* and other Latin American superhero movies, namely, the use of parody and the representation and working-through of specific national politicoeconomic anxieties. Parody and its accompanying tone of comedy broaden the cultural specificity of representing contemporary Central America, away from the registers of testimony, detective, and noir genres that have tended to guide the literary and cinematic depiction of the region. The violence that characterizes these prevailing narrative modes is cautiously light in comparison to the lived experience of Honduras and San Pedro Sula, which is sanitized, as there is no murder or torture in the film. In fact, we only hear of the murdered victims of violence through the backstories of different characters such as Pedro and Hipólito. We may thus view Padilla and Chí's film as a sort of allegory of violence, following Joanne Hershfield's idea that "cinematic allegories portray situations and events, as well as abstract ideas, through symbolic material objects, persons, and actions. . . . Allegory may also refer to a way of reading a film in which the viewer understands the story as a metaphor of an historical or contemporary event or process" (177). That is, *Chinche Man* can be read centrifugally, within the spatial and narrative confines of the plot, but also exegetically, where the characters and their actions allegorize a broader concern. In this regard, Don Manuel and his goons are symbolic stand-ins for the real gangs that have decimated the country; the real criminal organizations that are responsible for the assassination of Igor Padilla and Edwin Rivera Paz, among many others.

Coda: Súper H

On June 8, 2016, an open letter directed to President Juan Orlando Hernández made waves in social media. The letter is written by "a Honduran that loves this nation" ("un hondureño que ama esta nación") and notes that "Honduras is changing since [the president] took office" ("Honduras está cambiando desde que [el presidente] entró al poder"). The author proceeds to outline how the country has changed since 2014:

> You see more extortions, more deaths, more massacres, more robberies are the order of the day, bus drivers and taxi drivers killed. Many entrepreneurs better close their businesses due to too much corruption, more poverty, less work, the charity bag, I tell you that bag only lasts a family 2 days to eat. A person is not gifted food. He is given work so that he is not waiting for politicians, he is given education. They are given opportunities. But you would have to be in the shoes of my people to realize their needs.

(Vea usted más extorsiones, más muertes, más masacres, más robos a la orden del día choferes de buses rapiditos taxistas asesinados. Muchos empresarios mejor cierran sus empresas mucha corrupción, más pobreza, menos trabajo, la bolsa solidaria, le cuento esa bolsa lo más que le dura a una familia son 2 días y luego que comerán. A una persona no se le regala comida. Se le da trabajo para que no esté esperanzado a los políticos se le da educación. Se les da oportunidades. Pero bueno tendría usted que estar en los zapatos de mi gente para que se diera cuenta de las necesidades que pasan; " 'Super H' envía carta al presidente de Honduras"; all errors in the original)

After listing the ways in which various indices of social, political, and economic wellbeing have fallen in the country, the author proceeds to make a personal connection:

Mr. President, you will ask yourself why the image of a mother with her son boarding a train, well, see, I tell you . . . the year that you took possession of the mandate of this beautiful country between the month of May and June, they emigrated to the United States and thousands and thousands of mothers with their children fleeing from violence, from the poverty, from the lack of opportunities, for a better future for our children, at this moment my tears fall, you know why Mr. President because that image reflects my son and his mother. They also emigrated looking for a better future, a better life because the one you promised was never going to arrive.

(Señor presidente usted se preguntara por que la imagen de una madre con su hijo subiendo un tren, pues vea le cuento . . . el año que usted tomo posesión al mandato de este hermoso país entre el mes de Mayo y Junio, emigraron a estados unidos y se fueron miles y miles de madres con sus hijos huyendo de la violencia, de la pobreza de la falta de oportunidades, de un futuro mejor para nuestros hijos, en este momento se me caen las lágrimas, sabe por qué señor presidente porque esa imagen refleja a mi hijo y a la madre de él. Ellos emigraron también buscando un futuro mejor una vida mejor por que la que usted prometió nunca iba a llegar; " 'Super H' envía carta al presidente de Honduras"; all errors in the original)

The letter concludes with a critique of Hernández's political aspirations: "And now you come to say that you want to be reelected. No, man, be more serious if we talk about reelection we are talking about the same things that you did in these 4 years, the same thing will happen with the next 4 years, and then we'd be really fucked" ("Y ahora usted me viene a decir que quiere reelegirse, No hombre, sea más serio si hablamos de reelección estamos hablando de que lo mismo que usted hizo en estos 4 años lo mismo va a pasar con los otros 4 años y como que ahí ya estamos jodidos verdad"). These words will be especially prophetic given the recent electoral debacle in the country. On November 26, 2017, Hondurans went to the polls in presidential elections that marked a referendum on the changes outlined in the social media letter. In the preliminary vote count, Hernández's challenger, Salvador Nasralla, held a five-point lead with over half of all votes counted. The Tribunal Supremo Electoral then froze all vote counts for over a day, before declaring that Hernández had somehow (quite magically) taken the lead. The incumbent was declared the winner on December 17, with massive protests and state violence escalating the conflicts between rival political factions, and independent surveyors declaring the results a farce.

The letter denouncing Hernández was written by Elmer Ramos, also known as Súper H, a self-fashioned superhero from San Pedro Sula, "who by means of his actions seeks to inspire a change in attitude and mentality to move the country forward" ("quien a través de sus acciones busca inspirar un cambio de actitud y mentalidad para sacar adelante al país"; Abedrabbo). Like Superbarrio in Mexico, or Menganno in Argentina, Súper H is a concerned citizen who mobilizes and deploys the superhero (character, icon, narrative) as a legitimate actor of social change. Akin to the fictive Chinche Man, Súper H stands up for the rights of the downtrodden, the invisible underclass left in misery by the political and economic elite, and their allies in organized crime. He wears a luchador mask (signaling an aesthetic debt to the Mexican tradition) and the uniform of the Honduran national football team (what better way to capture the attention of a football-mad country?), but "doesn't fly or have any superpower" ("no vuela o tiene una fuerza fuera de lo normal"; Abedrabbo). In an interview with Richie Abedrabbo, Ramos states that he fashioned the persona to raise awareness about social issues such as homelessness, hunger, and littering, and that his ultimate goal is to create an NGO, "since the country has many needs" ("pues las necesidades del país son muchos").

Like Chinche Man, Mirageman, and Capitán Centroamérica, Súper H maintains a strong social media and Internet presence: his principal Facebook account has almost 5,000 friends (with other contacts scattered in earlier accounts), while his character page has more than 20,000 followers. The latter page describes him as a "Public Figure in San Pedro, Cortes, Honduras," lists his phone number (should a concerned citizen be in need of a superhero), and states that he is "very responsive to messages." Súper H uses the platform to post links to news stories and videos, political memes, and over one hundred videos. The videos are composed of messages to his followers, chronicles of different charity events and benevolent acts, and calls for help in particular cases identified as needy by the superhero. He has become so popular, in fact, that he appears in a cameo role in Juan Funes's *4 catrachos en apuros* (2017), and was even offered a character in the *Chinche Man* comic drawn by Orellana. His popularity makes it clear that a superhero does not need a fancy vehicle, superhuman powers, or even a sartorially inspired costume—maybe all a superhero needs today is a reliable Internet connection, social media account, and smartphone or tablet to effect tangible social change and betterment.

Chapter 5

YouTube, Parody, and Neoliberal Critique in *Capitán Centroamérica*

In the discussion in chapter 4 regarding *Chinche Man*, I highlight the presence of parody within the narrative, sartorial, and genre choices made by Padilla. The Honduran character parodies conventions of the superhero movie genre, but does not engage with a specific origin-text or figure. This, however, is not the case in *Capitán Centroamérica* (2011 web series; 2013 television series), where the mode of parody is evident from the very name of the protagonical hero. While parody is at its poietic core, I want to suggest that *Capitán Centroamérica* is more than a simple spoof of Marvel's Captain America franchise (and the Avengers by extension), as its characters and narrative arc establish cogent relationships with extant and palpable topics in Central American studies. Like *Chinche Man*, the crux of *Capitán Centroamérica* is not the superhero genre per se (though parody may suggest this), but instead tangible social, political, and economic issues and anxieties that are developed and discussed by means of the genre, and not in spite of it.

The character made his debut on the Internet in Puyaweb's YouTube channel on July 4, 2011.[1] With over 215,000 views (over 2,800 "I like this" and only 55 "I do not like this" clicks), "Capitán Centroamérica—El comienzo" is one of the channel's highest-ranking clips.[2] Puyaweb is composed of Andrés Díaz (producer and director), Darwin Martínez (sound engineer), and Adolfo Marinero (cameraman, screenwriter, and social media manager), a group of web video aficionados from El Salvador who create and market content through their dedicated YouTube channel. *Capitán Centroamérica* is the brainchild of Díaz, who studied social communication at the Universidad Centroamericana José Simeón Cañas, and made the sketch as a parody of *Captain America: The First Avenger* (2011), "which, in a dictatorial way, appropriated the name of the continent to use as a surname, although its jurisdiction is limited to the land of Uncle Sam" ("el cual, de forma dictatorial, se apropió del nombre del continente para utilizarlo como apellido, pese a que su jurisdicción se limita a la tierra del Tío Sam"; Mata Blanco).[3] Díaz's disdain for the US superhero underscores the same tension between Latin America and North America that we saw with the character Super Sam in *El Chapulín Colorado*.

After receiving substantial positive feedback, Díaz directed and uploaded the *Capitán Centroamérica* web series in the same year. Composed of five episodes ranging between ten and twenty minutes, the series has garnered over 400,000 views since its original emission. The cast is composed of amateur and relatively unknown actors, Díaz himself in a cameo role, and André Guttfreund, who won an Academy Award in 1976 as the producer of the short *En la región del hielo*. The proliferation of the episodes in social media views and shares (via other platforms such as Facebook and Twitter) gave Díaz enough clout to make the next logical jump: in 2013, *Capitán Centroamérica* made its small-screen debut on VTV Canal 35, "an open-signal channel not as privileged as others" ("un canal de señal abierta no tan privilegiada como otros"; Espinoza).[4] Writing in *Diario1*, Karla Espinoza characterizes *Capitán Centroamérica* the televisions series as "a series that captivated Salvadorans every Wednesday, a comedic program that touched on themes of corruption, violence, and other social phenomena that affect the country" ("una serie que miércoles a miércoles mantuvo expectantes a los salvadoreños, un programa cómico que tocaba temas sobre corrupción, violencia y diferentes fenómenos sociales que afectan al país"). Composed of twenty-two episodes with a screening time of between twenty and twenty-five minutes, the television series develops the principal characters and plot points of the web series. The extended screen time also allowed Díaz to flush out some of the narrative knots in the series. Puyaweb uploaded the entire series to its YouTube channel after the initial run on local television; the web and television series were thus available simultaneously and in their entirety to anybody with a decent Internet connection.

Capitán Centroamérica, the television series, made its international debut in fall 2017. The web series, after all, was always available to a global audience, thanks to the platform of free streaming media. In May 2017, Puyaweb attended LA Screenings, an international television market held annually in Los Angeles, and sold US viewing rights to two companies: the Televideo Latino Network (mitvlatino.pivotshare.com) and Mundo Flix (mundoflix.com). Both website services emulate Netflix, but focus instead on "serving Spanish-dominant and bilingual consumers in the U.S. by offering a broad range of top film and television entertainment appealing to multi-generational households" (Mundo Flix). The Mundo Flix mission statement, furthermore, specifies, "These consumers, who navigate a bifurcated emotional existence between their adopted U.S. homeland and countries-of-origin, seek Spanish and English-language programming that reflects their culture and/or language-of-origin" (Mundo Flix). As a result of both companies securing rights to the television series, Puyaweb removed the twenty-two episodes from their YouTube channel.[5] A US and El Salvador-based audience can now only access *Capitán Centroamérica*, the television series, for a monthly subscription fee ($3.99 for Televideo Latino; $5.99 for Mundo Flix).[6]

Both web and television series are based on the same protagonist, Chuzito, the nickname of Carlos de Jesús Cruz, a university student that is shot by two common criminals when he tries to stop a robbery. He is a "tan and slim" ("moreno y delgado") young man who after several scientific experiments gains superpowers (Espinoza). Alonso Mata Blanco adds that the protagonist, "an exemplary, honest and hardworking citizen, is the key soldier of the Ministry of Central American Unification to fight organized crime. His battle is against gangs and drug trafficking, but then, in the most painful way, he will realize that the real villain is within the government and is called corruption" ("un ciudadano ejemplar, honesto y trabajador, es el soldado clave del Ministerio de Unificación Centroamericana para combatir el crimen organizado. Su lucha es en contra de las maras y el narcotráfico, mas luego, de la manera más dolorosa, se dará cuenta de que el verdadero villano está dentro de los Gobiernos y se llama corrupción"). While *Chinche Man* obliquely suggested that the law was ineffective in dealing with crime, *Capitán Centroamérica* parts from the position that the law itself is criminal and complicit in organized crime.

Given the different production, emission, and circulation mechanisms in which the web series and television series operate, I will undertake a chronological examination of *Capitán Centroamérica*, that is, by beginning with the commentary of the web episodes before tackling the television broadcast. Research into Latin American web video production and distribution is relatively scarce, especially given the vertiginous pace at which media and technology have accelerated in the early twenty-first century.[7]

Writing in 2007 in Claire Taylor and Thea Pitman's *Latin American Cyberculture and Cyberliterature*, that is, before sites such as Netflix and Hulu became the global phenomenon that they are today, Debra Castillo astutely observed that

> given the inherently conservative nature of feature films, which increasingly need to respond to the requirements of international cooperative agreements, it can no longer surprise us that some of the most exciting and innovative work in cinema in contemporary Latin America will never be found in cinemas; instead, it is available for viewing and downloading, on thousands of sites, to a wide, appreciative, if highly segmented, potential audience. (35)

More recently, Jorge Ruffinelli notes that "our relationship with the cinema has changed in recent years. As a result, there is a before and after" ("nuestra relación con el cine, ha cambiado en los años recientes. En consecuencia hay un antes y un ahora"; 57), and that "today the cinema has left theaters and has entered the home. And at home we tend to watch movies and television in screens that are becoming bigger or smaller, like the tiny screens of the iPod" ("hoy el cine ha salido de la sala para entrar en el hogar. Y en el hogar tendemos a ver cine y televisión en pantallas cada vez más grandes o más pequeñas, como las minúsculas del iPod"; 64).[8] Though Castillo and Ruffinelli discuss cinema in particular, they also highlight the ways in which the medium and circuits of the Internet have impacted the consumption of audiovisual material; that is, these same observations may be extrapolated to other formats such as the short and serial. To this effect, Gonzalo Aguilar, Mariana Lacunza, and Niamh Thornton argue that the digital revolution "arrived quickly to the region and became an essential part of film culture" (359), and that "with the advent of streaming, film viewing has become increasingly mobile; instead of being tied to public exhibition venues or domestic spaces, spectators can now watch films on their cell phones while traveling on the subway" (359).

The rapid adoption of technology and its diverse mediums of circulation occurred in Central America from the 1980s onwards: television, cinema, and—later—the Internet would become omnipresent in many households (Cuevas Molina 8). Writing specifically on television, Cuevas Molina notes that, starting in the 1970s, "television began its ascendant career; became a true protagonist of social life . . . and positioned itself as an important way to configure social identities along with the school system and the family" ("la televisión inició su carrera ascendente; se convirtió en verdadera protagonista de la vida social . . . y se posicionó como una vía importante para la configuración de las identidades sociales junto a la escuela y la familia"; 132). In a Central American cultural terrain characterized by mass migrations and displacements, the verb of travel takes on a far broader meaning, wherein viewers may follow favorite shows from their native country outside its national borders. I am interested in the circuits and platforms of web-based moving images (and the potential for mobility it promises) because *Capitán Centroamérica*, unlike *Chinche Man*, was broadcasted first as a web show before making the leap to television; that is, the poietics of the series and character are inflected by the production and dissemination platform of the Internet, and, in this case, YouTube, and not vice versa.[9] In other words, the circuit of distribution and the succinct format of the web video is essential in understanding the content, affect, and impact of the series.

YouTube has radically changed the way culture is produced and circulated, engaging and encouraging a participatory economy that dynamically links fictive and nonfictive representation to the real in almost simultaneous temporality. Our access and participation are mediated by relatively cheap and low-tech devices: a simple smartphone or tablet (or barebones laptop or desktop computer, or even a smart television or fridge) and basic Internet connectivity are all we need to direct our browsers to the website or its app. It is a multipronged phenomenon, which Anandam Kavoori argues "may be many things—a platform, an archive, a library, a laboratory, a medium" (1). William Uricchio furthers that "Youtube stands as an important site for cultural aggregation . . . the site as a totality where variously sized videos, commentaries, tools, tracking devices and logics of hierarchization all combine into a dynamic seamless whole" (24). For Thomas Mosebo Simonsen, "It is also a melting pot of content where traditional genre conventions in many ways are inadequate. Fiction and non-fiction, television content, home-movies of pets and creative animations are placed in the same categories" (73).

This mix of media, a smorgasbord of images, stories, clips, interviews, and vlogs, has a "double function as both a 'top-down' platform for the distribution of popular culture and a 'bottom-up' platform for vernacular creativity" (Burgess and Green 6). An example of the former is Igor Padilla's broadcasting of *Los Verduleros* content on his YouTube channel that makes "the products of commercial media widely popular, challenging the promotional reach the mass media is accustomed to monopolizing" (Burgess and Green 6). YouTube gave Padilla a new venue and mechanism by which to reach viewers, and to extend the shelf life of the feature-length film beyond its run in local theaters. The latter, however, describes Puyaweb's success in making a sketch and then five-episode web series. It is a bottom-up phenomenon, delinked from the financial ecospheres of cinema and television, where all it takes to produce and circulate material is a catchy idea, some friends willing to appear as actors, and a decent resolution camera (most likely on a cell phone) that gains clicks and shares.[10]

The *Capitán Centroamérica* web series is a coherent set of webisodes built around a specific set of characters, plot lines, and spaces; that is, it is not a viral, one-off video of a dog dancing to the beat of bachata or a teenager accidentally setting their bangs on fire. The series instead operates following the linear logic of television, where each webisode is a progression in the narrative arc. In a sense, the YouTube web series is a blood descendant of television, but relies on advertising and views instead of advertisers to sponsor content and network executives to pick up a season. There are other ontological and phenomenological differences; Kavoori, for example, argues that "watching Youtube is fundamentally different from watching television or film: You make time to watch television or film, you watch Youtube when you have little time" (3). This brings us back to my earlier claim about accessibility, since YouTube is built around quick, cheap, and mobile access. Each webisode, furthermore, is at a manageable length, ideal for a short bus or taxi ride, or even between work shifts or classes. As a result, plot structures are condensed, as action and dialogue are privileged over long setting shots or inane transitions between scenes.

Another intrinsic difference between YouTube and television series is the former's possibilities along what Henry Jenkins, Sam Ford, and Joshua Green call "spreadable media." Unlike exclusively-for-TV shows that are subject to broadcast times, cable or satellite subscriptions, or over-the-air availability—in what can be called a distribution model—web series operate on a circulation system that is dynamic, organic, and largely barrier free.[11] Jenkins, Ford, and Green argue that this shift "signals a movement toward a more participatory model of culture, one which sees the public not as simply consumers of preconstructed messages but as people who are shaping, sharing, reframing, and remixing media content in ways which might not have been previously imagined" (2). They argue that the "spreadability" of media refers "to the potential—both technical and cultural—for audiences to share content for their own purposes" (3). They juxtapose the term to the concept of "stickiness" in web media, which describes "media texts which engender deep audience engagement" (4). While "stickiness models focus on counting isolated audience members," "spreadability recognizes the importance of the social connections among individuals" (4–5). This personalized platform and interface is an evolution of Lisa Parks's ideas on flexible microcasting, "where computer and television technologies are combined to produce the effect of enhanced viewer choice in the form of a stream of programming carefully tailored to the viewer's preferences, tastes, and desires" (135). I say evolution because television is only a vestigial medium in YouTube, as referenced in its very name (You*Tube*) and in the original logo from 2005 that had the word "Tube" within a rounded rectangle that represented a television screen.

This terminology is propitious for discussing *Capitán Centroamérica*'s progression from sketch to extended series: the superhero, after all, is a sticky body and genre (see the discussion of masks in *Mirageman*), promising for audience engagement and identification (an affirmation made clear by the more than four hundred user comments tallied on the sketch's YouTube page). It becomes spreadable when placed within a media framework that allows viewers to share its content across a wide variety of other web and social media portals, such as Facebook, Twitter, Google+, Blogger, Reddit, Pinterest, and LinkedIn. Users without accounts on these third-party sites (an increasingly shallow demographic pool) are even given the option to email the media or embed it within their own site or blog. YouTube, furthermore, allows viewers to share content starting at a particular moment in the clip, thus allowing user participation in what specific parts or dialogues of the narrative are spread.[12]

All this is important in understanding the development of *Capitán Centroamérica* because it allows us to frame the show and character as a bottom-up, sticky, and spreadable production, quite unlike any other superhero in the Latin American (and perhaps global) mediascape. It is not born from a large production budget or (transnational) studio set on monetizing the hero, but from the everyday views, likes, and shares of viewers who arrive at the show from word-of-mouth reviews. These viewers and sharers in fact also participate in the making of the series—webisode 2's ending credits include a special thanks to "our fans who appear as extras or actors!" (¡nuestros fans que salieron de extras o actuando!"). The web series is primed for spreadability due to YouTube's architecture that encourages social interaction among users. This would not be the case for other web-based platforms, such as Netflix, for example, that are more top-down in production and distribution. The company is notorious for not releasing viewership information and for maintaining a strict control on who gets to watch what, where, and when. The character and series therefore are contingent on their ability to stick to viewers across platforms, national borders, and time frames, their existence intrinsically linked to consumption by an audience willing to click and perhaps share.

Cicatrices

The first webisode, "Cicatrices," uploaded on September 3, 2011, opens with a young woman walking the streets of San Salvador. She is talking on her cellphone when two crooks attempt to rob her at gunpoint. Carlos tries to be a Good Samaritan by confronting the two men, who quickly neutralize him. The fisticuffs come to a climax when, in a close-up, one of the criminals reckons that "nobody acts like a hero here" ("aquí nadie se hace el héroe"), before unloading three rounds at the would-be savior. The decisive "here" of this early dialogue establishes the spatial template of the narrative, as a Central America rife with crime and unfriendly to anyone wanting to make a change. Díaz uses a slow-motion technique in this early scene, in what can be considered the origin vignette that explains how Carlos becomes the title character. To note is that this scene differs from the prototype YouTube sketch that already had its own origin for the hero, as a young soldier who volunteers to become Capitán Centroamérica to fight crime. Multiple origin narratives are nothing new in the superhero film genre (or even comic genre, for that matter), as evidenced by the multiple and frequent reboots we have seen in major US productions.

Returning to the scene, the director plays with the frame rate here, speeding up and slowing down the action in a subtle manner that evokes thousands of similar fight scenes from Hong Kong to Hollywood, from the futuristic nodes of science fiction to the story of a bunch of Spartans fighting in the Persian Wars. The fight scenes in the webisode, however, do not use the slow-motion technique to solely somehow amplify the action (as is the case with the CGI examples above), but rather to provoke a pause in the viewer, to slow down the perception processes vis-à-vis the moving image. This phenomenological slowing down permits the eruption of a reading of the audiovisual (as opposed to a simple consumption of the action), wherein the narrative mode is made plainly clear. In other

Figure 5.1. There are no heroes in the streets of Central America.

words, the slow-motion images appearing at the first minute of the webisode—the exaggerated action incongruent with the relative mildness of the mugging, and the fact that they so heavily mimic blockbusters such as *The Matrix* and *300*—establish the parodic nature of this superhero. Yet also important in this montage is the effect on the characters on screen and their role in the plot. What happens to the body in frame when the image is slowed down?

The image of the thug landing a punch and the slowed image of Carlos spitting up saliva evoke the corporality of the body in frame, as not a two-dimensional plate but rather a complex assemblage of politics, ethics, and sociocultural currents. The sputum slowly erupting from his lips provokes an affective reaction in the viewer, in that the viscous substance engages a correlative bodily process in the audience. Carlos's visceral reaction to the punch provokes an empathic reaction or a somatic reflex, aligning our bodies with the bodies on screen. This orientation is important as it sutures the viewer to the hero-in-waiting, posing an identification that is at the core of every superhero film—as the hero is only a superhero when he or she gains the empathic and ethical alignment of the audience.

A dissolve transition between this opening montage and the next scene underlines the importance of the corporality of the hero, as after all, and, as Scott Bukatman reminds us, "the central fascination in the superhero film is the transforming body, whether of hero or villain. Much attention is given to the body's discovery of its own transformation, which explains why superhero films are even more obsessed with origin stories than the comics themselves" (121). Now Carlos is no longer the skinny student but an engineered crime-fighting machine. He has become Capitán Centroamérica thanks to the Ministro de Unificación Centroamericana (MUC), played by Guttfreund, we see on the television screen announcing the creation of a United Central America. Seated on a bed with a female friend (whose amorous advances he is too naive to acknowledge), his gloved hand rests over the bloodied wound suffered at the hand of the thieves in the first montage, reminding himself and us of the corporality of the becoming montage.

The image proposes the scar as a record of the change into a superhero, but also the notion of the body as a somatic register of the scars of everyday violence. The MUC meanwhile announces that today is a day to celebrate as Capitán Centroamérica will clean up the streets of the region's capitals. He says it is a day to celebrate, not because the price of gasoline has gone down or that people have stopped migrating for better economic opportunities to El Norte (issues seen at the very end of *Chinche Man*), but because it is a day of the "rebirth of the Republic of Central America" ("renacimiento de la república centroamericana"). He encourages the citizens—including the Capitán—to look at their cicatrices and to be proud of them. Herein we see the explicit stitching together of the body, politics, and the citizenry through the affective register of the wound, an alignment made possible by the kinesthetics of the opening, albeit parodic, fighting montage.

The initial minutes of the web series condense the becoming of the hero and the physical wound within the framework of a political gesture; that is, Carlos is now Capitán Centroamérica and not Capitán El Salvador—his transformed self and heroics are linked to a regional identity and process over a strictly national identification, expanding the parameters of the "here." The coining of a Central American Republic inserts the web series within a broader discussion of regional cultural production and identity, in a more explicit fashion than that seen in *Chinche Man*, a film firmly entrenched in San Pedro Sula. *Capitán Centroamérica*, instead, participates in what Ana Patricia Rodríguez calls the production of culture "under the aegis of neoliberalism" ("bajo la égida del neoliberalismo"; 27). Rodríguez argues that Central American cultures today "are not the national cultures *imagined* by the liberals and federalists in the nineteenth century, nor are they the revolutionary cultures projected in the last decades" ("no son las culturas nacionales *imaginadas* por los liberales y federalistas decimonónicos, tampoco son las culturas revolucionarias proyectadas en las últimas décadas"; 27; emphasis in the original). She suggests that they are also not "strictly localized within geographic national borders" ("estrictamente localizadas dentro de las fronteras geográficas nacionales"), suggestively posing instead that "Central American cultures have spilled over from their national confines to spaces in the South and the North" ("las culturas centroamericanas se han derramado de sus confines nacionales hacia otros espacios en el Sur y el Norte"; 27).[13] This osmotic leakage results in the confluence of national veins within a broader identification with a conglomerate Central American culture.

The idea of a unified Central America—whether as nation or identity—as developed in the web series is nothing new, as there were already designs for a unified state in the nineteenth century. In fact, the Ministerio in the series may be seen as the latest incarnation of the drive for a common sense of political identity, even if the matrices of cultural identity already overlap and evolve in unison.

In identifying Central America as a union in the naming of the superhero, Díaz emphasizes the common character of the region as anchored in the histories of the six countries dating from independence to the *repúblicas bananeras* (banana republics) and civil wars during the Reagan Doctrine, to the neoliberal present as *repúblicas maquileras* (sweatshop republics).[14] The hero and the series are thus positioned at the crossroads between the national and supranational, where the latter guides the direction and trajectory of the narrative. The latter, furthermore, allows Puyaweb to produce and market a series that breaches national and digital barriers to a globalized audience that identifies as Central American over a specific identity. To be Central American here means belonging to a (digital) community, an imagined community that is not "restricted to specific geographic spaces but can be widespread as the tentacles of computer-mediated communication" (Mitra 55). This is not to say, however, that the narrative is entirely dislocated from the national, as Díaz in the very first sketch reminds the audience that "the superhero we need will be born in El Salvador" ("en El Salvador nacerá el superhéroe que necesitamos"). By underlining the national (El Salvador) within the regional (Central America), the series effectively poses the former as a metonym of the sociopolitical ethos of the latter; that is, we can understand the countries of Central America through the specificity of El Salvador within the narrative, as with a limited production budget, Díaz and company were unable to splurge on foreign locations for filming.

Unlike the Honduras of *Chinche Man* that was relatively unscathed by civil conflict during the 1980s and 1990s, El Salvador withstood a violent assault on its peoples during a civil war that took place in the tail end of the Cold War. Between 1980 and 1992, hundreds of thousands were killed, tortured, or wounded by the internal conflict, leading to the mass exodus to the United States. The psychological and physiological relics of the war remain very much in the present given the lack of institutions and laws that promulgate human rights.

What happens in the series—and in other cultural artifacts such as the novel—is the extrapolation of a national bellicose history onto analogous contexts that are geographically contiguous; that is, the specificity of the Salvadoran context is blurred as it is stretched over the terrain of countries (such as Guatemala and Nicaragua) with similar histories. Mario Lungo and Roxana Martel adopt this metonymization in an essay on social citizenship and violence in postwar Central American urban centers. They begin with a general survey of crime and impunity in the region, before focusing specifically on the Salvadoran case, arguing that the current state of affairs is a legacy of violent conflict and unresolved social and political frictions. Lungo and Martel note that, though peace treaties were initiated in countries affected by civil conflict during the 1990s, this did not lead to a reduction in violence; in fact, indices of social violence shot up (394). What they describe rings true for much of Central America, including countries such as Costa Rica that did not experience war, but now are also victims to high indices of crime. They pose the following paradox in understanding the Central America that the Capitán is tasked with saving:

> Central America is a paradox. With greater democracy comes higher levels of violence. . . . We propose . . . the hypothesis that the explanation is complex because, despite the widespread democratization experienced by the Central American countries formerly subjected to dictatorial regimes, the histories and cultures themselves have created contexts that explain the persistence of violence, and that despite their current manifestations, are similar, these contexts are particular, as an example that globalization cannot erase national specificities despite transcending the borders of countries. (396)

(Situación paradójica entonces la de Centroamérica. A mayor democracia mayores niveles de violencia. . . . Planteamos . . . la hipótesis que la explicación es múltiple debido a que, a pesar de la generalizada democratización experimentada por los países centroamericanos sometidos antes a regímenes dictatoriales, las historias y las culturas propias han creado contextos que explican la persistencia de la violencia, y que a pesar de que sus manifestaciones actuales sean semejantes, estos contextos son particulares, en un ejemplo de que la globalización no puede borrar las especificidades nacionales a pesar trascienda las fronteras de los países; 396)

Important in this hypothesis is the tensile relationship between the local and the global, between historical factors and lived conflict, and the supposed smoothening out of liberal markets and trade mechanisms. We thus have a general landscape in which to read the diegetic events and extradiegetic gestures in a web series that engages a viewer to delve deeper into the cultural and political matrices of Central America as a whole.

Let us return to the becoming scene. The scar on his shoulder is a polyvalenced sign: within the narrative, it serves as a vestige of his past and a reminder of what Lungo and Martel call the harsh criminality of urban life; that is, the scar is an embodied representation of violence. It also, however, functions outside the plot lines of the webisode and series, serving as metaphor of the cultural landscape of Central America entering the twenty-first century. It metaphorically reminds the viewer (and the diegetic characters) of the lesions of war, and of the resistive abrasions produced by the local-global dyad.

Parting from these conditions, Alexandra Ortiz Wallner argues that "the Central American scenarios of the late twentieth century are fissured scenarios. They are places disrupted by the effects of an accelerated globalization, neoliberal ideology and discursive battles that have been undertaken to name the asymmetries and the state of fragmentation of the nation's foundational narratives" ("los escenarios centroamericanos de finales del siglo XX son escenarios fisurados. Son lugares trastocados por los efectos de una globalización acelerada, del ideario neoliberal y de batallas discursivas que se han emprendido para nombrar las asimetrías y el estado de fragmentación de las narrativas fundacionales de la nación"; 63). She knits this cultural tapestry to deploy the metaphor of the fissure to describe contemporary Central American cultural production, arguing that "the fissures are understood as a programmatic task and not as a need to overcome them, eliminate them or cover them up; the fissures are a constant, they are part of the communicating vessels that make up Central American literary and cultural productions" ("las fisuras se comprenden como una tarea programática y no como una necesidad de superarlas, eliminarlas o taparlas; las fisuras son una constancia, forman parte de los vasos comunicantes que componen las producciones literarias y culturales centroamericanas"; 65). Though Ortiz Wallner focuses on literature, and what she calls a *literatura friccional*, she does leave the door open for the inclusion of other cultural texts within the metaphor of the fissure. Television, after all, is, as Paul Julian Smith reminds us, "the first medium to engage with urgent contemporary social issues, working through them week by week for audiences in their millions" (1). These urgent issues are at the core of the fissure; the scar on the Capitán's body is thus both a literal fissure, a previously open incision now held together by the overexpressed collagen of fibrous tissue, and a metaphor for reading the series within a cultural landscape.

Capitán Centroamérica is beckoned to meet with the MUC and other high officers of the Ministerio. There is an element of comedy in this segment, a mode of satire when he receives a missed call and states: "A missed call. . . . That can only mean two things: they need me and they don't have any minutes left" ("Una llamada perdida. . . . Sólo puede significar dos cosas: me necesitan y no tienen saldo"). The image cuts to a setting shot of the Plaza Francisco Morazán located in the historic center of San Salvador. The plaza is evocative of the notion of a unified Central America, as it houses a statue of Francisco Morazán, president of the failed Federal Republic of Central America from 1827 to 1838, and other monuments representing the five nations that formed the Federal Republic: Honduras, El Salvador, Guatemala, Nicaragua, and Costa Rica. The camera pans downward on a vertical axis, going below ground to show the MUC in a subterranean room. In this scene, the superhero and the audience are informed of his powers; ironically, "he technically doesn't have superpowers, but has the strength of twelve masons who do heavy manual labor" ("técnicamente no tiene superpoderes, pero tiene la fuerza de doce albañiles que hacen obra pesada"). A high-ranking aide, the General, adds, "You have superhuman immunological abilities: you can even eat trash; even your scars from the past will slowly disappear" ("Tenés habilidades imunológicas sobrehumanas: hasta puedes comer basura; hasta tus cicatrices del pasado se irán borrando"). This last point is

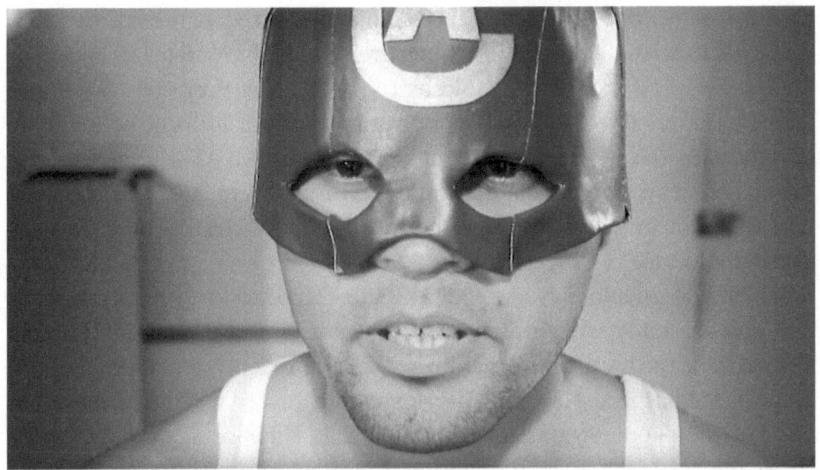

Figure 5.2. Parodic aesthetics and powers.

significant, given the import of the scar as somatic and metaphoric register, suggesting that its erasure will come only when the hero accomplishes the utopic mission of uniting Central America and ridding its streets of crime.

We also learn in this scene that the Capitán will work with two sidekicks, both of whom are ex-military. López García (also known as "Toño el mudo") was trained in Nicaragua, whereas Rodríguez (codename: "Marimba") is a Costa Rican soldier trained by Hondurans. The MUC informs Capitán Centromerica that the two will be under his charge during "the war" ("la guerra"). He moves to an interactive touchscreen to go over the history of Central America and how it was once originally a republic. An accelerated timeline features different historical moments, culminating in Carlos becoming Capitán Centroamérica, as a decision by the MUC to "invest in a superhero" ("invertir en un superhéroe"), "our last hope in the war against evil" ("nuestra última esperanza en la guerra contra el mal"). The war here in question evokes the infamous war against (the axis of) "evil" that has defined global geopolitics in the post-2001 world, an epistemic shift that is at the substrate of the boom in Hollywood superhero films. By delinking the adversary from a state or organization, the war against evil or "el mal" is a war in perpetuity, a war against an abstraction that is shape-shifting and malleable to the immediate needs of political and economic capital. Evil is intangible, and a victory over it comes only at the behest of the warmonger who can reassign it to multiple enemies. This is made clear when an excited

Capitán states that he is ready to take on "organized crime, bureaucrats, money laundering, killers" ("el crimen organizado, burócratas, el lavado de dinero, asesinos"), only to be told by the MUC that they will take things "slowly, it's not the time for that right now" ("no a lo loco, no es ahora tiempo para eso"). The General informs that the MUC will take care of the big fish, and that the Capitán's mission instead is to "hit the streets and take the fight to where it is right now, to the Salvadoran people, to all of Central America" ("salir a las calles [y] llevar la pelea a donde ahorita la pelea está, al pueblo Salvadoreño, a todo el territorio centroamericano"). The episode ends with grandiose theme music and a caption "Capitán Centroamérica: La última esperanza" ("Capitán Centroamérica: The Last Hope"), leading the viewer to ask for whom or for what? Is he the last hope of the people against urban and social crime, or against the bigger issues the MUC is reluctant to address? Or perhaps he is the last hope for one final push towards a unification that has been centuries in waiting. By leaving the first episode as an open ending, Díaz effectively sets the stage for multiple and complex narrative lines, which is proper for and characteristic of the serial medium.

Parody and Captain America

In addition to planting an origin narrative for the superhero, the first webisode effectively and transparently signals the presence of parody as a narrative, sartorial, kinesthetic, and aesthetic mode. While the parodic character is a staple of the Latin American audiovisual superhero, it also stands at a propitious crossroads within the horizon of Central American cultural production. The superhero links the present to the past, indicating a historicity and genealogy of the present that transgresses the supposed free-flowing nature of globalization and neoliberalism. The superhero conversely allows an engagement with global culture, wherein the local enters into dialogue with transnational artifacts of cultural production.

The terrain in which *Capitán Centroamérica* participates is complex; in broad brushstrokes, Ortiz Wallner argues that

> the Central American space is . . . a social and historical product. . . . Palimpsest, mosaic and marginality are forms through which an attempt has been made to define a constant within this

social and historical product that is Central America. . . . This constant can be defined as the transgression of borders both in the sense of transgressions of legality and in the reality of population flows, the mobility of national territorial limits, mass displacements, exile and migration.

(El espacio centroamericano es . . . un producto social e histórico. . . . Palimpsesto, mosaico y marginalidad son formas a través de las que se ha intentado definir una constante dentro de este producto social e histórico que es el espacio centroamericano. . . . Esta constante se puede definir como la transgresión de las fronteras tanto en el sentido de las transgresiones de la legalidad como en la realidad de los flujos de población, la movilidad de los límites territoriales nacionales, los desplazamientos masivos, el exilio y las migraciones; 43)

Ortiz Wallner's deployment of the palimpsest and mosaic as tools for understanding Central America is built upon a gesture towards both the textual (as epistemology and phenomenology) and the postmodern continuum of (de/re)codification. This gesture is a favorable condition for the mode of parody, as it confirms Hutcheon's idea that parody—"often called ironic quotation, pastiche, appropriation, or intertextuality—is usually considered central to postmodernism, both by its detractors and its defenders" (*Politics* 93). Hutcheon does not view parody as other scholars of postmodern culture (such as Frederic Jameson) that consider it "a symptom of the age, one way in which we have lost our connection to the past and to effective political critique" (Felluga 207).[15] Instead, she argues that postmodern "parody signals how present representations come from past ones and what ideological consequences derive from both continuity and difference" (Hutcheon, *Politics* 93).[16] Parody, in other words, is not solely representational but rather ultimately ideological. This is evident in Ortiz Wallner's explanation of the palimpsest and mosaic, as they are not acts of pastiche or vacuous recodifications (so prevalent in the postmodern mediascape), but rather "epistemological metaphors by which one has tried to explain the conditions of a politically, socially, and culturally fragmented Central America" ("metáforas epistemológicas con las cuales se ha querido explicar las condiciones de una Centroamérica política, social u culturalmente fragmentaria"; 43). These metaphors do not suggest "some infinite regress into textuality" (Hutcheon, *Politics* 95), but rather enable a multifaceted questioning of ideological positions within the terrain of cultural production.

To parody Captain America is to engage with an omnipresent and blockbuster character in the contemporary global/local mediascape, and to engage the politics and ideology of this particular superhero. First appearing in 1941 for Timely Comics, Captain America was a wartime favorite, as it metonymized the spirit of one bloc of World War II.[17] The character made its Marvel debut in 1964, and has remained in print, television, and the cinema ever since.[18] The politics of the hero are not ambivalent, and do not require deep close reading; in fact, the character punches Adolf Hitler in the very first issue! The comic book version has gone on to fight Nazis, the Japanese, and communism through its evolution over the decades, though what interests me here is the foray of the character (and, by extension, the United States) into Central America.

The region first appears in a narratively significant role in issue 206 of volume 1 (1977), as the metonymic space of Rio de Muerte (*sic*), a small country bordering Guatemala, Honduras, and El Salvador, yet also metonymic of Central and South America as a whole within the worldview of the Cold War.[19] It is the location of a prison camp commanded by Hector (*sic*) Santiago, the Swine, a megalomaniac warden/military general who brazenly submits his inmates to psychologically and physically intricate feats of torture. In retrospect, it is ironic that the South American dictator should be portrayed as a vicious torturer and murderer, especially since much of this training and support was done by the Captain's real-life superiors! Captain America is kidnapped and brought to Rio de Muerte by the Swine's henchman in a plane after the former interferes in their abduction of a restaurant waiter who was once a prisoner in the camp. Over three issues, Captain America battles the Swine on his own turf, ending in issue 208 with the latter's defeat.

The narrative arc over the three issues is insignificant in the broader trajectory of the superhero, but it does give us clues as to the relationship between the Centroamérica of our parodic web hero and the origin text of Captain America. The issues were published during the Central American crisis of the 1970s, during a flashpoint of the Cold War and the war by proxy that took the bloodshed and massive violations of human rights to the global south. Central America was a hotbed of conflict, including movements by the leftist Frente Sandinista de Liberación Nacional (FSLN) in Nicaragua, the Frente Farabundo Martí para la Liberación Nacional

(FMLN) in El Salvador, and other groups in Guatemala that resisted military governments installed and upheld by the United States. Occurring in the proverbial backyard, Central America was a strategic site of anti-communist efforts, and thus a natural terrain for Captain America to enter. This characterization of Rio de Muerte is blatant in its depiction of a backwards, barbaric, and prehuman space, needing the Captain to come and civilize it. In addition to the lack of townships and urban development (the idea of a wild Latin America, incongruous with reality), it is inhabited by prisoners worked into a zombie-like state (shackled by the authoritarian regime and not allowed to enjoy the "freedoms" of US capitalism) and a river monster called the Man-Fish, a beast that ends up killing the Swine. The depiction of Santiago also merits comment. His facial features are exaggerated to conform to an indigenous phenotype, and he is dressed in full military garb, quite unlike a prison warden and more like a dictator.

The Swine and Rio de Muerte are not the only instances in which a fictional Central America has appeared in the Marvel universe. The Republic of Costa Verde to the north of Rio de Muerte was the setting of *Avengers* #35 (1966). Here, the Avengers (including Captain America) come to the rescue of a country facing a dictatorial regime. They come to the aid of army troops in support of a democratic government and free elections modeled on US politics. The Republic of Santo Rico, another cognate space, is similarly the center of attention in *Tales to Astonish* #54 (1964), where the Wasp and Henry Pym defeat a communist dictator, El Toro, to then hold democratic elections. Control of the Republic of San Gusto is at the heart of the plot in *Fantastic Four* #21 (1963), where the villain, the Hate-Monger, creates civil conflict and riots in a country that is important for US interests in the Cold War. In all these cases, Central America is the setting for Cold War policies and politics, its nations and peoples fictionalized and relegated to the realm of objectification. They have no agency, no control over their political sovereignty, and no right to self-determination. Importantly, Central America in these earlier examples, and especially in *Captain America*, requires the intervention of US superheroes to fight evil.

The Cold War enemy in these comic strips brings us back to the ending vignette of webisode 1 of *Capitán Centroamérica*, as the hero is also charged with fighting this abstract, omnipotent enemy. Herein we see the narrative acceptation of parody, as the Capitán will also fight off the bad guys like his *tocayo* (namesake), the Avengers, and other heroes of the

Marvel universe before him. But unlike the Swine and other villains—who stand in for macroeconomic and macropolitical entities and issues—he is to fight the small fish, that is, the common crook who subscribes to criminality as a tactical way of life. Parody lies in the fact that his duty lacks the grandiose missions of the US superheroes; it lacks the possibility of real (or even metaphoric) systemic change.

In this gesture, the web series follows Hutcheon's notion that "parody is doubly coded in political terms: it both legitimizes and subverts that which it parodies" (*Politics* 101).[20] The series legitimizes the origin text by subscribing to the notion of the superhero as far-reaching agent, as viable actor within the unviable political theater of Central America, but subverts it by rejecting the possibilities of geopolitical incursions of the state: Capitán Centroamérica and his lack of real superpowers is a superhero for the layperson, and not an ideological metonym of (supra)national interests. The parodic mode is a postcolonial gesture, where the colonial is not the Iberian empire but the more recent hegemony and empire of the United States during the twentieth century. This subversion aligns the web series with a long tradition of parodic texts in Latin American audiovisual production, following Paulo Antonio Paranaguá's idea that "parody, as one already knows, is the ambiguous weapon of the colonized, an intertextual relationship typical of a culture subjected to matrices of being an object of derision, confirm both its universality and, therefore, its superiority" ("la parodia, ya se sabe, es el arma ambigua del colonizado, una relación intertextual típica de una cultura sometida a matrices que al ser objeto de escarnio confirman al mismo tiempo su universalidad y por lo tanto su superioridad"; 265). Roberto Ferro adds to this characterization or weaponization of parody as a postcolonial affront, noting that it is

> a way in which deliberate gesticulation dismantles the sacralizing presuppositions of all protocols of precedence and privilege of the model; that in the dissemination of the senses, in overacting and cross-dressing, it undoes the univocal direction of the metropolis/colony and contaminates, through the multiplicity of meanings, the restraints imposed by the institutional fabric and its symbolic mortar in all facets of Latin American life.
>
> (Un modo que en la gesticulación deliberada desmonta los presupuestos sacralizantes de todos los protocolos de anterioridad y privilegio del modelo; que en la diseminación de

los sentidos, en la sobreactuación y el travestismo deshace la dirección unívoca metrópolis/colonia y contamina con la multiplicidad de las significaciones las sujeciones impuestas por el tramado institucional y su argamasa simbólica en todos los órdenes de la vida latinoamericana; 7)

Capitán Centroamérica can thus be framed within the narrative mode of parody (as an intertextual reference to a specific superhero amid a long tradition of superheroes in Central America), and within the political and ideological networks that parody and these texts engage with. It is not a simple spoof of a Captain Central America—as he has appeared in other comedic media—but a serious and thoughtful reflection of the dialectic between the present and the past, between autonomous self-determination and foreign intervention.[21] This is clear in Díaz's assertion that the hero parodies Captain America, "which, in a dictatorial way, appropriated the name of the continent to use as a surname, although its jurisdiction is limited to the land of Uncle Sam" (Mata Blanco). Note the use of "jurisdicción" and its politicoeconomic connotations in the matrix of the superhero narrative—by parodying Captain America, the hypertext, Díaz's *Capitán Centroamérica*, effectively "undoes the univocal direction of the metropolis/colony" (Ferro 7).

Fighting Crime in El Territorio Centroamericano

Let us now return to the remaining entries of the web series. Webisode 2, "Gloria," was first uploaded to Puyaweb's YouTube channel on December 22, 2011, that is, three months after the premiere of webisode 1, but was quickly met with an obstacle faced by even casual users who do not have monetized channels: the infamous "Content ID claim." The site has an integrated automated system wherein uploaded content is "scanned against a database of files that have been submitted . . . by content owners. Copyright owners get to decide what happens when content in a video on YouTube matches a work they own. When this happens, the video gets a Content ID claim" (YouTube Support). The black credits of the video open with the following: "On 12/22/11 / the premiere of this / episode / was blocked. / Thanks to some fans / on that day they managed / to override the block / and many managed to see it, / and others did not" ("El 22/12/11 / el estreno de este / episodio / fue bloqueado. / Gracias a algunos fans / ese dia [sic] lograron / saltar el bloqueo / y muchos lograron verlo, / y otros no"). This opening statement is followed by: "The next day / it was / everywhere, / but our official version / reedited / was still needed" ("Al día siguiente / ya estaba / en todos lados, / pero faltaba / nuestra versión oficial / re-editada").

In a Facebook Messenger exchange I held with Puyaweb's social media admin, Adolfo Marinero, he explained that the video was initially blocked due to the use of copyrighted background music, a common culprit in Content ID cases. The producers reedited the video and uploaded it a month later on January 7, though they claim that it was available "everywhere." Unlike a large movie or television studio with a dedicated legal team and content specialists—or even media produced by smaller outfits specifically for television—web producers such as Puyaweb are far more susceptible to stumble on the minutiae of production, which in this case temporarily hampered the dissemination of the episode.

The introductory credits mimic Marvel Studios' opening (akin to Enchufetv's opening for "Superhéroes en Latinoamérica" and "Superhéroes en Latinoamérica 2"). The flipping of comic book pages sutures the clip to Jeffries's idea of "comic book film style," and evokes the aesthetics of parody in framing the series. The latter is clear in the composition of the flipped pages. Unlike Marvel's montage that introduces characters in print and dialogue that will later appear in the movie or television episode, the montage here is a postmodern pastiche of multimedia images and content, ranging from President Barack Obama giving a speech, to the cover art of Rockstar Games' influential *Grand Theft Auto* series. These images are not random, but rather evoke the politics of the origin film (and their relation to an early twenty-first-century global culture) and the ways in which the hypertext (the web series) may or may not engage them.

The narrative picks up from the concluding dialogue of webisode 1, as the Capitán and his sidekicks take to the streets. In slow motion, the Capitán confronts a band of criminals, using his shield to neutralize them as they attempt to flee. Díaz employs CGI for the first time, distorting the image in an amplification effect as the shield makes impact. With the crooks languishing in the middle of the road, the superhero hovers over them with shield in hand, before looking at the camera. The image freezes into a photograph, and pans out to the front page of a fictitious print newspaper, "The Happy Press: Serious News" ("La prensa felíz: Noticias en serio") under the headline "Criminals Afraid to Rob. The Captain Cleans the Streets" ("Delincuentes temen salir a asaltar. El Capitán limpia las calles"). The cover page is in relief against a backdrop of printed interior pages. The camera then moves inwards and downwards, focusing on a second front page that is juxtaposed to others in this digital tableau.

This image, also from a Salvadoran newspaper, affirms that children now feel safe in Central America, next to a boxed subhead stating that now everybody wants to buy Capitán Centroamérica T-shirts. These images exist in a multimedia, digital tableau, in a parallel dimension of multivalenced realities where his crime fighting immediately appears across a news media space in a variety of spreadable, shareable, and sticky articles and platforms.

The image then cuts back to a young woman nervously clenching her purse as various men loom in, presumably to rob her. Their intentions, however, are cut short as a rapid blur makes short work of them. CGI is used again to emphasize the powers of the superhero in fighting crime, an about face as in the ending of webisode 1, the MUC noted that the Capitán didn't have any real powers. The blur then stops in front of the three beat-up thugs, and the Capitán looks on defiantly at the camera. This image also freezes into a photo that transforms into a headline page in the tableau format, this time form a Guatemalan newspaper. The camera moves to another paper from El Salvador detailing the political repercussions of these microvignettes: the president completely supports the superhero, and the populace can now rest easy with their front doors unlocked. The opening montage goes on to show the superhero fighting off other social ills, including domestic violence, gang-related executions, and bus robberies.

The montage provides the viewer with a snapshot of criminality in Central America, emphasizing the point that crime and violence are part of everyday life and spaces, and not isolated to specific demographic groups or geographic neighborhoods. The images alternate with headlines from the news tableau, including "USA decides to open borders with Central America" ("EU decide abrir fronteras a Centroamérica") in a Nicaraguan paper, thereby proving two points: that the superhero is indeed a transnational hero; and that his actions are resulting in the reduction of crime. That being said, he is still relegated to symptomatic action, that is, fighting villains in media res, and not at the source of their criminality, a source that the MUC seemingly wants to protect.

The opening montage of webisode 2 is significant in that it moves beyond the origin story and into the substantive plot elements of the series' narrative arc. It presents the viewer with the principal characteristics of the hero, what makes him a superhero, in addition to extending a time frame for his actions to take effect. Importantly, it signals how the character is identified within the diegesis as a superhero, identification being a primal characteristic of the archetype. Díaz uses CGI in these images to highlight the "superness" of the hero and his physique, which is radically different from the petite lankiness of Carlos before his transformation. Indeed, his physique is highlighted in one tableau page where, instead of showing him in the act of fighting criminals, the main image features the Capitán flexing his well-developed biceps and deltoids.

The physical stature of the hero presents another parodic dialogue between the superhero and the origin text. The "CA" on his helmet and the shield are obvious sartorial calques of Captain America. But the star-studded emblem on his undershirt, and the cargo pants and work boots that characterize his uniform clearly differ from the blue and red suit worn by the North American hero: Capitán Centroamérica is a superhero despite being dressed as a construction worker. His visual composition is thus a parody of the original—not unlike the famed yellow and red leotard—but this is not to say that the character does not maintain compositional elements of the latter. Though his physical appearance subverts the mission and gravitas of the Marvel superhero, it does legitimize the notion that the superhero is a bastion of physical, hegemonic masculinity.

Writing on recent superhero parodies and masculinity, Jeffrey Brown correctly notes that superheroes "have always represented the pinnacle of American cultural ideas about masculinity, and have served for generations as a key power fantasy for male adolescents. The superhero is stronger than anyone, defeats every villain, is always in the right, and gets the girl" (131). I would add to Brown's observation that these (North) American cultural ideas have been successfully exported through the global ubiquity of the twenty-first-century superhero movie. In a global, and increasingly transnational and neoliberal world, culturally popular and visible masculinities smooth over local and regional hegemons; they do not replace local masculine structures, but pose a parallel matrix of power. This is the case of the North American superhero that circulates across borders, posing particular physiological and behavioral standards for masculine idealization, as seen in Capitán Centroamérica's bicep curls. In addition to the qualities outlined by Brown, I would add that the contemporary superhero (with a few exceptions, of course), is self-aware and reflexive of his muscularity. This is evident in the various gratuitous shirtless scenes in films featuring Mirageman, Batman, Superman, and the X-Men; whether it be Marko Zaror, Hugh Jackman, or Ben Affleck, the contemporary filmic superhero is a physical specimen, happy to flaunt his bulging biceps, impeccable pectorals, and symmetrical abdominals to a gawking audience. This is perhaps most evident in DC's recent *Justice League* (2017), where the sheer physical mass of Henry Cavill and Jason Momoa often substitutes for dialogue and narrative depth throughout the two-hour runtime.[22]

Though his attire subverts the superhero, Capitán Centroamérica's physical attributes and muscular preening maintain the ideology of gender hegemony so prevalent in the genre. This is highlighted in the juxtaposition presented in the first scene in webisode 2, immediately after the introductory montage of crime fighting and newspaper headlines. Soft music (unlike the high-octane action soundtrack in the montage) accompanies the camera as it pans to the MUC performing dumbbell presses on an inclined bench. His physical attire is also quite unlike the day-laborer costume worn by the Capitán, as he wears a polo shirt with the emblem of the University of Texas–Austin that suggests that he was educated in the United States. Like the Chilean Chicago Boys before him who brought neoliberal policies to Latin America, we may infer that the MUC is also tied to US geopolitical interests and ideologies. Two bodyguards flank him and assist with the weights; they are not, however, conventional spotters who stand in attention should the lifter lose strength and coordination, but actually lift the weights, though the MUC seemingly struggles with each repetition. The viewer is to glean from this scene that the political head is radically different from the superhero in all aspects, thus posing a countertype that only heightens the masculine ideal.

In the subsequent scene, the viewer gathers further information about the characters' development. Given the brevity of the format (and the limited production funds behind pro-amateur video production), the producers utilize creative techniques to condense multiple stories and plot points into the short runtime of each webisode. We see the superhero and his sidekicks resting in the outskirts of San Salvador and learn through the dialogue that the exploits featured in the newspaper tableau took place over the course of three months. Their dialogue also opens to the audience a little-discussed detail about superhero work: financial compensation. Though most heroes have a day job (Mirageman is a bouncer, El Man is a taxi driver, Superman is a journalist), one does wonder how full-time heroes that are not billionaires subsist—even El Santo, with his gadgets and sports cars earned checks from fighting in the *cuadrilatero*. The three characters mention the paycheck they will receive at the end of the month and discuss how they will spend their wages. Their work, however, is not solely for capital gain, as the Capitán is quick to reference their patriotic fervor for fighting crime: "It is always a pleasure to serve this country" ("Siempre es un placer servir a este país").

The informal chat is interrupted by something that the Capitán spies in the distance—a well-dressed, heavier man with a leather briefcase surreptitiously entering a house accompanied by two armed bodyguards. The protagonist affirms that they should investigate though Marimba seems reticent to act. The superhero, however, insists that they act ("Duty never rests" ["El deber no descansa"]). The image cuts to an interior shot where we see the three men enter a room with armed bodyguards surrounding another well-dressed (and armed) man eating pupusas. He, like the other with the briefcase, belongs to a criminal organization known as La Red. The Capitán and his sidekicks come upon the lair just as the longhaired boss is about to supply drugs in exchange for cash. A battle ensues between the three different factions; the Capitán fights with his superhuman skills whereas El Mudo and Marimba shoot to kill. The fight scene is graphic and lethal—criminals are killed and not neatly tied up to then be delivered to the authorities. *Capitán Centroamérica* is unlike *Chinche Man* in that the series is verisimilar in its depiction of violence. It rejects the notion of superhero as an agent of the judiciary, for a model where the superhero is the enactor of justice, however violent that justice may be.

Webisode 2 ends with the capture of both criminals, albeit in very different circumstances. The longhaired narco is confronted by the Capitán, and refuses to disclose any details about the criminal organization. When threatened with jail time, he laughingly replies that he will be free in 72 hours, thus signaling the inefficiency of the criminal justice system in deterring future behavior, and the impunity in which criminals may operate (not unlike what happens with the death of Igor Padilla). The other crook, the heavier gentleman wishing to purchase drugs, escapes the superhero, but is interrogated in a closed chamber by a mysterious off-screen voice, who now decides to target the Capitán, as he has interfered in the drug transaction. The viewer is told that this voice is a heavy hitter in La Red, the antithetical villain to the superhero, who up till this point only had to deal with common criminals.

The insinuations of corruption and moral and civic decay present in the first two webisodes are taken to fruition in the third, "La caída," where the superhero falls from grace. This is a repeated trope in the genre, a key point in the narrative arc wherein the hero must seek redemption after suffering public scorn and ridicule (see *Zenitram*, for example), which occurs at the midpoint of the web series. The episode opens with the radio news reporting that the superhero busted a drug deal (of cocaine, marijuana, and glue) worth 30 million dollars. In the next scene, the Capitán meets with officials from the MUC in the Teatro Nacional of San Salvador. The MUC participates in the scene through teleconference, instructing his aides to give the superhero a check for his labor: a measly $256.25. The hero is then escorted to a throng of waiting journalists and fans (holding printed posters). When asked about the 30 million dollars, an aide quickly interjects that the amount was only 15 million (as the other half was in counterfeit currency), and that the bills were all burnt with the seized drugs. The assembled journalists murmur and smirk in disapproval—a not so veiled reference to the cynicism that Beatriz Cortez argues characterizes much of postwar Central American fiction—evidencing to the diegetic characters present and to the viewer the open secret that the authorities have seized the funds and drugs for their own enrichment. This was hinted at in the earlier scene, immediately after the Capitán received his pay, when the MUC asks his aide if *his* salary has been processed. The viewer can easily tie together the loose ends to arrive at the conclusion that the drug money (and any profits made from selling the drugs) are all now lining the pockets of the MUC and other top government officials. The series thus explicitly critiques local and regional governments in their role in fostering a climate of corruption and lack of civic trust in institutions of law and order.

The press conference ends with a celebration, as members of a local ensemble dressed in traditional attire and masks perform a folkloric dance. The superhero is presented with a Capitán Centroamérica cake and other desserts made by Paladarte, a real pastry business that sponsored the web series. The protagonist tries one of the pastries and expresses his approval, effectively endorsing the bakery should a YouTube viewer be interested in quelling a craving. As in the case of *Chinche Man*, *Capitán Centroamérica* features local sponsors that advertise their wares and services, in what may be viewed as another characteristic of bottom-up production. This practice is in opposition to the presence of product placement in top-down productions, where companies are featured in a seemingly innocuous fashion, entering the audience's subconscious through the ubiquitous placement of products and logos. In *Chinche Man* and *Capitán Centroamérica*, advertisers are featured in shots that highlight their phone number, address, and even web presence. There is no effort to camouflage their patronship, as they are important contributors to the production of each superhero.

The jovial scene is interrupted when one of the dancers breaks character and attacks the superhero with a machete; unbeknownst to the Capitán and the viewer is that three of the dancers are in fact "Los 3 Zanates," a band of assassins hired by La Red. The only characters who seem unsurprised by the act are the MUC's aides who coordinate the press conference. They quietly slip away, suggesting that they are complicit with the attack. The inference to be made is clear: either the MUC is La Red, or is working closely with the criminal organization, suggesting that institutions of the law are indeed subservient or equal to the principal institution of criminality in this diegetic Central America. Though outside the genre conventions and aesthetics of the detective movie, the web series does follow in the vein of a wider swath of Central American cultural production (especially narrative, and, to some extent, film), that cultivates the detective genre as a critique of the sociopolitical present. Following this idea, the series engages in a cross-genre hybrid, in what Misha Kokotovic calls a "noir sensibility characterized by a pervasive sense of corruption, decay, and disillusionment, in which the social order itself, and particularly the state, is the ultimate source of criminality, rather than of justice" (15). By leaving the superhero to the mercy of the assassins, the MUC (by proxy of his surrogates) establishes himself as a key player within the operations of La Red.

What follows is a lengthy fight scene between the superhero and the assassins, replete with CGI effects, slow motion capture, and bungee-assisted aerial stunts that are all associated with the visuals of the superhero film genre. The negative connotations associated with parody are sidestepped in this scene, as the use of digital technology elevates this YouTube superhero to the expectations of an audience saturated with action sequences in the genre. The Zanates also possess superhuman strength, a characteristic that raises them to the level of supervillain, unlike the earlier scenes with common criminals and narcos. Their status as worthy adversaries is highlighted early in the fight scene when they manage to remove (in slow motion) the Capitán's mask.

As I argue in the chapter on *Mirageman*, the mask is a key affective element and form in the superhero film genre, potentiating feelings and emotions surrounding the character and key narrative plot points. Díaz uses slow motion in this scene to further emphasize its import vis-à-vis the narrative and the villains. The removal of the mask in defeat also signals the mortality of the superhero. Superheroes become sticky characters imbued with the empathic investment of the audience when they manage to elicit deep emotive changes in the viewer. There is no more efficient way to do this than to dangle the hero's body over the prospect of death. The removal of the mask denudes the superhero's body to the realm of the human, momentarily relegating the character to the conditions of humanity that are otherwise exceeded in the genre. The removal also sets in motion a cyclical effect, wherein the hero moves from victory to defeat, and then eventually to victory; superhero films, after all, would be narratologically vacuous if not for the pathos of the victory-defeat-victory cycle.

The move towards victory takes place in the same fight scene, as the protagonist manages to put on his mask before taking on the three villains. They move through the spaces of the building in a choreographed exchange of blows and kicks, culminating in the Zanates (who also have teleporting abilities) tying the superhero up. One of them seasons the edge of his machete with a raw onion and is about to kill the Capitán when El Mudo and Marimba, who were previously MIA, throw a flying tortilla in his defense. The two unhurt Zanates scurry away in defeat, as the superhero collects himself with the help of his sidekicks and interrogates the fallen crook. At her deathbed, the unmasked villain tells the protagonist that her boss does not belong to La Red, with her final words being "Tricked fool . . . I was just like . . ." ("Bicho engañado . . . yo era igual que . . ."). The unnamed female assailant's last words pose added intrigue to the return to victory in the cycle, as it introduces several unknowns, including the identity of the kingpin, and the origin story of the Zanates. Were they also superheroes enlisted by the MUC? How did they transform into the bad guys? What role do they play in curtailing the activities of the superhero? These are some of the questions left unanswered, inducing the viewer to click on the link for the next webisode. In a platform and distribution model based on clicks and shares, YouTube serials must quickly and efficiently engage the audience to click on (or to subscribe), and do not enjoy the build-up of commercials and other paratextual media that television shows rely on to keep viewership up.

The mystery surrounding the events at the press conference and its aftermath intensifies in the following scene. A quick setting shot brings us to the Ministry of Central American Unification, where the MUC's senior aides meet with one of the scientists (played by Díaz) who created the Capitán (the cameo by the creator—which is also seen in *Chinche Man* and *Mirageman*—is reminiscent of the Stan Lee cameos in Marvel films). They discuss covering up everything that happened and to explain away the attack by the Zanates to maintain the positive public perception regarding criminality and the role of the MUC in creating a united region. Their task is made difficult by the actions of a journalist in the fight scene (the same journalist who asked about the missing $30 million), who recorded the events with his cellphone camera. Akin to the real-life death of Igor Padilla after *Chinche Man*, these first-person amateur images make their way into print, television, and Internet outlets, reflective of how mobile digital devices have changed circulations and epistemologies of journalism. The episode concludes with a disheveled and disoriented protagonist awakening in the brush of the jungle. He is without mask and shield, adding intrigue to just what transpired after the meeting among the MUC's aides in the previous scene. The webisode thus concludes with an added air of mystery, hooking the audience into subscribing to the channel (to receive updates on a new episode) or into directly clicking on the next episode if already available.

Released four months later, webisode 4 ("El encuentro"), begins in media res, as the MUC gives a television interview regarding the superhero and the events from the press conference. He notes that though initially a success (by reducing crime by over 300% or more in the past three months), the officers of the Ministerio now feel cheated. When prodded by the reporter as to why the superhero failed, the MUC replies with a dismissive "he's lost his mind" ("se ha vuelto loco"). The image cuts to a shot of the Capitán making his way through the forest as the audio of the interview continues, then back to the studio, as the journalist asks if the Capitán is somehow connected to La Red. The MUC's answer is one of incredulity, blaming the media for supposedly inventing La Red. Any semblance of honesty and truth on the part of the minister are rendered moot by this outburst that seeks to discredit the news media, as the viewer already witnessed the actions of La Red in the previous webisodes, thus suggesting that the MUC is also covering up the existence of the organization. The interview does, however, give details as to how and why the protagonist is now in the jungle: the MUC states that Marimba, the only surviving member of the unit, confirmed that no battle occurred between them and the Zanates. His testimony amps up the mystery factor of the web series (and its noir sensibility) as we now also question his (Marimba's) involvement in the cover-up. The journalist then follows up the interrogation with details from the cellphone video, which contradicts the official line that the Capitán killed El Mudo before going AWOL. When faced with the facts, the MUC resorts to demagogy and a now well-known tactic of screaming "fake news" and "alternative facts" (though the series was uploaded in 2012), asserting that the ministry will "make him pay for betraying our people, the people of Central America" ("hacerlo pagar por la traición y el engaño a los pueblos nuestros, al pueblo centroamericano"). Though webisode 4 opens with more questions, it does provide some answers surrounding the fate of the exiled hero and the role played by the institutions of law.

The exiled hero is another trope familiar to audiences in the superhero genre, and occurs when the character recovers from the initial defeat before returning to victory. The return is a multifaceted trope, where a physical and psychological (and at times spiritual) mission must be completed before the superhero can return to the metropolis and fight the archvillain. This is set in motion as the two remaining Zanates ambush the protagonist in a clearing. He fights them in a weakened state, and is about to be defeated when a mysterious man dressed in traditional white linen clothing comes to his help. This newcomer also has superpowers (similar to the moves of various characters from the Japanese anime *Dragon Ball*, and Capcom videogame, *Street Fighter*) and makes short work of the two villains, who teleport away when they realize they are no match for his powers.

The scene ends with an exhausted protagonist losing consciousness, and then transitions to a composite flashback scene. In this montage, we first see a young Carlos playing soccer with friends before his Aunt Berta puts the Capitán's helmet on him instructing him to fight crime. The return to childhood in a flashback is another tropic convention that Díaz identifies and uses; like the CGI fights, the flashback here moves the character away from parody and into a serious engagement with the genre. This sequence is followed by images of his transformation into Capitán Centroamérica in the first origin video, and images of the MUC's aides laughing. The camera then cuts to the superhero awakening in a rural hut, and follows him as he exits and approaches the mystery man, the "Maestro," who is seen meditating outside with the *Popul Vuh* cradled in his crossed legs. The Maestro instructs the protagonist that he has forgotten who he is and where he comes from, and that much training is needed. What follows is the training montage typical in the genre, with the difference here being that the Capitán gains his strength and skills from the wisdom of his indigenous ancestors, with the end goal of "sacar el indio," or to harness the native powers that the Maestro dominates. In addition to incredible strength and the use of energy ions as a weapon, the Capitán masters super speed, gaining the ability to dodge bullets.

The webisode concludes with a band of soldiers ambushing the superhero as he flirts with the Maestro's daughter. Uploaded two weeks later, webisode 5 ("La Traición") begins with a recap of the previous installments.[23] The montage both brings the viewer up to speed on the plot and creates a sense of expectation, as we anticipate an answering of questions and the return of the hero to victory over the villains. Our suspicions as to who was behind the cover up are quickly appeased: Marimba enters the scene as the leader of the military unit. He informs the protagonist that "orders are orders" ("órdenes son órdenes"), and that he was instructed to never take on the upper echelons of power. The image cuts to another flashback, which is the visual representation of the hero regaining his memory. In this image, we see Marimba turn on El Mudo and the superhero as they were taking the fallen Zanate to the authorities. Back in diegetic time, the superhero takes on the soldiers and Marimba with his new skills and powers. Just as he is about to defeat them, a Zanate and Marimba teleport away with the Maestro's daughter. The webisode ends with the Capitán making his way back to San Salvador, Aunt Berta being kidnapped, and the viewer learning that the leader of La Red is indeed the MUC and his top aide. The upper echelons were thus none other than the supposed institution of the law, now turned into the source and axis of criminality. The series thus ends its five-webisode run with an open ending, as, with his love interest kidnapped, the superhero must make a triumphant return to victory, defeating the villains to overcome affronts on ethical (MUC) and emotive (his kidnapped lover) terms.

From YouTube to Television

By leaving the ethical knots neatly wound, Díaz and his partners in Puyaweb effectively create significant buzz around the webisodes, so much as to merit the jump to television. The web series thus is not a complete narrative set, but an appetizer for a fully developed arc to take place over twenty-two episodes. The producers acknowledge this in the comments section of webisode 3. A viewer asks (in 2016) what the difference is between the television and web series, to which the channel administrator replies that "the webisodes are just a base. The real canon of the series is the 22 episodes" ("los webisodios son una base nomás. El verdadero canon de la serie está en la serie de 22 capítulos"). The administrator also adds the caveat that, "if you want to know what happens in Panama, then you will have to wait for the movie, which does not have a production date as of yet" ("y si quieres saber más de lo que pasa de Panamá tendrás que esperar la película, de cual aún no hay fecha de producción").

The popularity of the web superhero is played out in a television format, first over the episodes aired on VTV Canal 35, and then later in the producer's YouTube channel. The principal story line of the television series is similar to the webisodes: Carlos becomes Capitán Centroamérica after being shot during a robbery, and is then charged by the MUC to rid the streets of Central America of crime. There are more similarities between both series: he is again accompanied in his adventures by El Mudo and Marimba; and the episodes conclude with an open ending wherein the real head of La Red is revealed to be part of the upper echelons of the government. There are, however, important differences between both shows, namely, the presence of various villains in the twenty-two episodes, the fact that Marimba is outed as a conspirator early on, and that the General of the Ministerio de Unificación Centroamericana and not the MUC is the leader of La Red. The narrative lacunae present in the webisodes are also largely resolved, as Díaz takes advantage of the longer runtime to flush out characters, origin stories, and plot twists.

Before touching on the narrative differences, I want to first draw our attention to the format of each episode. Airing weekly, without the viewer having the privilege of a mouse to click pause or on a previous episode, each entry begins with an extensive recap of the plot. This transitions into a theme song where the actions from the original trailer are now drawn in Japanese anime style, another hypotext to the character that was alluded to in the Maestro's superpowers. Completing the transformation into the television format is the fact that acting credits are also used in the introductory sequence. The montage changes throughout the course of the season, but concludes with a narratologically symbolic image. These images include a shot of a young Carlos anachronistically wearing the hero's mask at the beginning, and a later image of the superhero kissing La Princesa de la Málaga, his first kiss and the series' first villain. Each episode ends with concluding credits, a bloopers section, and—following the conventions of the medium—an *adelanto*, or images from the following episode. The latter is particularly important for the weekly format of the show, as it hooks the viewer into continuing to watch episodes. This, of course, is not needed in a streaming medium where viewers simply binge watch several episodes at a time (if not the whole series). I, for example, watched the twenty-two episodes on Televideo Latino, and simply clicked through the recap and *adelanto* sections after several episodes. The ending montage also includes social media information (such as the twitter handle and hashtag for the show), and a YouTube link to view the episodes online, thus enabling the convergence of web and television viewers. By explicitly linking to the Internet (as medium and its availability of the episodes and webisodes), the ending credits delink the episodes from the mechanisms of television, effectively decentering the dialectic of viewer–television set in favor of a plural experience characterized by a multitude of interactive possibilities. *Capitán Centroamérica* is thus an example of what Michael Strangelove calls "post-TV," where "television is not a discrete object or a privileged device. It is visual content that emanates from a wide variety of production systems . . . and flows across multiple types of screens and into all manner of electronic gadgets" (13).

Episode 1 delves into the conditions in which the Nueva Esperanza project (rechristened from "la última esperanza" in the webisodes) is born. An opening montage showcases a slew of criminal activity in Central America, including robberies, rapes, and gang-related killings. In one scene, two police officers attempt to stop a band of criminals, but their pistols are no match for the automatic and semiautomatic rifles brandished by the bad guys (the audience invariably has to wonder where they procure these weapons). Accompanying the action is a voiceover of the MUC discussing the state of affairs with the General, and that the continued existence of the Ministerio de Unificación Centroamericana and the División de las Fuerzas Unionistas is contingent on the reduction of social violence. The other key player in the Ministerio is the Head of Science, a doctor-in-training played by Díaz. He explains that several soldiers have undergone the procedures of the Nueva Esperanza project, but that none have been stabilized as a super human. Some have died, while others demonstrate an unnamed mutation. The doctor argues that he needs someone with "a spirit of service . . . a pure heart" ("espíritu de servicio . . . corazón puro") to become the super soldier. The scene is reminiscent of uncountable instances in the wrestler-superhero archive where a mad scientist attempts to create the perfect super warrior, usually finding such raw material in the pure and wise protagonist.

The exemplar specimen is none other than Carlos, who is seen performing acts of kindness and honesty among his neighbors. He lives with Aunt Berta, a maternal aunt with whom he stays when his mother leaves him at a young age to migrate to the United States. Orphanhood is a repeated trope in the superhero genre, but it is given a Central American flavor in *Capitán Centroamérica*, as Carlos is orphaned by the lack of economic opportunity and increasing violence, which has forced so many to leave. The episode concludes with a scene taken from the web series, where Carlos attempts to stop a robbery and is shot in the process. The episodes are thus built around the narrative core of the webisodes, filling in and extending characters and plot lines to complete the diegetic universe.

Another important aesthetic difference in the television episodes is Díaz's use of transition images between scenes and setting shots that depict the spaces of *Capitán Centroamérica*. The brevity of quick, online media does not cultivate a logic of continuity, favoring instead fragmentation and pastiche, not altogether different from the hands-on experience of navigating web content. The episodes, however, are enriched by the montage of setting images and specific transition techniques that situate the series within a political gesture that is developed in the plot. The setting images often produce a microscopic effect, in that the compositions move from the regional to the local. In episode 1, for example, an image of beautiful countryside with the caption "América Central" cuts to another image of "El Salvador," then "San Salvador," before finally settling on "a common neighborhood" ("un barrio popular"). In progressing from the macro to the micro, the setting images both focalize the politics of unity that I discuss earlier, and the notion that everyday violence (and any other issue that may impact the subject) stems from broader institutions and processes (a reading gleaned from the topologic zoom-in effect). The setting montages and transition shots also share another quality: the use of a time-lapse technique that produces the effect of a sped-up image. Unlike the slow-motion technique used in the fight sequences that served to generate an affective reaction in the viewer, the time-lapse evokes the uncontrollable speed and hubbub of urban life. Díaz uses these images throughout the twenty-two episodes, continually reminding the viewer of where the action is taking place, and at what speed.

The physical transformation from Chuzito to the Capitán is drawn out in the series over the first five episodes, as we learn that the doctor and other officials of the Ministerio essentially con a hesitant Carlos to undergo the treatment by telling him that Berta is being threatened by the crooks who shot him: "Aunt Berta is in danger . . . all of Central America is in danger" ("La tía Berta corre peligro . . . Centroamérica entera corre peligro"). After enduring the process, he emerges with super human skills.

Importantly, he is not yet a superhero or Capitán Centroamérica, but a crime-fighting soldier under the employ of the MUC. He notes that he is much darker in complexion, "more mestizo" ("más mestizo"), to which the doctor replies that the super soldier must "vindicate the mestizo in Central America" ("revindicar el mestizo en centroamérica") in addition to fighting criminals, introducing a cultural politics of race that was gestured to in the Maestro reading the *Popul Vuh*.

The first proper bad guy appears in episode 6, as the Viceministro de Bienes Públicos is attacked and killed in the compound of his office by El Hondillero, a well-dressed villain armed with a slingshot. We learn details of his biography through the local news: he is a transnational bad guy that was caught by Guatemalan authorities, but then somehow managed to escape. He attacks and kills government officials that he deems are corrupt throughout Central America, thus playing the role of the ethically questionable cleanser in the moral universe of the superhero. Also occurring in episode 6 is the development of Chuzito as a soldier in the MUC's army. He begins to train with two others who are ex-Special Forces in several scenes throughout the episode. The trio then proceed to investigate the murder, and are ambushed by El Hondillero in the process. In this first battle, Chuzito outperforms his companions, but the villain manages to escape. Importantly, Chuzito is unlike his companions in that he refuses to use guns or to kill the bad guy, as he believes that punishment falls under the purview of the judiciary and other institutions of the law. The superhero, at this stage of the series, still holds faith in the institutions of the state.

Given the exceptional qualities of their super soldier, the MUC and his aides decide to pair him up with new sidekicks who will better complement his talents: El Mudo and Marimba. They are also developed in the television series: El Mudo is shown to be loyal, whereas Marimba becomes a double-agent almost immediately, thus removing the element of surprise present in the webisodes when he confronts the amnesiac protagonist in the jungle. The two Special Forces officers have their own fate: they will become Zanates in later episodes after undergoing the same procedure that Chuzito was subjected to. Their transformation, however, is different, as their body chemistry and cellular structure is unbalanced, allowing them to teleport but to also be dependent on "chichaína," a chemical compound distilled from "chicha," a fermented alcoholic beverage.[24] In adding El Mudo and Marimba to the team, the MUC decides that the super soldier needs to be rebranded. In a long discussion with the doctor, the General, Teniente Morales, and Tati (the project's image consultant and the MUC's goddaughter), he decides to rechristen the hero as Capitán Centroamérica. They are aware that the name blatantly copies one of the stars of *The Avengers* (Tati acknowledges that he is "based on a super cool US superhero" ["basado en un superhéroe estadounidense super cool"]), but that a known name is needed to generate positive buzz around the project, and that foreign imports sell better in El Salvador. The MUC affirms that the new superhero "is going to be a great hit!" ("¡va a ser un hit enorme!").

Episodes 9 and 10 reuse scenes from webisodes 1 and 2, where the initial exploits of the Capitán are chronicled in the region's newspapers. Their first mission—as part of the fight against "evil" (and not against the "altas esferas")—is to ensure that disabled parking is respected in supermarkets and malls. It is an absurd mission, but one that permits Tati to begin to compile photos, videos, and selfies to use in the Capitán's Facebook page. The Latin American superhero, after all, is acutely aware of the role played by social media, technology, and web communication in the fabric of modern society. Given their later creation and emission dates (as compared to North American characters), contemporary Latin American superheroes are digital natives, coming into being in an age where the interconnectivity of the Net and its multiple platforms and mediums is axiomatic to the role of the hero in fighting crime. This is evident in *Mirageman*, as Maco uses email to communicate with the public, and even clearer in *Capitán Centroamérica*, as the trio take selfies commemorating their exploits for the public to follow. In a sense, the diegetic use of social media is parallel to the paratextual deployment of spreadable media by Puyaweb to generate interest in their character. The Capitán, after all, is "a great hit" if we consider that a short YouTube trailer then made its way to national television and international web distribution through video-on-demand (VOD) portals.

The second villain in the series appears in episode 10. La Princesa de la Málaga is one of the most powerful and vicious criminals in El Salvador. She is an intertextual character (like the protagonist), an explicit reference to "La Reina del Sur" and other female narcos who appear in literary and cinematic texts. She functions in *Capitán Centroamérica* as both an antagonist and a love interest—at the conclusion of their first encounter, she counteracts the superhero by giving him his first kiss before quickly escaping. Like the Zanates who remove the Capitán's mask, their kiss establishes La Princesa as an important counterbalance to the superhero, as in doing so she peels away the veneer of the superhuman, exposing below the humanity of the character. Defeating her thus becomes an ethical impasse, as to do so would also negate the hero's amorous impulses; yet these impulses cannot supersede the mission of justice.

A third supervillain makes his first appearance in episode 11, which is centered on an informal gathering of mayors in a house. They eat, drink, and ingest *chichaína*, while professing the importance of being not only "loyal to the party" ("fiel al partido") but more importantly "loyal to money" ("fiel al dinero"). Like the Ministro killed by El Hondillero, they are corrupt politicos at the core of the state in detritus. They are ambushed by a masked and caped character that attacks them with a neurotoxin that emanates from a spinning top. While the local news will later report that the politicians died in a fire caused by a gas leak, the MUC suspects that the attack was carried out by terrorists who had previously operated in Costa Rica.[25] Tati charges the crime-fighting duo (Marimba mysteriously disappears before this scene) to take on the villain she dubs "Trompo," who we find out in the next scene extorts money from politicians so that he and his sister may emigrate to Panama. The superhero and villain clash in episode 13, when the Capitán tracks down Trompo in the outskirts of San Salvador. The latter throws a gas-emitting top that transports the two characters to an alternate universe where the superhero's powers are rendered moot. In one of the first actions in the fight scene, he throws a "trompo" or spinning top that dislodges the Capitáns mask, repeating for the audience a visual trope of villainy in the genre. He also specifies that their fight is a battle among superheroes. Importantly, Trompo views himself as a superhero and not supervillain, as he steals from the rich and corrupt. Like La Princesa, his character posits an ethical twist in the placeholder of the villain, as his actions explore an ontological grey area within the ethical horizon of the genre. The battle ends with the Capitán and El Mudo in a coma as Trompo escapes with the help of his sister. The difficulty in situating Trompo in ethical opposition to the superhero is part of the broader ethos of Central American cultural production, problematizing what should be simple axial poles. In other words, contemporary Central American cultural production is flush with characters that evade the black-and-white ontologies of good and bad, hero and villain, posing instead complex ethical positions that require the reader/viewer to dig deeper into the many layers that underlie the conflictive present.

Episode 14 marks a change in the series towards a darker and grittier tone. This is set in motion by Díaz using an aerial setting shot of the city at night to replace the earlier time-lapse montages. In their place, the nocturnal shot visually evokes the shift from parodic comedy and satire towards a more serious engagement with the issues plaguing the sociopolitical milieu. The episode opens with the camera panning towards the left in a desolate forest before resting on a slingshot: El Hondillero returns with a vengeance. The protagonist wakes from the coma to be greeted by Marimba, who is unable to explain his absence (El Mudo remains under the effects of the neurotoxin). The viewer, however, knows that he is being dishonest, as he is a double agent for the MUC and La Red. He informs the Capitán that El Hondillero is back and is targeting ex-Ministros. They tend a trap for the villain in a scenic resort, hoping to draw him out before arresting him.

Episode 15 begins with a battle between the Capitán, Marimba, and El Hondillero. After a lengthy brawl, the two good guys corner the villain and ask him to surrender. The standoff is a favorable tropic scene for politicoethical engagement in the superhero genre, as it permits characters who metonymize multiple ethical positions to engage in a dialectic pivot. When told to concede, El Hondillero (who is played by the same actor as Trompo) asks the protagonist if he is also being separated from his family, suggesting that he is familiar with the MUC's tactics and that he too was once in the employ of the Ministerio. The Capitán naively retorts that El Hondillero "is evil" ("es malo"), and is playing mindgames to escape. The villain irately responds, "The man you are covering for is evil. The system is evil. Your bosses are evil. This detritus we are living in is evil. . . . All of this is a lie. Open your eyes . . . this lie of a last hope is useless" ("Malo el hombre que estás encumbriendo. Malo este sistema. Malo tus jefes. Malo todo esto podrido en lo que vivimos. . . . Todo esto es una mentira. Abrí los ojos . . . esta mentira de la última esperanza no sirve"). His impassioned speech is cut short as Marimba unloads multiple rounds and kills him. The superhero is immediately thrown into confusion, as he believes his partner's actions to be excessive, though the viewer knows that Marimba silences El Hondillero to maintain the facade of the Ministerio as an institution of good. He kneels to check that the villain is dead, but is stabbed multiple times as El Hondillero clings to his life. Seeing his sidekick in danger, the Capitán reacts instinctively and kills the villain with a punch, thus going against his values of not killing bad guys.

By challenging the superhero to examine the power matrix in which he operates and forcing him to kill, El Hondillero poses an ethical exercise that dislodges the character from preassigned axial metonyms. The villain becomes what Stanford Carpenter calls a "superior" villain: "Whereas regular villains prey on, and therefore need, the structure and institutions of their society, superior villains both critique and threaten the positive values of the culture and society that the superhero represents. . . . Superior villains challenge superheroes by externalizing their internal struggle to be responsible" (89). Carpenter argues that "superheroes need *superior* villains to raise the stakes of the heroic struggle by putting culturally defined value systems in high relief" (89; emphasis in the original). El Hondillero is undoubtedly one such superior villain, as he calls into question the "evil" in the ethical tableau of *Capitán Centroamérica*. This is highlighted in the following scene as a despondent Capitán sits alone in El Parque Cuscatlán and questions his role as a crime-fighting superhero.

His doubts, however, are quelled in episodes 16 and 17 as he manages to save La Princesa from La Red, as she unwittingly steals an important shipment of *chichaína* hidden in plastic balls. He saves her from certain death at the hands of La Red's assassins by arresting her, thereby realigning his actions with the values he espouses in the opening episodes prior to the ethical interjection posed by El Hondillero. With two villains resolved, the Capitán confronts Trompo in episode 18, who is now contracted by La Red to avenge the loss of face suffered at the capture of La Princesa. In true super villain fashion, he engineers an improbable and overly complex hostage situation that intellectually challenges the superhero to save the hostage (Tati). Just as the superhero is about to give up, El Mudo makes a triumphant return and kills Trompo, before Marimba disables the bomb.

Now, with all three villains neutralized (either through death or arrest), the series reverts to the true source of criminality—La Red—and the events of the webisodes. Episodes 19 through 22 develop the events from webisodes 2 through 5, as the Zanates attack the hero and are defeated. There are some important extras in the television episodes, namely, that the MUC is not the chief of La Red, though the Ministro "is in cahoots with the drug traffickers" ("está casad[o] con los narcos"), as La Red has financed his presidential campaign—the real boss is the General who masquerades as the MUC's aide. Also to note is that the rural area in which the Capitán trains with the Maestro is in Panamá. Episode 22 concludes with the superhero defeating the Zanates and Marimba, and returning to the city to seek justice. Disoriented, he asks a local woman for directions. When she asks him his name, he replies: "I am Cap . . . I am Carlos Jesús de Cruz, ready to serve the nation" ("Soy el Capi . . . Soy Carlos de Jesús Cruz para servir la nación").[26]

Importantly, the protagonist now identifies with his prehero name, though he maintains the physical appearance and costume of Capitán Centroamérica. Rejecting the moniker is a rejection of the institutionality of the hero, that is, a rejection of the Ministerio, the MUC, and the political drive to unify Central America under a government that is beholden to the drug trade. Rejecting the given name is also an acknowledgement that the superior villains in his narrative path left an imprint in his psyche, forcing an ethical reevaluation of the role and place of the "hero" in the superhero. It is an action that implies an acknowledgment of the corruption at the core of the state, the source of the social and political ills of the region. In this regard, *Capitán Centroamérica*, the television series, aligns itself with the noir sensibility and cynicism that Kokotovic and Cortez respectively theorize, inserting the popular superhero genre (and the popular medium) within the critical cultural landscape of Central America, moving the character and the medium beyond the parameters of kitsch and parody. Ultimately, the name change suggests that superheroes are not viable agents of good in the Central American landscape, and that justice can only be achieved by the common citizen.

Post Data

"Un pibe . . . un boludo más . . . nos vino a salvar"[1]

This book has attempted to fill a void in global superhero and Latin American cinema studies vis-à-vis the Latin American superhero. In broad strokes, *Capitán Latinoamérica* argues that the contemporary Latin American superhero—across a wide spectrum of media outlets, platforms, and circulatory mechanisms—is a hybrid character, a confluence of three distinct archetypes, that is, the Anglo superhero, the wrestler-as-superhero, and the parodic hero par excellence, El Chapulín Colorado. Unlike hegemonic incarnations, Latin American superheroes are deeply entrenched in their national contexts, playing out and meditating on critical ethical, political, social, and economic issues. In other words, they channel specific local anxieties that already dominate the cultural horizon of their respective national contexts. Importantly, the Latin American superhero is not a conservative bastion maintaining the status quo (see the principal Anglo archetypes), but rather challenges systems of power, injustice, and the law.

In this book I have analyzed a variety of heroes from Mexico to Chile, underscoring points of contact and disjunction within the category of "Latin American" cultural production. That is, I recognize that it is at best complicated to lump together countries, contexts, and cultures within a singular moniker, but I find value in building connections within this corpus. The project could easily have focused solely on Mexico, given its plethora of superheroes, or even Central America, given recent productions; yet I believe the broader argument is strengthened by a transnational approach. The latter, in turn, may cyclically allow for deeper introspections into national superheroes, thus providing a centripetal critical framework for future research. As I hope to have shown in the preceding pages, there are salient and distinct characteristics of the Latin American superhero that separate it from global and Anglo trajectories. It is these idiosyncrasies that can be harnessed, reconfigured, and even challenged in future work.

This broad methodological approach further applies to the corpus studied, in that I have combined an analysis of film, television, and web series. The methodology is informed by the fact that the contemporary Latin American superhero is a digital native, his or her origin story firmly rooted in the Internet and smartphone age. The superhero is diegetically and extradiegetically deployed across media platforms and channels, connecting to a diverse and transnational public through multiple screens of engagement. In other words, these superheroes are no longer cordoned off to a singular media, such as the cinema, but rather move seamlessly across mediums. To solely focus on cinematic heroes would unproductively ignore the plethora of bottom-up characters that display the wide engagement between the superhero archetype and Latin American audiences and creators. Yet to solely focus on the opposite, that is, web or television heroes, would also ignore the cinematic superhero, which is often the mediatic yardstick for comparing cultural production across traditional geonational fields.

Every superhero film is an unfinished story, a strategic window left open where the plot leaves untouched a myriad of narrative possibilities. Indeed I have not covered every superhero film, television show, or web serial made in Latin America. Most obviously missing are the animated shows made for younger audiences of such characters as El Chapulín and El Santo, and newer *luchador* films, many starring the "Son of" pantheon of wrestlers or others that feature original superheroes such as *El Alambrista* (2005 and 2014), that have attempted to resuscitate the genre but to little success. Also missing are the films from the Mil Máscaras trilogy that were filmed and produced in the United States. I have also not seriously examined the appropriation of North American superheroes as pop culture icons recycled and redeployed in a variety of contexts (for example, Paulina Rubio wearing a Wonder Woman costume in live concerts). All these examples round out the broader interstices between superheroes and Latin American cultural production that *Capitán Latinoamérica* attempts to elucidate.

Also missing are characters from countries and contexts that I have left untreated, including more adult-oriented characters such as the Brazilian animated series *Super Drags* (2018) that was produced exclusively for Netflix. In an aesthetic that evokes the now cult *The Powerpuff Girls*, the show stars three drag queen superheroes that come to the rescue of the LGBT community and its rights as they enter a phase of precarity and survival under a right-wing regime in the country. As one may imagine, the animated series is a treasure trove for exploring both queer issues in Latin America and Brazilian politics in an age of right-wing populism. Indeed, a dissection of the short series may be undertaken in consonance with an examination of earlier Brazilian superheroes such as *Capitão 7* (television, 1954–66), a character that successfully moved from moving images to print. The title character was a sort of Superman calque with a twist; that is, a young Carlos is taken to an alien planet and then returned to Earth as Capitão 7. His superhuman speed and strength were clear allusions to the North American archetype, adapted for a local audience and politicocultural substrate. Perhaps a better point of analysis for *Super Drags* would be the recently released action blockbuster *O Doutrinador* (2018), which was adapted as a television series in 2019. Based on a homonym comic book, the film stars Kiko Pissolato as a federal police officer transformed into a vigilante superhero—after suffering an irreparable trauma, of course. With his characteristic glowing red gas mask, O Doutrinador unleashes a passionate takedown of corrupt politicians and the upper echelons of a self-serving oligarchy. As is the case with *Super Drags*, it is quite easy to see the extradiegetic allusions to and critique of a post–World Cup Brazil and the government of recently elected president Jair Bolsonaro.

Conspicuously absent as well are productions from Argentina that could very well form an entire book! We could begin this hypothetical "Super Argentina" project with the massively popular Patoruzú comics and their animated adaptation, where a Tehuelche *cacique*, Patoruzú, fends off thieves and conmen with his superhuman strength and speed. Conjugating sociopolitical anxieties and ideologies that draw in issues of race, immigration, political reform, and social movements, the character is a bounty for analysis. Patoruzú, importantly, predates the paragon of North American superheroes by some eight years, suggesting that the center-periphery schematic of world superheroes may not be as axiomatic as one may think.

Also included in this project would be an examination of the Cybersix franchise. First published as comics in the early 1990s, the female superhero was adapted to a live-action series in 1995, and then a multinational animated series in 1999. The heroine, Cyber-6, originates as a Nazi experiment gone wrong, forced to adopt a male persona by day, and face the threat posed by the Nazi doctor who created her (Dr. Von Reichter) by night. The live-action series ran for eight episodes, but the animated series was more successful, as it appealed to a wider audience due to its manga aesthetic and science fiction themes, though the more adult themes of the Nazi past and sex scenes were suppressed for a younger viewership.

Appearing a decade later, Luis Barone's *Zenitram* (2010) is cut from the same cloth as Trompetero's *El Man* in being a one-off production that tackles cogent contemporary social issues through the register of parody. Starring Juan Minujín and Verónica Sánchez (as Laura), and based on a short story by Juan Sasturain, the Argentine-Spanish coproduction addresses issues relating to the neoliberal state, the privatization of public resources, and the disenfranchisement of the population as multinationals commoditize natural resources in the year 2025. Minujín plays the role of Rubén Martínez, a young man from a peripheral neighborhood of Buenos Aires that works as a trash man. A voice-over relates that the city is reeling from drought created by climate change, and that the capitalist appropriation and exploitation of water sources has led to widespread suffering and economic depression. But hope springs from the rubble of a civilization in decay, from "the middle of fucking nowhere" ("el culo del mundo"), "a kid ... another moron ... came to save us" ("un pibe ... un boludo más ... nos vino a salvar"). Dressed in an *albiceleste* shirt of the *selección* (or national soccer team), Rubén becomes Zenitram, or Martínez spelt backwards, through a quick origin moment that sees a mysterious stranger inform him in a bathroom that he is a superhero. He simply has to say the name Zenitram while clutching his testicles to activate his powers, which include the ability to fly and superhuman strength.

The film reuses many of the familiar tropes of the genre, including comic book sketches and aesthetics, the presence of an older male mentor, self-reflexivity vis-à-vis the superhero film and the superhero genre at large, the proliferation of other diegetic media such as comic books starring the titular character, and sartorial references to the national that efficiently suture the hero to the state and its populace. But *Zenitram* also recycles plot points and strategies from El Chapulín, including the exaggerated, almost comical, machismo of clutching one's testicles to trigger powers, and the presence of a superhero union that has specific rules for its members to follow. The character also parodies Superman when he flies with his love interest, Laura, as she vomits upon landing, as the extreme G-forces of flying naturally produce nausea.

The principal antagonist is a foreign multinational, WaterWay, headed by Daniel Durbán, whose prominent Peninsular Spanish accent evokes

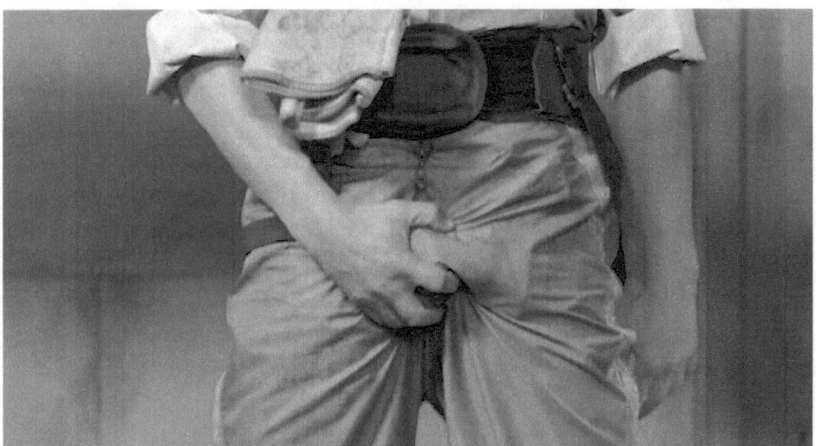

Figure P.1. Zenitram and Argentina in crisis.

the economic *reconquista* or reconquest of Latin America in the 1990s by Spanish companies. Not only does he steal the city's water, but he also has designs on Rubén's love interest. The private and public collide—in another trait of the superhero genre—leading Zenitram to take on WaterWay and to free the population from the economic shackles of the conqueror. The film does not solely adopt an us-versus-them mentality, but rather is also centrifugal in its critique. In one scene, Zenitram laments that "this country destroys its heroes" ("este país destruye a sus héroes"), leading him to want to emigrate to Miami.[2] We also evidence the inefficiency and absurdity of Argentine bureaucracy, as the superhero is given the duty of Minister of Special Affairs, which in reality is a job inundated by endless paperwork. Throughout the movie, moreover, various exchanges between Rubén, Laura, and Durbán criticize the evolution of the Left in Argentina.

As the film proceeds with kitschy special effects and comic relief, Durbán becomes a de facto dictator, and engineers the public collapse of the superhero. As Zenitram is left out of commission, the mantel of justice is taken over by Laura, who leads an urban guerrilla movement called Círculo Rojo that explicitly evokes the Dirty War. When Zenitram returns, he joins forces with the *guerrilleros* to take down Durbán, WaterWay, and a Cuban-American superhero who comes to Buenos Aires to protect the interests of the dictatorship.

In the climax, Zenitram and Círculo defeat Durbán, though the superhero pays the ultimate price by sacrificing himself to fix the ecosystem and bring about an unceasing rain to end the drought (which, as the voice-over indicates, creates a whole other slew of problems in the future). Importantly, when the superhero is questioned for joining the guerrillas and fighting against the government and military, he retorts that the rule of law only applies in the North, where superheroes are, ironically, not needed. Herein we see the film's principal addition to the Latin American superhero archive, as the character explicates the conservative nature of the superhero while gesturing towards the revolutionary possibilities of a local iteration.

The following chapter of "Super Argentina" would study Nicanor Loreti's award-winning 2015 homonym adaptation of Leonardo Oyola's novel *Kryptonita* (2011). Based on the DC Comics paradigm of Elseworlds, that permit readaptations and imaginations of archetypal characters and storylines to alternate contexts and universes, the film transposes the famed superheroes of the Justice League to a gritty contemporary Buenos Aires. Each character is reborn as a local superhero, yet maintains defining personality and super traits of the original: Nafta Súper is Superman; El Federico is Batman; Faisán plays the Green Lantern; Ráfaga has the superhuman speed of Flash; Cuñatai Güirá is a Guaraní Hawkgirl; and Lady Di rounds out the band as a trans Wonder Woman.

The film takes place over the course of a single night in a hospital located in a working-class neighborhood, where a pill-popping nightshift doctor is met by the Nafta Súper gang who seek medical care for their injured leader. They are pursued by the corrupt police who quickly surround the hospital, led by two villains who are the local incarnations of the Joker and Doomsday. Loreti's feature favors deep, introspective dialogues and monologues over fast-paced action sequences, resulting in a film that may be slow for some audiences but a treasure trove for viewers keen on seeing just how different well-known characters would have turned out in an alternative sociocultural milieu. *Kryptonita*'s success was followed up by an eight-episode television series, *Nafta Súper*, that premiered in 2016, and is now available for free through the producer's website (naftasuper.spacego.tv). The series takes off from the events of the film, as the superheroes now have to fight off the police and a new drug gang seeking inroads in the La Matanza barrio of the city. *Kryptonita* and *Nafta Súper* are quite unlike anything else in the Latin American mediascape, as their characters and narratives move from novel to film, and then to television/web platforms.

The final chapter of this project would address the film *Capitán Menganno*, based on the real-life exploits of Menganno, a superhero from

Lanús covered by such media outlets as the popular Radio Ambulante podcast, in addition to local and international television channels. Menganno, like Súper H in Honduras or Superbarrio in Mexico, is a normal citizen who puts on a mask to fight crime and raise awareness about critical social issues impacting his community. Produced by Metrópolis Films, 153 Producciones, and Cinema Digital, the project is—as of March 2020—in late filming and production stages. All in all, these Argentine superheroes critique and destabilize the episteme of politico/economic/mnemonic crisis that has come to characterize depictions of the national in recent Argentine cultural production.

Aside from these Argentine superheroes, fans may also be interested in characters that attempt a transnational identification. Nicolás López's

Figure P.2. Fictionalizing the lay-hero in *Capitán Menganno*.

Santos (2008), for example, is set in a smoothed out "Latin American" space. The audience is told that a grand seismic event results in the flooding of Western Europe and East Asia, leading to the mass migration and settling of these peoples in the New World, specifically in a fictive space called Capital City that is a sort of technological utopia, whose ordered streets and even development are unseen in the megalopolises of the continent. Starring Javier Gutiérrez, Elsa Pataky, and Leonardo Sbaraglia, López's film fuses Japanese and Anglo traditions and aesthetics, with clear allusions to El Chapulín Colorado (the yellow and red leotard worn by the hero, Santos, and the film's self-reflexive nature). The plot revolves around the unlikely hero saving the universe from a foe from outer space. Like most López films, the humor is often sexist and sophomoric, and fails to tackle any serious issue, perhaps explaining its failure in the box office.

Another pan–Latin American hero is Zambo Dende. Produced by 7GLab (based out of Colombia, Panama, and the United States), and starring Marko Zaror, the trailer for the film premiered in 2016. The character debuted in a print format and was slated to appear in an animated and live-action series, in addition to the film. The action takes place a few centuries ago, even before El Santo's ancestor donned the mask and took up a sword against heretics, during the early colonization of the New World. Zambo Dende is the alter ego of Azúk, an indigenous warrior committed to freeing slaves and avenging the death of his father at the hands of "Six Deaths" McGloin, a merciless Scot who gets his kicks from torturing indigenous and African prisoners. The comic (and assumingly the series and film) recounts Zambo's exploits in fighting the injustices of colonialism and racism in Latin America, as a sort of originary avenger against the foreign forces of evil. The foreign here is somewhat ahistoric and exoticized, reminding the reader/viewer of Kalimán, as Zambo's principal enemies are a band of delinquents hailing from China, Ireland, Russia, Arabia, and a cannibal "pigmy from a distant land." As of March 2020, the producers have put the film and series on hold, astutely waiting to build a broader fan base from the print medium before embarking on a big-budget production.

In a piece on Zambo Dende for *Remezcla*, Andrew Vargas notes, "For better or for worse, it usually takes Latin America a few years to catch up to cultural and political trends coming out of El Norte—which means it was only a matter of time until we got a Latin American superhero movie." The journalist is seemingly unaware of the variety of films, series, and characters that have already been produced and gained popularity in Latin America, as Zambo Dende is nowhere near being the first Latin American superhero, as this book would attest. That being said, however, the future looks bright for the Latin American superhero, as projects are in motion and creators are taking advantage of a wide variety of local and global platforms and circulatory mechanisms to populate the mediascape with autochthonous heroes. As I hope to have shown throughout *Capitán Latinoamérica*, these superheroes require a serious critical study, both within the optic of specialized cinema studies and through a more generalized cultural approach.

Notes

Introduction

1. This number is now at four, with the record-breaking ticket sales set by *Avengers: Endgame*.

2. Similar statistics are evidenced in Argentina, Bolivia, Peru, Colombia, and Chile for yearly numbers during the last decade. All ticket sales data gleaned from boxofficemojo.com.

3. A pleasant break from this trend occurs in 2017, as the top grossing film was *Coco*, with the closest superhero competitor coming in at number 6 (*Spider-Man: Homecoming*).

4. Superhero studies are part of a broader examination of pop culture, genre film, and print mediums in a global context, often simply called comic studies or comics and popular culture. The University of Mississippi Press, the University of Texas Press, and the University of Arizona Press are among several that have series dedicated to the field.

5. Fernández L'Hoeste and Poblete, for example, explain that "comics have constituted one of the important media in [the] connection between socio-economic modernization, cultural matrices, and mass-mediatization" (3). See their *Redrawing the Nation: National Identity in Latin/o American Comics*; Jorge Catalá Carrasco, Paulo Drinot, and James Scorer's *Comics and Memory in Latin America*; Dorfman and Mattelart's *Para leer al Pato Donald*; and several books by Foster, that include an analysis of graphic novels.

6. This idea evokes Néstor García Canclini's discussion of the popular in the era of globalization, as a cultural manifestation not necessarily sutured to a national territory but rather as a glocal phenomenon (85–86).

7. See Richard Slotkin's *Gunfighter Nation* for a detailed analysis of how the hero in the US imaginary must often work outside the law to uphold the very rule of law (10–12).

8. This idea resonates with the front cover art of Eduardo Mendieta's *Latin American Philosophy: Currents, Issues, Debates*, which is taken from Guillermo

Gómez-Peña, Enrique Chagoya, and Felicia Rice's *Codex Espangliensis: From Columbus to the Border Patrol*. The image shows the Man of Steel and Wonder Woman battling an indigenous warrior, as the latter gains the upper hand and Superman exclaims, "Whoof! No Good!" I thank my colleague Mauro Caraccioli for pointing this out.

9. Their bottom-up production and circulation model follows an exciting new paradigm in cultural production, where relevancy and continuity are defined by consumption and not politico-aesthetic gatekeeping, though we may equally critique this "democratic" model as another symptom of a neoliberal episteme.

10. There is of course a sense of academic pigeonholing when we use the term "Latin America" to describe a series of films that are not necessarily bound together by any underlying conditions of unity. I revert to Deborah Shaw's argumentation that "*Latin American cinema* is a generalized term . . . clearly used and useful to discuss films from Latin America" (3). Alberto Elena and Marina Díaz López, furthermore, argue that the term should not be viewed as "fossilized and immutable" (10) but as a fluid designation that is useful in framing and situating analyses.

11. All translations of quotes from printed sources and media are my own.

12. For more information on the masculine aesthetics of Superman, and how this may be evidenced in Latin America, see the chapter on "Glocalized Masculinities" in my *The Body as Capital*.

Chapter 1

1. His source of inspiration is not altogether different from Peter Parker coming upon a luchador poster in *The Amazing Spider-Man* (2012).

2. This idea follows a line of thinking forwarded by Arjun Appadurai in *Modernity at Large*, where the transnational flow of cultural forms and productions provoke local reconfigurations to such a degree that the center powers that once dictated these very forms are no longer in a position to determine peripheral reappropriations and meanings. See chapter 5 and the analysis of Capitán Centroamérica.

3. By genre film, I am referring to Barry Keith Grant's definition of "genre movies [as] those commercial feature films that, through repetition and variation, tell familiar stories with familiar characters in familiar situations" (xvii). Thomas Schatz's ideas on genre are also useful, providing more nuances than Grant's definition. Schatz understands genre film as "part of a limited number of story forms that have been refined into formulas because of their unique social and/or aesthetic qualities" (16). Genre films have a "specific grammar or system of rules of expression and construction" (19) that provide a "range of expression . . . [and] of experience" (22).

4. For more on the Mexican Golden Age, see Andrea Noble's *Mexican National Cinema* and Emilio García Riera's indispensable *Breve historia del cine mexicano: Primer siglo, 1897–1997*. Also see Maricruz Castro Ricalde and Robert McKee Irwin's *El cine mexicano "se impone."*

5. The DC and Marvel cinematic boom started, as we know, after the events of September 11, 2001, and the so-called War on Terror. More recently, the increasing polarity of US politics, the assault on civil liberties, and the election of Donald Trump have also become important intertexts in these cinematic universes.

6. Mexico hosting the 1968 Olympics and 1970 FIFA World Cup is perhaps the apotheosis of the Miracle.

7. Roger Bartra notes that 1968 is both a "sign of defeats" and "marks the beginning of an age of transition" away from authoritarianism and towards democracy (134), which will only culminate in the 2000 presidential election. Samuel Steinberg provides nuance to this reading, noting that the concept of transition is "still quite obscure" and intrinsically "extremely violent" (8–9).

8. For Evan Lieberman, "The mask might well be considered the defining icon of Mexican culture. Dating back to the earliest pre-Columbian civilizations, Mexico has had an extremely rich tradition of ceremonial masks, representing demons and deities in the form of animals such as bats, lizards, birds, and monkeys, which were originally used to costume dancers performing religious and social rites" (3).

9. I particularly enjoy the poetry of Juan Villoro's definition of the *rudo* and *técnico*: the *rudo* "lives for the trap, the breaking of the rules, the elbow of treason, the lemon in the eyes of the innocent adversary. His salary is outrage; his tip, the jeer" ("vive para la trampa, la ruptura de las reglas, el codazo a traición, el limón en los ojos del inocente adversario. Su salario es el ultraje; su propina, el abucheo"). On the other hand, the *técnico* "is ironclad in his kindness. He performs masterful holds, dominates the 'quebradora,' the 'rana,' and the 'tapatía,' but when the opponent is on the canvas and the public demands: 'Blood!, blood!,' he does not render the definitive blow" ("está acorazado por su bondad. Aplica *llaves* terribles, domina la 'quebradora,' la 'rana,' y la 'tapatía,' pero cuando el oponente está en la lona y el público exige: '¡San-gre!, san-gre!,' no propina el golpe ruín y definitivo"; 16).

10. Anne Rubenstein affirms that he changed his name at the suggestion of a referee who, "spotting his star potential, convinced Guzmán to name himself after the referee's favorite comic-strip character, the Saint" (571).

11. This is a disputed date. Lieberman and Hegarty have 1952 as a start, while Illescas Nájera and Rubenstein point to 1951 and 1953 respectively.

12. Indeed, the comics Santo originally had nothing to do with the world of wrestling. His origin story was "reminiscent of other comic characters like Batman: Santo's parents were killed by criminals, and he became a crimefighter to bring the murderers to justice, then decided to help other people with their problems" (Wilt 213).

13. See Francisco Illescas Nájera's article for a deeper analysis of the sociopolitical and ideological role of El Santo during the critical transformations of the twentieth century.

14. We may also add Susana Distancia, the superhero tasked by the Mexican government with fighting off the COVID-19 virus, though she is more akin to the US superhero than the Mexican luchador trope.

15. Hegarty adds that "El Santo's iconic status is evidenced by the fact that for the past six decades, his image has been cross-marketed to millions of fans through comic books, action figures, and wrestling-mask replicas, and it still continues to be highly marketable today, with his son" (4).

16. See Greene and Levi for greater detail on the television ban, its ideological basis, and cultural ramifications. Levi suggests that the government only really wanted to remove *rudos*, which was largely successful, as their role was then taken upon by monsters and nonhuman super villains (181–84).

17. It is not only well-known superheroes that endorse products; local businesses are notorious for creating "super" characters whose sole purpose is to sell used cars, insurance, or the services of an exterminator.

18. Coogan adds, in *Superhero: The Secret Origin of a Genre*, that "despite the attention currently given to superheroes, the superhero genre is little studied. Typically it is either taken for granted or dismissed as a genre and marked as subset of other genres—science fiction primarily" (23)

19. See Kohut (16–17) for a further tracing between the superhero and Greek mythology. Importantly, Kohut argues that the superhero trope "should not be considered a mere extension of the Greek word heros in terms of its meaning but rather as a standalone cultural category that needs to be defined beyond the original meaning of the stem of the word" (17).

20. The recognition by peers as a super-character is fundamental to the genre, and a detail that critics have not fully underlined. Superman is a superhero because the multitude in the streets of Metropolis point to him and describe him as more than human; Buffy the Vampire Slayer is not a superhero (though her abilities and actions would suggest otherwise) because the diegetic characters that interact with her (both directly and indirectly) do not single her out as a superhero.

21. Comics and superheroes are vessels of US ideology and propaganda. The reader may also consult the work of Ariel Dorfman and David William Foster on comics, superheroes, and Disney characters as they circulate in Latin America.

22. See chapter 5 on *Capitán Centroamérica*, where I trace the politics and ideology of Captain America as he adventured throughout Central America.

23. The Santo of the Turkish film, however, is quite unlike the Mexican superhero, in that he spends much of the film with his mask off.

24. Mexploitation as a critical and aesthetic moniker denotes a cinema popular in the Mexico of the late 1950s to late 1970s that "consisted of horror films featuring an array of vampires, Aztec mummies, mad scientists, ape-men,

and various other macabre menaces" (Greene 1), many of which incorporated real-life and fictive characters from the world of lucha libre.

25. Genre and exploitation cinemas have long been unfavored in critical studies on cinema, considered lower, popular, and vulgar forms that do not demand a serious analysis. Paul Schroeder Rodríguez's recent but quickly indispensable *Latin American Cinema: A Comparative History*, for example, very briefly mentions El Santo's films in a discussion of the crisis of the Golden Age (116) and the production of *churros* to compensate for its economic woes. Schroeder Rodríguez lumps the wrestler films together with comedic features starring Cantinflas and Tin Tan, but only analyzes the latter. Jorge Ayala Blanco's *La aventura del cine mexicano: En la época de oro y después*, Charles Ramírez Berg's *A Cinema of Solitude: A Critical Study of Mexican Film, 1967–1983*, and Andrea Noble's *Mexican National Cinema* fail to analyze the wrestling films, a surprising detail given their ubiquity both in domestic and international theaters. Ignacio Sánchez Prado's also canonical *Screening Neoliberalism*, undertakes an archaeology of contemporary Mexican film, but limits itself to describing the wrestler films as "targeting urban popular classes," having "a cultural iconicity of their own," and being "essential instruments for understanding Mexico City's marginalized urban populations" (5).

26. Greene and others such as Hegarty focus on Carl J. Mora's eviscerating critique of the state of the industry at the heyday of the wrestling movies. Hegarty notes that Mora "calls the era in which their production began . . . 'the darkest days' of the nation's film industry," and that "other recent histories of Mexican cinema simply ignore El Santo's movies altogether, thus avoiding the awkward business of denouncing the most profitable Mexican movies made from the 1950s until the release of *Like Water for Chocolate* in 1993" (574).

27. Evan Lieberman makes a similar claim. He argues that, though the films were "ignored or reviled by critics of the Mexican cinema because of their folkloric character," they "are important texts for understanding the transitions taking place in Mexican culture in the 1960s and 1970s" (3). Importantly, their "representations of technology, modernity, and most significantly gender relations mark a decisive shift away from traditional formulations to point towards a contemporary engagement of these issues that, contrary to the claims of most scholars, acutely reflect the social dynamics of this turbulent period in Mexico's development" (3). Also see Lieberman's extensive discussion of the negative perception of wrestler films in Mexican film and critical circles (7–8).

28. A genre and its corresponding character tropes are cemented as such only when a parody is made possible; there are several pornographic parodies of the luchador and luchador genre (see for example Gustavo Subero's essay "Gay Pornography as Latin American Queer Historiography").

29. Hegarty argues that "we might better understand the popularity of the films' awkwardly low production values if we see them as filmic extensions of the

semantics of the comic book rather than attempts to translate the comic-book series to the language of narrative film" (8–9).

30. Levi adds that films in the genre were "an exercise in collective suspension of disbelief" (188).

31. Hegarty convincingly argues for an alternative, though not mutually exclusive, theory. She poses that the fantastical may have given audiences "a sort of liberation from the constraints of conventional (Hollywood) narrative film language in favor of a more autochthonous cultural expression" (10). Importantly, the critic links these films to the magical realism of the literary world, "forming part of a broader cultural network" that provided "an escape from dominant paradigms of representation rooted in notions of the rational and the linear, and projecting instead an idealized world in which the modern and the folk, the technological and the indigenous, the real and the surreal, all exist simultaneously" (10–11).

32. I am here adopting Richard J. Gray II and Betty Kaklamanidou's reading of the contemporary superhero movie in Hollywood. They "consider the filmic adaptations of literary or comic sources as autonomous narratives," as "it is much more fruitful to consider the sources as a kind of database from which the film team draws a sum of directions which they should handle cinematically" (2).

33. Many have called these films *churros*, as a reference to their cheap nature and lack of aesthetic and narrative nutrition. While I understand that aficionados of a more "serious" cinema may ignore luchador films, I think there is always a time and place for churros, even if they are often reviled as vulgar *fritanga*.

34. Greene adds that many of the films of the era, including films starring El Santo, were "ostensibly serials designed for television; however, their marketability on that medium was so restricted that producers turned to combining the separate serials into one or more full-length features" (7).

35. Rafael Aviña contends that 1952 is a key year in the luchador genre as it saw the screening of four important films that, he argues, lay the foundation for the genre: *La bestia magnífica*, *El luchador fenómeno*, *Resortes*, and *El enmascarado de plata* (21).

36. See Cotter's extensive discussion of this film and his speculations of why El Santo decided to not appear in the film (23).

37. The character did, however, successfully transition to a career in lucha libre.

38. Release dates for these films are taken from David Wilt's excellent database *The Films of El Santo*. Created over twenty years ago, Wilt's website is a veritable treasure chest of information for the Santo aficionado, and includes documentaries made by the author in addition to commentary on individual films. In regards to the latter, Wilt includes screening dates, ratings, and ticket sales.

39. See Hegarty (14).

40. See Illescas Nájera for a theoretical exploration of this argument (62).

41. As Rubenstein notes, "El Santo became a working-class hero at the precise moment when Mexico's urban industrial working class reached the peak of its power and prosperity" (571).

42. Several critics have commented on the ideological purpose of the Santo films within the terrain of media and politics in twentieth-century Mexico. See Illescas Nájera (51–52), for example, or Greene (56–57). Both critics argue that the character may be viewed as a sort of national allegory within times of vertiginous change.

43. The gender expression of El Santo's masculinity has been studied by several critics, though most notably by Rubenstein, who defines the character as a sort of counter-macho to the *charro* archetype that dominated popular culture (576). Lieberman adds that the superhero "may be seen as a model of the new masculinity, and a figure through whom is constructed a modern mythology of technology, intelligence, science, urban internationalism, and equal treatment of women" (6). There is a lot to say about the systems and positions of masculinity in these films, but I will leave that to future research.

44. Greene argues that the juxtaposition of past and present in tension is "a pivotal conflict . . . [a] struggle between progress and modernity, represented by the forces of *the present* (such as popular wrestlers . . .) verses [sic] the supernatural evils and dangers of *the past*" (21; emphasis in the original).

45. See Ramírez Berg (2).

46. Cotter summarizes his wrestling and acting careers: "Although he only made about half as many films as Santo, and never quite attained the somewhat mythical aura which surrounds the Silver-Masked Man, Blue Demon could be content with the knowledge that he was a better technical wrestler than the Saint (he always pointed out in interviews that he had taken two out of three championships from Santo)" (94).

47. The symbolic weight of the Church and Catholicism in these films merits its own study. While "the Catholic religion is one of the cornerstones of Mexican national identity" (Hegarty 17), it is to note that the religious in these films is an official Church that is not associated with the Catholicism of the masses, which at the time, was moving staunchly to the Left. By focusing on devil-worship and not indigenous religions, Santo maintains himself as a defender of populist values.

48. The Spanish colony is vilified in these movies, as is Aztec civilization, "by virtue of being part of an obsolescent past . . . [that] threaten[s] modern Mexico" (Greene 22).

49. See Pedro Ángel Palou's incisive *El fracaso del mestizo* for a detailed analysis of the system of political representation in Mexican cinema (13).

50. For a complete summary of the plethora of films and characters that dot the landscape of luchador cinema, see the filmographies compiled by Criollo, Návar, and Aviña.

51. Superzán was played by Alfonso Mora Veytia, and appeared in several other films as part of an ensemble cast of wrestlers such as *El Investigador Capulina* (1973), *El castillo de las momias de Guanajuato* (1973), and *El triunfo de los Campeones Justicieros* (1974).

52. Johnny is, however, Afro-Mexican, but we must remember that Afro-Mexicans fall outside the mestizo continuum of whiteness and indigeneity that was cultivated in post-revolutionary Mexico.

53. As Greene thoroughly argues across a wider spectrum of films from the era, the monsters and aliens of Hollywood would be resurrected "with an ideological agenda reflecting two primary cultural concerns in Mexico in the twentieth century: *mexicanidad* and *modernity*" (19). To note, I am not exploring the multifaceted matrix of these two terms in this chapter (as others have already done so in detail), but am rather more interested in how these films dialogue with the superhero genre to produce a Latin American model to follow.

54. The film succeeds *Las luchadoras contra el médico asesino* (1963) and *Las luchadoras contra la Momia* (1964). That being said, there are other female-led films that appear within this timeline, such as *Las mujeres panteras* (1967). The most famous luchadoras duo was played by Lorena Velázquez and Elizabeth Campbell, but a new pairing of Regina Torne and Malu Reyes appears in *Contra el robot asesino*.

55. This endgame is repeated throughout the wrestler-superhero genre, and even appears in other adaptations such as Kalimán. It merits longer analysis; that is, why the focus on mind control and losing one's free will? Is this a reaction to the perceived threat of communism and its promise of economic/ideological/social parity?

56. The stereotype-countertype dynamic is central to any symbolic associations made between the masculine ideal and subordinate gender positions within the tableau of a national imaginary. For an idealized stereotype to come into existence, Mosse argues that an efficient system and hierarchy of countertypes must first be erected. The masculine stereotype is to be strengthened by "the existence of a negative stereotype of men who not only failed to measure up to the ideal but who in body and soul were its foil, projecting the exact opposite of true masculinity" (6). Chava is not a pure countertype in that he is not a negative stereotype, but he does play the role of the foil to Arturo's swashbuckling display of masculinity.

57. The "science" scenes are especially ridiculous, even within the suspension of disbelief paradigm that is demanded by the genre.

58. All historical data can be found on the dedicated Kalimán Wikia.

59. More recently, Kalimán has been featured in museum and festival exhibits in Puebla, Mexico City, and Querétaro. In 2017 a private company called Superhéroe promised to develop a new thirteen-episode series and video game. Regarding the series, a granddaughter of one of the creators adds that "we are designing it for a streaming platform like Netflix or Blim" ("Lo estamos diseñando

para una plataforma de streaming y está siendo analizado por Netflix o Blim"; Zubieta), and that the idea is to then segue into a feature film.

60. Fernández L'Hoeste affirms that "Mexicans learned to be Mexicans not only by going to the cinemas . . . but also by reading comics" (70).

61. The opening montage of every Marvel Cinematic Universe film reaffirms this strategy, as the flipping through of a material comic book reveals to the reader the origin text of what will shortly appear on the screen. Again, we may watch the film with no prior knowledge of said characters and narrative twists, or we may delve deeper into the source texts. Such a move is an inclusive strategy, as it reaches out to an already established fan base while reaching towards newer audiences who may be unfamiliar with the print/radio source.

62. Kalimán, like the archetypal superhero, reaffirmed the status quo, and was "supportive of oligarchic and patriarchal structures" (Fernández L'Hoeste 63).

63. Scholars wishing to pursue an analysis of orientalism and internal colonialism will have a field day with this film. In addition to the eroticized and exoticized Xiomara, the representation of zombies as brutish and animalistic indigenous peoples is particularly jarring.

64. There are, however, several instances of a Cold War–era Eastern European antagonist in the Santo oeuvre, including villains in *Santo y Blue Demon contra los monstruous* (1969) and *Santo contra la magia negra* (1972).

65. The shockwaves and legacies of the massacre at Tlatelolco in 1968 are a field of study in themselves and merit much more space than I have given them here.

66. See Palou's *El fracaso del mestizo* for a thorough overview of the connections between race and ideology in twentieth-century Mexico, especially as it is deployed in the cinema. Also see Dalton's work on the Santo films and mestizaje.

67. For further reading on whiteness in Mexican film, see Mónica García Blizzard's work.

68. Indeed, Carlos Aguasaco's *¡No contaban con mi astucia! México: Parodia, nación y sujeto en la serie de El Chapulín Colorado* is of utmost importance in any analysis of the show.

69. Conspiracy theorists have traced the familial connections between Gómez Bolaños and the principal culprit behind Tlatelolco, President Gustavo Díaz-Ordaz, a cousin of the comedian's mother. Gómez Bolaños's rise in the ranks of the media corresponds to a parallel rise in the politician, leading some to argue that the latter benefited from his political connections (Aguasaco 60).

70. I thank David Dalton for these pictures.

Chapter 2

1. Suárez adds that questions of spatiality are secondary in Colombian cinema, and that "films set in rural zones are characterized by the creation of a

symbolic imaginary of violence, while films set in urban zones favor Bogotá as a location and merely use the city as a backdrop to locate the consequence of violence" (45).

2. This is not to say that Trompetero has only made comedies, as his *Violeta de mil colores* (2005) is quite profound and visually appealing. In fact, I wonder if he has moved on from the comedic fare of *El Man*. Unable to find *El Man* on DVD or stream, I tweeted the director explaining the *Capitán Latinoamérica* project and hoping that he could find me a copy. Unlike Nicolás López and the production teams behind *Capitán Centroamérica* and *Zambo Dende* (who sent DVDs or answered any question I had about their films/series), Trompetero replied with a curt "you can find it on YouTube." When I informed him that the film was no longer available and asked if he had a DVD he could spare or a web link, I received no reply.

3. This is in stark contrast to the Central American superhero films/series I analyze later that are closely aligned with the zeitgeist of contemporary literary and filmic production outside the genre.

4. Though originally created by Johnston McCulley in 1919, the character is Mexican and lives in California during the Spanish colonial era.

5. Currie was an economist and director of the first foreign project of the World Bank (then known as the International Bank for Reconstruction and Development). As James Brittain notes, Currie proposed a blueprint to reshape Colombia's economy and to weaken the guerrilla forces that were taking up positions in the rural countryside. See Brittain for a complete overview of Currie's impact in the 1960s and the continuation of the internal conflict.

6. For a more detailed reading of *Buscando a Miguel*, see my article on the filmic representations of Bogotá, Medellín, and Cali vis-à-vis urbanization.

7. While I discuss Rosenberg's ideas here, we can equally apply them to the superheroes and origin stories that appear in later chapters.

8. Rosenberg further classifies all origin stories along three main categories: trauma, destiny, and chance (9). *El Man* clearly follows the final model of chance, as Felipe becomes El Man due to El Coronel having previously fashioned a costume for a party, and needing some sort of (ethical) intervention to stave off the workers. Felipe is never destined to be the hero, nor is he traumatized into adapting the persona, as is the case of Maco in *Mirageman* for example.

9. Coogan notes that "there are four additional sub-types of supervillain—the alien, the evil god, the femme fatale, and the super-henchman. These subtypes are character tropes that appear in any number of genres. In superhero stories they serve as supervillains, and typically toward one of the main types in their characterization" (74). La Princesa in *Capitán Centroamérica*, the television series, is an excellent example of the femme fatale, while the Zanates in the same storyworld are representative of the superhenchman.

10. Coogan adds, "But most supervillains fit pretty firmly into one of these categories. All these types—except the inverted-superhero supervillain—predate the superhero" (61).

11. See the literature overview in the introduction and chapter 1.

12. The effeminate countertype also appears in *Chinche Man*. In both cases, the character simply appears for comic relief and is never developed or problematized in a thorough manner.

13. See my *The Body as Capital: Masculinities in Contemporary Latin American Fiction* for discussions on global masculinity versus local, Latin American models.

14. Connell adds that "the growth of global mass media, especially electronic media, is an obvious 'vector' for the globalization of gender" ("Masculinities and Globalization" 10), in which the superhero genre invariably participates, given its continued success in the global box office.

15. The populist, leftist nature of the superhero is rather odd, given Trompetero's career in media, advertising, and affinity for commercial films (such as *El Man*).

16. Caña Jiménez theorizes what she calls "somatic neoliberalism" ("neoliberalismo somático") through a tracing of affect and emotion vis-à-vis discourse of healthism. This somatic manifestation, however, is largely absent from *El Man*, given Trompetero's preference for a narrative, scopic cinema over a strongly pronounced affective register.

17. The physical body is an important vector in contemporary Colombian cinema, tending to illustrate the human consequences of violence. María Victoria Uribe, for example, asserts that films that have focused on recent Colombian history have tended to theorize and depict the body as an easily dismembered and ephemeral presence (95), indicative of the violences that run through the nation's social fabric. In comedies and other lighter, commercial fare, the body is a site of sexual identification and objectification, often used as a prop for comedic and erotic effect.

Chapter 3

1. For more information about the director in his own words, the reader may wish to view Blanca Lewin's interview of Díaz Espinoza in an episode of *Filmografías del Nuevo Cine Chileno*.

2. There is a historical presence of the superhero genre in print culture. In comic books, see characters who were in print before the coup, such as Rakatan (1966) and Capitán Júpiter (1966). After the dictatorship, Supercifuentes appeared in 1978, but more as a parody of the genre. Also, who can forget the character Baticóndor from the *Condorito* series. In novels, one may find traces

of the superhero in texts such as *Barrio Alto* (2005) by Hernán Rodríguez Matte. Enrique Lihn's *Batman en Chile* (first published in Argentina in 1973, and then reprinted in Santiago in 2008), however, is an experimental work that recounts how Batman walks the streets of Santiago immediately before the coup. Written in a satirical and parodic tone that critiques the immediate past and present of 1973, the novel is a must-read text.

3. Discussing contemporary Chilean cinema and critique, Antonio Traverso notes that "since the return of parliamentary democracy in 1990, the activities of independent Chilean filmmakers, both in Chile and abroad, have been supported with the establishment of Fondart (the National Fund for the Arts) in 1992, the Film and Audiovisual Development Law in 2004, and the National Film Archive in 2006. Government financial support combined with private investment and sponsorship have resulted in an ever-increasing number of fiction and documentary films and videos made each year, with an approximate 100 programmes made in 2008 alone. Alongside this exponential increase in the number of films produced in the past 20 years, there has been a growing literature in Spanish, currently establishing the scholarly coordinates of what may become the field of Chilean national cinema studies" (179).

4. A final condition for establishing a filmic movement is, according to Cavallo and Maza, the existence of "a critical apparatus that recognizes it" ("una aparato crítico que lo reconozca"; 16).

5. Translated in Risner.

6. Though taxis in Buenos Aires adopt the same colorway.

7. As Dan Hassler-Forest reminds us, "The figure of the superhero is inextricably interwoven with the landscape and architecture of the modern city. . . . As 'vehicles of urban representation,' they have embodied popular fantasies of navigating the daunting environment of the metropolis" (113).

8. Founded originally at the beginning of the Francoist years in Madrid in 1942, Passapoga Santiago opened on May 30, 2002. The original business, Pasapoga Music Hall, was located in the famed Gran Vía and was a center for the high life of postwar Spain. International artists frequently played at the Music Hall. In its later years, the business evolved into a *discoteca*, becoming at a time a center for gay life in Madrid. Passapoga Madrid closed a year after the opening of the Santiago location.

9. Viewers familiar with Tim Burton's 1989 *Batman* starring Michael Keaton will recognize this narrative device, as Batman, toward the conclusion of the film, realizes that Jack Nicholson's Joker is indeed the same thug who killed his parents in an armed robbery. A converse relationship plays out in *The Dark Knight Rises* (2012), when Talia al Ghul avenges her father by attacking Batman and attempting to destroy Gotham.

10. Note the relationship with the press, another feature of the superhero narrative. What good are heroes, after all, if they do not appear in the collective consciousness through the media?

11. Antonella Estévez notes that "the process of recognizing the abuses of human rights and the deaths caused by the dictatorship was made impossible by the conditions imposed by the military regime itself to give power and the creation of a democracy of consensus . . . where the real possibilities for truth and justice are out of question" ("el proceso de reconocimiento de los atropellos a los derechos humanos y las muertes causadas por la dictadura fue imposibilitado por las condiciones impuestas por el mismo régimen militar para entregar el poder y la creación de una democracia de consensos . . . en donde quedan fuera de cuestión las posibilidades reales de verdad y justicia"; 19). Sergio Villalobos-Ruminott adds that "the terms of the transitional governments were, in reality, extremely ineffective, being reduced to tinkering with the market and constitutional model of 1980 with two kinds of discursive interpellations: on the one hand, those that tended to exaggerate the democratizing and modernizing intentions of the government in power, and on the other, those that promised to resolve a key problem of post-dictatorial societies, the problem, that is, of an alternative historical memory to the official one" (232).

12. Another hindrance was, of course, the economic prosperity enjoyed by the country during Pinochet's rule. At the staging of the coup, Chile's economy was in shambles, largely due to US-backed interventionist policies that aimed to strictly punish Allende's attempts at reform—attempts that were seen as too leftist by Henry Kissinger and Richard Nixon. After assuming control, Pinochet embarked on a series of policies that were guided by the Chicago Boys, a group of some twenty-five Chilean economists trained under Milton Friedman at the University of Chicago. In what would anticipate the adoption of neoliberal policies throughout the continent following the crises of the 1980s, the Chicago Boys oversaw the reduction of public spending, the privatization and deregularization of services and the economy, and the liberalization of trade barriers. The Chilean Miracle describes a period from 1977 to 1982, and it then emerged again in 1985, albeit in a more reined-in fashion as the country attempted to recover from the global crisis. Why was this a hindrance for the transition? Simply because many were quick to turn a blind eye to human rights abuses with the excuse that some sacrifice—especially of the "Communist" element that supposedly brought about the crisis of 1973—was needed to maintain a healthy and prosperous country.

13. Elizabeth Lira adds that "throughout Chilean history, impunity had provided the foundation for social peace and appeared to be installing itself once again" (123–24).

14. This was done with the aid and coordination of the US-led Operation Condor in Latin America.

15. Ana Ros notes that "almost thirty films, mostly documentaries, were produced since the late 1990s. . . . The production reached a peak in 2003 and 2004 in the context of the thirtieth commemoration of the coup; these films creatively address different aspects of the repression and also the resistance, the

generational experience, and the continuities between the dictatorial past and the present" (121).

16. Bridget Franco adds, "The concluding scene encapsulates the political tension of the transition years: on the one hand, there is a recognition of the violation of human rights and a superficial, empathetic alignment with the victims, but at the same time the protagonist must accept the limitations of the fragile postdictatorship democracy in order to move forward with his own life" (411).

17. Regarding the former, Stefan Rinke traces a genealogy of the absent or lost father in Chilean cinema of the 1990s. Covering films by directors such as Silvio Caiozzi, Andrés Wood, and Miguel Littín, Rinke argues that the "overwhelming presence of the dictatorship" in the cinema of the transition may be read in the "use of the father figure in many recent films" (187).

18. Documentary film in the transition and beyond has always been more progressive. See Antonio Traverso's excellent overview in "Dictatorship Memories."

19. Kara Kvaran reminds us that "almost all modern superheroes are orphans. They lose their parents in sudden, awful acts of violence, which cause them future angst and spur epic heroics" (219).

20. The media channels and magazines, however, are all fictional.

21. The resignation only came due to increased international pressure on Pinochet's government, which eventually led to the plebiscite of 1988.

22. In *The Untimely Present*, Idelber Avelar explains that allegorical narratives predominate in dictatorship and postdictatorship culture: "Allegory emerges not because in order to escape censorship writers have to craft 'allegorical' ways of saying things that they would otherwise be able to express 'directly.' Allegory is the aesthetic face of political defeat . . ." (69). It may be useful to situate the film within the poetics that Avelar traces, but I believe the director's use of genre slyly deviates the film from a dialectic trajectory with mourning, which is imperative to Avelar's survey of recent Latin American literature.

23. I understand "working through" as Dominick LaCapra defines it: "Working-through, of which mourning is one prominent form, should not be conflated with utopian optimism or total liberation from the past and its melancholic burdens; instead, it should be seen as a supplement and counterforce to melancholia and acting out" (138).

24. The unexpected reemergence of these images (and their corresponding lived experience for the protagonist) undoubtedly evokes Cathy Caruth's theses on trauma and memory, and the persistence of the wound within the psyche.

25. Jean Franco adds to this by posing that surviving a life-and-death moment (such as an execution) "separates lives into a 'before' and long and cruel sequel in which the very notion of 'closure' is a mockery" (171).

26. Zaror's acting, in fact, can be best characterized by a lack of acting, evoking the early Santo days.

27. Wilde clarifies that "the events considered here are 'public' in the sense both that they receive extensive coverage in the media and involve the authority of public institutions and of the elites responsible for them. They involve a period of recent national history notably framed by conflicting political memories—of the acts of leading figures of the dictatorship; of the blame born by politicians for the conditions that led to the coup; above all of the massive violation of fundamental human rights under the dictatorship" (475). We may include the recent deployment of the military to the streets of Santiago as an example of an irruption. The cover image of this book is from a protester who decided to dress as El Chapulín while fending off the authorities.

28. The connection here being important if we are to consider the protagonist as an irruption vis-à-vis the role of institutionality in unearthing the past during the Rettig and Valech processes.

29. The Lagos government was in the process of asking for Pinochet's release from British authorities. The inauguration ceremony itself was marred by a series of protests from both Left and Right. See Katherine Hite's "Resurrecting Allende."

30. In fact, I strongly believe that Allende would actually be a superhero character in a hypothetical Chilean version of Álex de la Iglesia's *Balada triste de trompeta*, a dark, funny, and grotesque film that caricaturized the Spanish dictator, Franco, and his dictatorship.

31. See Marianne Hirsch's definition in *The Generation of Postmemory: Writing and Visual Culture after the Holocaust* (2012) and in earlier works.

32. In discussing the place of the river in the immediate aftermath of the coup, Elizabeth Lira notes that "the lack of information propagated rumors. . . . The number of bodies seen floating along the rivers multiplied by hundreds every day" (115).

33. The bodies of many of those killed were taken along with others and clandestinely buried in the infamous Patio 29 in the Cementerio General de Santiago. For further reading, see Peter Read and Marivic Wyndham's *Narrow but Endlessly Deep: The Struggle for Memorialisation in Chile since the Transition to Democracy*. Also see photographs in Macarena Gómez-Barris's *Where Memory Dwells* (9).

34. One headline states: "Has the Chilean Chapulín Withered?" ("¿Arruga Chapulín chileno?"), referencing the famed El Chapulín Colorado.

35. While the diegesis is set in Chile, the presence of a disappeared child clearly alludes to the Argentine dictatorship that ran parallel to Pinochet's reign of terror.

36. Avelar adds that "one of the calculated effects of torture is to make the experience a non-experience" ("uno de los efectos calculados de la tortura es hacer de la experiencia una no experiencia"; 184). The emergence of Mirageman and his agency in solving crimes that are analogous to the originary trauma reignite

Tito's psyche, engaging him verbally and kinesthetically to come to terms with the torture he suffered at the hands of the criminals. In effect, the superhero provokes a phenomenological and mnemonic relationship between Tito (and the thousands of other survivors) and the wave of crime ransacking Santiago in the early 2000s, thus giving him the tools to make the "no experiencia" a lived memory once again.

37. Moli's role in all this is rather problematic and not easily reconciled. He is supposedly helping save the kidnapped girl by handing Mirageman confidential information, but is also engaged in censoring information. His complex narrative position in the plot is left unresolved, perhaps alluding to the ethically complex position of the institutions of law that were responsible for the atrocities and who are now tasked with rendering justice.

38. The girl, importantly, is in a sort of *secuestro permanente* or permanent kidnapping in the film, as she is not pawned off to a pedophile, murdered, or disappeared. The allusion here is to the legal concept of the *secuestro permanente* that was introduced in the transition to circumvent the legal constrictions of the amnesty law.

39. The killing of the criminal evokes William Acree's suggestion that cultural artifacts may perform a retrial when the normal channels of the law fail to bring about justice. While Acree builds this idea around Southern Cone theater, I believe it is equally applicable to other popular manifestations such as the superhero genre.

40. Again, *Mirageman* uses a visual semantics that evokes the events of the dictatorship. The body of water, combined with the lack of a body and the seeming death of the character is analogous to the experiences of the many *desaparecidos* during the coup and its immediate aftermath. By lingering over its calm surface, the film evokes the mnemonic qualities of the water-image, as what lies below its murky stillness is open for searching and interpretation.

41. We may extrapolate this analysis to other global markets wherein superhero narratives are being produced.

42. Aaron Taylor, for example, has examined embodied phenomenology, whereas Dana Anderson forwards a phenomenological definition of the trope in Robin Rosenberg and Peter Coogan's *What Is a Superhero?* Here, Anderson argues that "as readers experience him or her, this gestalt relationship begins to form around those encounters, generating a group dynamic through which the superhero evolves into an icon" (65).

43. See my and María del Carmen Caña Jiménez's "Affect, Bodies, and Circulations in Contemporary Latin American Film" for further reading on affect in Latin American cinema.

44. Ahmed alludes to this when she notes that "affective economies need to be seen as social and material. . . . In other words, the accumulation of affective value shapes the surfaces of bodies and worlds" ("Affective Economies" 121).

45. As a side note, the police officer who turns in this piece of evidence is "J. Kerr," a recognizable pseudonym of the Joker. We thus know that the character has already infiltrated the police force at the end of the first film in the trilogy.

46. This montage is another repeated trope in the superhero genre, where characters engaged in becoming go through a series of prototypes, often to comic relief, before finessing a final look. Superheroes are, after all, products of pragmatism and perfection.

Chapter 4

1. Several news and travel outlets have named the city as the most dangerous in the world.

2. Reports from *El Heraldo* include journalist photos of the crime scene and medics transporting a deceased Padilla in a body bag. They also include graphic cellphone images taken by bystanders of Padilla laying wounded on the ground and in the back of a pickup truck as he was taken to hospital.

3. In addition to his work in television, Padilla also contributed to radio and print venues. In 2012, he stood for local elections as a member of the Partido Nacional, but failed to garner sufficient votes.

4. The presence of the luchador mask speaks to the cultural import of the El Santo films as a truly Latin American phenomenon and reference for the superhero genre.

5. A quick sampling of the YouTube video's comments gleans the following excerpts that demonstrate that the viewership is transnational: "yo soy de Honduras pero vivo en Estados Unidos me enkanta estos videos me recuerdan m hermosa Honduras viva mi Honduras catracho 100%"; "yo vivo en orldano floridA y estoy en busca de tipos que sean asi de locos"; "Saludos desde virginia me encanta sus vídeos"; "HONDUREÑO Y YO CONOSCO LOS LUGARES DONDE EYOS ESTAN." The popularity of the sketch evokes Claire Taylor's thoughts on digital cultures: "The internet nowadays, rather than being a (solely) globalized, placeless medium, in fact offers ways of allowing people to make important connections to, and re-affirm their affiliations to, their physical, offline location" (1).

6. Padilla was indeed already working on *Chinche Man II*. In an interview with Karen Mendoza of *La Prensa* two months after *Chinche Man*'s theatrical release, Padilla and José Zaldívar (who plays the title character) discuss the plot of the second film. In the sequel, Chinche Man rescues a rich businessman from a band of kidnappers. As a reward, the businessman finances a more powerful costume, weapons, and vehicle for the hero, who is now joined by a sidekick, K-Tracho (a stylized *catracho*, or Honduran male). The movie was to be filmed in August 2016, and then premiered in the US before playing in local theatres. Padilla also planned to release a comic book created by Jhony Orellana and other

branded fan paraphernalia such as clothing. The second film and comic book, however, are in limbo given Padilla's assassination.

7. A *maquila* is a tax-advantaged production operation that imports raw materials and then exports finished goods. The working conditions and salaries in these factories have been heavily and rightfully criticized by human rights and labor groups. Cuevas Molina furthers that the *república maquilera* "is the legacy of the war, which left open, infected scars that still spread their pustules to the social body of Central America" ("es el legado de la guerra, que dejó cicatrices que aún supuran, infectadas, y esparcen sus pústulas en el cuerpo social centroamericano"; 2). The terminology chosen of course reflects the early nomenclature of Central America as a group of *repúblicas bananeras*.

8. Cortez and Caña Jiménez's concepts work across literature and film.

9. See Sánchez Prado's *Screening Neoliberalism* for a thorough examination of the dialectic between cinema and the Mexican neoliberal state.

10. Also see Arturo Arias (121).

11. It is also telling that studies on superheroes and globalization have tended to heavily focus on North-Other relationships, that is, how North American superheroes largely from the DC and Marvel franchises engage with world politics and movements. Richard J. Gray II and Betty Kaklamanidou's *The 21st-Century Superhero: Essays on Gender, Genre, and Globalization in Film*, for example, only deals with US heroes. Denison and Mizsei-Ward's anthology, however, does explore the trope of the global within non-US narratives.

12. See chapter 1 on Mexico for a detailed analysis of El Chapulín.

13. See Super Manco (Peru), El Man (Colombia), the Enchufetv skits of "Superhéroes en Latinoamérica," and Condorito's super avatars of Súper Cóndor and Bati-Cóndor.

14. In studying parody in Latin American cinema, Ana López argues that "more often than not, parody is defined as a kind of imitation designed to make the thoughts or style of another seem ridiculous, ludicrous, or comic" (63). She argues, following the ideas of Gerard Genette, that parody is hypertextual, a kind of intertext borne from the transformation of a hypotext. Parody as mode, as hypertext, "is also special because it is a critical practice, a form that by challenging an antecedent text or a prevailing mode of thought, can disturb preconceptions and prejudices and can give rise to new forms of consciousness" (63).

15. Liam Burke argues that "the newfound freedoms of digital cinema, coupled with the representational overlap comics and cinema enjoy, has led many in the industry, and beyond, to characterize comics as idle storyboards waiting to be shot" (170).

16. In discussing comic book movies, Burke notes that "a comic book movie does not need to actually be based on a comic book to be included in this genre; it simply needs to adopt elements synonymous with the comic book movie" (99).

17. Jeffries provides an exhaustive definition for comic book film style, including: "comic book film style thereby goes against the grain of 'good' adaptation practice by retaining, if not privileging, the aesthetics of the original medium at the expense of cinematic convention" (3); "comic book film style's interest in remediating comics and its concomitant emphasis on intermedial aesthetics represent a nonclassical approach to film style" (4); and "comic book film style is not motivated by narrative but instead by an intermedial relationship to and aesthetic interest in comics" (4).

18. Following Hutcheon's ideas of parody and the political in *The Politics of Postmodernism* (93–95).

19. The exaggerated femininity of this character is setup as a countertype to the heterosexual, macho protagonist. As several critics have noted (which I examine in greater detail in chapter 2), superhero films often revert to the reification of heterosexual hegemonic masculinity over all other forms of gender expression.

20. In his seminal "The Myth of Superman," Umberto Eco argues that Superman choses to maintain the status quo instead of pursuing a utopian ideal, which he seemingly should be able to attain given his extraordinary powers.

21. This distinction reminds me of the opposing views of Judith Hess Wright and Jean-Loup Bourget as reprinted in Barry Keith Grant's *Film Genre Reader IV* (2012). Hess Wright notes that genre films "assist in the maintenance of the existing political structure" (68), whereas Bourget affirms that "genre conventions can be either used as an alibi (the implicit meaning is to be found elsewhere in the film) or turned upside down (irony underlines the conventionality of the convention)" (76).

Chapter 5

1. The irony of parodying Captain America on July 4, Independence Day in the United States, is not lost on a viewer in the know.

2. Puyaweb's other viral character is the parody reggaetón act Power Flow. The singer's debut video, "Bun bun," has over 1.8 million views.

3. This is the fifth film in the Marvel Cinematic Universe (MCU). Captain America is a core character in Marvel's Avengers films, and has appeared in several MCU features, including *The Avengers* (2012), *Captain America: The Winter Soldier* (2014), *Avengers: Age of Ultron* (2015), *Ant-Man* (2015), *Captain America: Civil War* (2016), *Spider-Man: Homecoming* (2017), *Avengers: Infinity War* (2018), and *Avengers: Endgame* (2019).

4. Telecorporación Salvadoreña (TCS), the largest television company in El Salvador, acquired VTV Canal 35 in September 2017. The channel was renamed TCS+. For a history of television in El Salvador, see Herrera Palacios.

5. Consequently, I am unable to provide the viewing statistics of these episodes.

6. Mundo Flix has a considerably larger catalogue of films and television serials.

7. Claire Taylor has developed a rigorous and prolific research portfolio on online Latin American culture. See the Taylor and Pitman anthology from 2007, and a later collaboration, Pitman and Taylor, *Latin American Identity in Online Cultural Production* (2013). Also see Taylor's single-authored *Place and Politics in Latin American Digital Culture* (2014).

8. Writing on new media, Lev Manovich argues that "today . . . the screen is rapidly becoming the main means of accessing any kind of information, be it still images, moving images, or text. . . . We may debate whether our society is a society of spectacle or simulation, but, undoubtedly, it is a society of the screen" (94).

9. For further reading on YouTube history and media, see Jean Burgess and Joshua Green's *YouTube: Online Video and Participatory Culture* and Henry Jenkins, Sam Ford, and Joshua Green's *Spreadable Media: Creating Value and Meaning in a Networked Culture*.

10. Carol Vernallis adds that "what separates YouTube from other media are the clips' brevity and the ways they're often encountered through exchange with other people: a clip's interest derives from its associations with colleagues, family, friends, and contexts within communities. Often clips get forwarded because there's an intensity of affect that can't be assimilated: humorous or biting, only forwarding it will diffuse its aggressiveness or power to hold us fast" (9).

11. Private, closed Wi-Fi networks can of course block certain sites, as can subscription fees.

12. I unfortunately do not have statistics as to the number of times each web episode has been shared by users.

13. This movement of production, dissemination, and consumption is evident in the YouTube comments section of each video, where persons of Central American origin residing in the Global South and North are able to identify and interact with their very local superheroes.

14. Central America is a designated region for area studies within the humanities and social sciences. This is seen in the marketing of novels and films (as an example of cultural production), and scholarly studies under the regional umbrella of Central America, where the singular takes a back seat to the general in terms of the social, political, and economic qualities of the member countries.

15. Hutcheon adds that "the prevailing interpretation is that postmodernism offers a value-free, decorative, de-historicized quotation of past forms and that this is a most apt mode for a culture like our own that is oversaturated with images" (*Politics* 94).

16. Postmodern parody differs from modernist parody in that "it is more willing to break down distinctions between 'reality' and 'fiction'" (Felluga 209).

17. Timely later became Atlas Comics, and was rebranded as Marvel Comics in 1961.

18. Captain America appeared in film for the first time in 1944, in a fifteen-episode serial.

19. One can and should analyze this space within the incarnation of the river imagery vis-à-vis barbarism in the production of a Latin American space.

20. Vieira and Stam argue that "parody stands at the point of convergence of multiple contradictions, serving at times a negative aesthetic based on self-derision and servility, and at other times becoming an instrument of carnivalized revolt against hegemony" (26).

21. Here I am referring to the creation of a Captain Central America in a vignette of the popular and somewhat offensive North American animated series, *Family Guy*. He is engineered akin to Captain America (and Captain Centroamérica in Díaz's *Capitán Centroamérica*), but his only superpower is an aptitude for painting houses.

22. One may also connect his hypermasculinity and musculature to the aesthetics of the action genre in the 1980s. The films starring such actors as Sylvester Stallone, Dolph Lundgren, Jean-Claude Van Damme, and Arnold Schwarzenegger are an important intertext to the contemporary superhero genre.

23. Some shots in the montage do not appear in the previous episodes, such as the scene where the superhero informs Aunt Berta that he is no longer Carlos.

24. Another intertext is revealed here, as the doctor exclaims that they can teleport like Goku in the popular Japanese anime *Dragon Ball Z (DBZ)*. *DBZ* also inspires the Maestro's fighting techniques.

25. The show demythifies the idea of Costa Rica as the Switzerland of Central America, with the MUC stating that the country has a "super-secret army" ("ejército súper secreto") to fight domestic terrorism.

26. This is not the final appearance of the character, even though development of the promised movie is stalled and the series was not picked up for a second season on local television. Capitán Centroamérica reappears in a Puyaweb's skit in the "Hora pico" series on January 20, 2017.

Post Data

1. "A kid . . . another moron . . . came to save us."

2. Keeping with the theme of soccer, as evoked by the superhero's costume, one need not look further than the headlines surrounding Lionel Messi after every collapse with the national team. Even I, as a staunch Real Madrid supporter, feel sorry for the Argentine superhero—La Pulga (The Flea)—after every big tournament.

Works Cited

Abedrabbo, Richie. "Súper H: El héroe sampedrano que está cambiando a Honduras." *Radiohouse.hn*, 11 July 2016, http://www.radiohouse.hn/super-h-el-superheroe-sampedrano-que-esta-cambiando-honduras/.
Acree, William G. "The Trial of Theatre: Fiat iustitia et pereat mundus." *Latin American Theatre Review*, vol. 40, no. 1, Fall 2006, pp. 39–60.
Aguasaco, Carlos. *¡No contaban con mi astucia! México: Parodia, nación y sujeto en la serie de El Chapulín Colorado*. Universidad Autónoma de Nuevo León, 2014.
Aguilar, Gonzalo, Mariana Lacunza, and Niamh Thornton. "Latin American Film in the Digital Age." *The Routledge Companion to Latin American Cinema*, edited by Marvin D'Lugo, Ana M. López, and Laura Podalsky, Routledge, 2017, pp. 358–73.
Ahmed, Sara. "Affective Economies." *Social Text*, vol. 22, no. 2, Summer 2004, pp. 117–39.
———. *The Cultural Politics of Emotion*. Routledge, 2004.
Alba, Francisco, and Joseph E. Potter. "Population and Development in Mexico since 1940: An Interpretation." *Population and Development Review*, vol. 12, no. 1, Mar. 1986, pp. 47–75.
Aldama, Frederick Luis. *Latinx Superheroes in Mainstream Comics*. U of Arizona P, 2017.
Anderson, Dana. "The Experience of the Superhero: A Phenomenological Definition." *What Is a Superhero?*, edited by Robin S. Rosenberg and Peter Coogan, Oxford UP, 2013, pp. 65–70.
Appadurai, Arjun. *Modernity at Large: Cultural Dimensions of Globalization*. U of Minnesota P, 1996.
Arias, Arturo. "Post-identidades post-nacionales: Duelo, trauma y melancolía en la constitución de las subjetividades centroamericanas de posguerra." *(Per) Versiones de la modernidad: Literaturas, identidades y desplazamientos*, edited by Beatriz Cortez, Alexandra Ortiz Wallner, and Verónica Ríos Quesada, F&G, 2012, pp. 121–39.

Avelar, Idelber. "La práctica de la tortura y la historia de la verdad." *Pensar en/la postdictadura*, edited by Nelly Richard and Alberto Moreiras, Cuarto Propio, 2001, pp. 175–91.

———. *The Untimely Present: Postdictatorial Latin American Fiction and the Task of Mourning*. Duke UP, 1999.

Ayala Blanco, Jorge. *La aventura del cine mexicano: En la época de oro y después*. Grijalbo, 1991.

Barraza Toledo, Vania. "Reviewing the Present in Pablo Larraín's Historical Cinema." *Iberoamericana*, vol. 13, no. 51, Sept. 2013, pp. 159–72.

Bartra, Roger. *The Mexican Transition: Politics, Culture, and Democracy in the Twenty-First Century*. U of Wales P, 2013.

Bolter, Jay David, and Richard Grusin. *Remediation: Understanding New Media*. MIT P, 2003.

Bourget, Jean-Loup. "Social Implications in the Hollywood Genres." *Film Genre Reader IV*, edited by Barry Keith Grant, U of Texas P, 2012, pp. 69–77.

Brinkema, Eugenie. *The Forms of the Affects*. Duke UP, 2014.

Brittain, James J. "A Theory of Accelerating Rural Violence: Lauchlin Currie's Role in Underdeveloping Colombia." *Journal of Peasant Studies*, vol. 32, no. 2, 2005, pp. 335–60.

Brown, Jeffrey A. "The Superhero Film Parody and Hegemonic Masculinity." *Quarterly Review of Film and Video*, vol. 33, no. 2, 2016, pp. 131–50.

Bukatman, Scott. "Why I Hate Superhero Movies." *Cinema Journal*, vol. 50, no. 3, Spring 2011, pp. 118–22.

Burgess, Jean, and Joshua Green. *YouTube: Online Video and Participatory Culture*. Polity, 2009.

Burke, Liam. *The Comic Book Film Adaptation: Exploring Modern Hollywood's Leading Genre*. UP of Mississippi, 2017.

Cabrera López, Patricia. *Una inquietud de amanecer: Literatura y política en México, 1962–1987*. Plaza y Valdés, 2006.

Cairns, Kate, and Josée Johnston. "Choosing Health: Embodied Neoliberalism, Postfeminism, and the 'Do-Diet.'" *Theory and Society*, vol. 44, no. 2, Mar. 2015, pp. 153–75.

Caña Jiménez, María del Carmen. "El asco: Reflexiones estéticas sobre la violencia neoliberal en Centroamérica." *Symposium*, vol. 68, no. 4, 2014, pp. 218–30.

———. "Neoliberalismo somático: Sentimientos y afectos en *Malos hábitos*." *Arizona Journal of Hispanic Cultural Studies*, vol. 20, 2016, pp. 183–202.

Carrigan, Tim, Bob Connell, and John Lee. "Hard and Heavy: Toward a New Sociology of Masculinity." *Beyond Patriarchy: Essays by Men on Pleasure, Power, and Change*, edited by Michael Kaufman, Oxford UP, 1987, pp. 139–92.

Caruth, Cathy. *Unclaimed Experience: Trauma, Narrative, and History*. Johns Hopkins UP, 1996.

Castells, Manuel. *The City and the Grassroots*. U of California P, 1983.

Castillo, Debra A. "The New New Latin American Cinema: Cortometrajes on the Internet." *Latin American Cyberculture and Cyberliterature*, edited by Claire Taylor and Thea Pitman, Liverpool UP, 2007, pp. 33–49.
Castro Ricalde, Maricruz, and Robert McKee Irwin. *El cine mexicano "se impone": Mercados internacionales y penetración cultural en la época dorada*. Universidad Nacional Autónoma de México, 2011.
Catalá Carrasco, Jorge L., Paulo Drinot, and James Scorer, editors. *Comics and Memory in Latin America*. U of Pittsburgh P, 2017.
Cavallo, Ascanio, and Gonzalo Maza. "Explicación de este libro." *El novísimo cine chileno*, edited by Ascancio Cavallo and Gonzalo Maza, Uqbar, 2011, pp. 13–16.
Cavallo, Ascanio, Pablo Douzet, and Cecilia Rodríguez. *Huérfanos y perdidos: El cine chileno de la transición, 1990–1999*. Grijalbo, 1999.
Conley, Tom. *Cartographic Cinema*. U of Minnesota P, 2007.
Connell, R. W. *Masculinities*. U of California P, 1995.
———. "Masculinities and Globalization." *Men and Masculinities*, vol. 1, no. 1, 1998, pp. 3–23.
Connell, R. W., and Julian Wood. "Globalization and Business Masculinities." *Men and Masculinities*, vol. 7, no. 4, 2005, pp. 347–64.
Coogan, Peter. "The Hero Defines the Genre, the Genre Defines the Hero." *What Is a Superhero?*, edited by Robin Rosenberg and Peter Coogan, Oxford UP, 2013, pp. 3–10.
———. *Superhero: The Secret Origin of a Genre*. MonkeyBrain, 2006.
Correa, Julián David. "Cine colombiano en el 2011: Persistencia en el debate." *Cinémas d'Amérique Latine*, vol. 20, 2012, pp. 110–21.
Cortez, Beatriz. "Estética del cinismo: La ficción centroamericana de posguerra." *Ancora: Suplemento Cultural de la Nación*, 2001, pp. 1–15.
Costello, Matthew J., and Kent Worcester. "The Politics of the Superhero: Introduction." *PS: Political Science and Politics*, vol. 47, no. 1, Jan. 2014, pp. 85–89.
Cotter, Robert Michael. *The Mexican Masked Wrestler and Monster Filmography*. McFarland, 2005.
Criollo, Raúl, José Xavier Návar, and Rafael Aviña. *¡Quiero ver sangre! Historia ilustrada del cine de luchadores*. Universidad Nacional Autónoma de México, 2013.
Cruz Kronfly, Fernando. "Las ciudades literarias." *Pensar la ciudad*, edited by Fabio Giraldo and Fernando Viviescas, Tercer Mundo, 1996.
Cuevas Molina, Rafael. *De banana republics a repúblicas maquileras: La cultura en Centroamérica en tiempos de globalización neoliberal (1990–2010)*. Editorial Universidad Estatal a Distancia, 2012.
Dalton, David S. *Mestizo Modernity: Race, Technology, and the Body in Postrevolutionary Mexico*. U of Florida P, 2018.
Denison, Rayna, and Rachel Mizsei-Ward, editors. *Superheroes on World Screens*.

UP of Mississippi, 2015.
DiPaolo, Marc. *War, Politics and Superheroes: Ethics and Propaganda in Comics and Film*. McFarland, 2011.
Dorfman, Ariel, and Armand Mattelart. *Para leer al Pato Donald*. Editorial de Ciencias Sociales, 1971.
Eco, Umberto. "The Myth of Superman." *Diacritics*, vol. 2, no. 1, 1972, pp. 14–22.
Elena, Alberto, and Marina Díaz López, editors. *The Cinema of Latin America*. Wallflower, 2003.
Enchufetv. "Superhéroes en Latinoamérica." *YouTube*, 28 June 2015, https://www.youtube.com/watch?v=HmETS5UVgcc.
———. "Superhéroes en Latinoamérica 2." *YouTube*, 23 Nov. 2015, https://www.youtube.com/watch?v=3SQoPMuWFyk.
Erazo, Vanessa. "13 Central American Films that Beat the Odds and Made It to Theaters." *Remezcla*, 15 Sept. 2015, http://remezcla.com/lists/film/13-central-american-films-that-beat-the-odds-and-made-it-to-theaters-in-2015/.
Espinoza, Karla. "Andrés Díaz, la mente detrás de 'Power Flow' y el 'Capitán Centroamérica.'" *Diario1*, 2 Nov. 2014, http://diario1.com/vida/2014/11/andres-diaz-la-mente-detras-de-power-flow-y-el-capitan-centroamerica/.
Estévez, Antonella. "Dolores políticos: reacciones cinematográficas. Resistencias melancólicas en el cine chileno contemporáneo." *Aisthesis*, no. 47, 2010, pp. 15–32.
Felluga, Dino Franco. *Critical Theory: The Key Concepts*. Routledge, 2015.
Fernández L'Hoeste, Héctor. "Race and Gender in The Adventures of Kalimán." *Redrawing the Nation: National Identity in Latin/o American Comics*, edited by Héctor Fernández L'Hoeste and Juan Poblete, Palgrave Macmillan, 2009, pp. 55–80.
Fernández L'Hoeste, Héctor, and Juan Poblete, editors. *Redrawing the Nation: National Identity in Latin/o American Comics*. Palgrave Macmillan, 2009.
Ferro, Roberto. Introduction. *La parodia en la literatura latinoamericana*, edited by Roberto Ferro, Universidad de Buenos Aires, 1993, pp. 7–12.
Foster, David William. *From Mafalda to Los Supermachos: Latin American Graphic Humor as Popular Culture*. Lynn Rienner, 1989.
Franco, Bridget. "Cinematographic and Political Transitions in *La redada* and *La frontera*." *Hispania*, vol. 98, no. 3, Sept. 2015, pp. 406–20.
Franco, Jean. *Cruel Modernity*. Duke UP, 2014.
García Blizzard, Mónica. "Whiteness and the Ideal of Modern Mexican Citizenship in *Tepeyac* (1917)." *Vivomatografías*, no. 1, 2015, 72–95.
García Canclini, Néstor. *Latinoamericanos buscando lugar en este siglo*. Paidós, 2002.
García Riera, Emilio. *Breve historia del cine mexicano: Primer siglo, 1897–1997*. Mapa, 1999.
Gómez-Barris, Macarena. *Where Memory Dwells: Culture and State Violence in Chile*. U of California P, 2009.

Gotto, Lisa. "Fantastic Views: Superheroes, Visual Perception, and Digital Perspective." *Superhero Synergies: Comic Book Characters Go Digital*, edited by James N. Gilmore and Matthias Stork, Rowman and Littlefield, 2014, pp. 41–56.
Grant, Barry Keith. Introduction. *Film Genre Reader IV*, edited by Barry Keith Grant, U of Texas P, 2012, pp. xvii–xxii.
Gray, Richard J., II, and Betty Kaklamanidou. Introduction. *The 21st Century Superhero: Essays on Gender, Genre and Globalization in Film*, edited by Richard J. Gray II and Betty Kaklamanidou, McFarland, 2011, pp. 1–14.
Greene, Doyle. *Mexploitation Cinema: A Critical History of Mexican Vampire, Wrestler, Ape-Man, and Similar Films, 1957–1977*, McFarland, 2005.
Hassler-Forest, Dan. *Capitalist Superheroes: Caped Crusaders in the Neoliberal Age*. Zero, 2012.
Hegarty, Kerry. "From Superhero to National Hero: The Populist Myth of El Santo." *Studies in Latin American Popular Culture*, no. 31, 2013, pp. 3–27.
Herrera Palacios, Antonio. "Un breve recorrido por la televisión en El Salvador." *Revista Latina de Comunicación Social*, vol. 12, 1998, http://www.revista-latinacs.org/a/02nherrera.htm.
Hershfield, Joanne. "Women's Cinema and Contemporary Allegories of Violence in Mexico." *Discourse*, vol. 32, no. 2, Spring 2010, pp. 170–85.
Hess Wright, Judith. "Genre Films and the Status Quo." *Film Genre Reader IV*, edited by Barry Keith Grant, U of Texas P, 2012, pp. 60–68.
Hinds, Harold E., and Charles M. Tatum. *Not Just for Children: The Mexican Comic Book in the Late 1960s and 1970s*. Greenwood, 1992.
Hirsch, Marianne. *The Generation of Postmemory: Writing and Visual Culture after the Holocaust*. Columbia UP, 2012.
Hite, Katherine. "Resurrecting Allende." *NACLA*, 25 Sept. 2007, https://nacla.org/article/resurrecting-allende.
Hutcheon, Linda. *The Politics of Postmodernism*. Routledge, 2007.
———. *A Theory of Parody: The Teachings of Twentieth-Century Art Forms*. Methuen, 1985.
Illescas Nájera, Francisco. "¿Hasta qué punto fue El Santo, 'El Enmascarado de Plata,' definido por la ascendente cultura popular mexicana del Siglo XX?" *En-claves del pensamiento*, vol. 6, no. 12, 2012, pp. 49–66.
Jaramillo Morales, Alejandra. *Bogotá imaginada: Narraciones urbanas, cultura y política*. Alcaldía Mayor de Bogotá, 2003.
Jeffries, Dru. *Comic Book Film Style: Cinema at 24 Panels per Second*. U of Texas P, 2017.
Jenkins, Henry, Sam Ford, and Joshua Green. *Spreadable Media: Creating Value and Meaning in a Networked Culture*. New York UP, 2012.
Kavoori, Anandam. "Making Sense of Youtube." *Global Media Journal*, vol. 13, no. 24, 2015, pp. 1–25.

Kohut, Miroslav. *Superheroes: The Philosophy behind the Modern Myth.* 2014. Masaryk U, MA thesis.

Kokotovic, Misha. "Neoliberal Noir: Contemporary Central American Crime Fiction as Social Criticism." *Clues*, vol. 24, no. 3, Spring 2006, pp. 15-29.

Kvaran, Kara M. "Super Daddy Issues: Parental Figures, Masculinity, and Superhero Films." *Journal of Popular Culture*, vol. 50, no. 2, 2017, pp., 218-38.

LaCapra, Dominick. *History and Memory after Auschwitz.* Cornell UP, 1998.

Lawrence, John Shelton, and Robert Jewett. *The Myth of the American Superhero.* William B. Eerdmans, 2002.

Lazzara, Michael J. *Chile in Transition: The Poetics and Politics of Memory.* UP of Florida, 2006.

Levi, Heather. *The World of Lucha Libre: Secrets, Revelations, and Mexican National Identity.* Duke UP, 2010.

Lieberman, Evan. "Mask and Masculinity: Culture, Modernity, and Gender Identity in the Mexican *Lucha Libre* films of El Santo." *Studies in Hispanic Cinemas*, vol. 6, no. 1, Dec. 2009, pp. 3-17.

Lira, Elizabeth. "Chile: Dilemmas of Memory." *The Memory of State Terrorism in the Southern Cone*, edited by Francesca Lessa and Vincent Druliolle, Palgrave Macmillan, 2011, pp. 107-32.

López, Ana. "Parody, Underdevelopment, and the New Latin American Cinema." *Quarterly Review of Film and Video*, vol. 12, no. 1-2, 1990, pp. 63-71.

Lungo, Mario, and Roxana Martel. "Ciudadanía social y violencia en las ciudades centroamericanas." *Istmo* 8 (2004).

Manovich, Lev. *The Language of New Media.* MIT P, 2002.

Martin, Jean-Clet. "Of Images and Worlds: Toward a Geology of the Cinema." *The Brain is the Screen: Deleuze and the Philosophy of Cinema*, edited by Gregory Flaxman, U of Minnesota P, 2000, pp. 61-85.

Martín-Barbero, Jesús. "La ciudad que media los medios." *Espacio urbano, comunicación y violencia en América Latina*, edited by Mabel Moraña, Instituto Internacional de Literatura Iberoamericana, 2002, pp. 19-35.

Martínez Abeijon, Matias. "*El Paseo* by Harold Trompetero: Approaching Popular Film from Colombia in a North American Classroom." *Cultural Encounters, Conflicts, and Resolutions*, vol. 2, no. 1, 2015, https://engagedscholarship.csuohio.edu/cecr/vol2/iss1/5/.

Massumi, Brian. *Parables for the Virtual: Movement, Affect, Sensation.* Duke UP, 2002.

Mata Blanco, Alonso. "Conozca al Capitán Centroamérica." *La Nación*, 20 Apr. 2014, https://www.nacion.com/revista-dominical/conozca-al-capitan-centroamerica/W7NEXLIZCFEQXJILUAXD64RUJA/story/.

Mattos, Carlos A. de. "Santiago de Chile, globalización y expansión metropolitana: Lo que existía sigue existiendo." *São Paulo em Perspectiva*, vol. 14, no. 4, Dec. 2000, pp. 43-62.

Mayolo, Luis Fernando. "El Man, el nuevo héroe nacional." *El Espectador*, 23 Jan. 2009, https://www.elespectador.com/articulo111019-el-man-el-nuevo-heroe-nacional.
Mosse, George L. *The Image of Man: The Creation of Modern Masculinity*. Oxford UP, 1996.
Mouesca, Jacqueline, and Carlos Orellana. *Breve historia del cine chileno: Desde sus orígenes hasta nuestros días*. LOM, 2010.
Murillo, Juan E. "Mirageman." *laFuga*, vol. 7, Fall 2008.
Ndalianis, Angela. "Do We Need Another Hero?" *Super/Heroes: From Hercules to Superman*, edited by Wendy Haslem, Angela Ndalianis, and Chris Mackie, New Academia, 2007, pp. 1–8.
Noble, Andrea. *Mexican National Cinema*. Routledge, 2010.
Ortiz Wallner, Alexandra. *El arte de ficcionar: La novela contemporánea en Centroamérica*. Iberoamericana Vervuert, 2012.
Padilla, Igor. "Los Verduleros HN—Chinche Man." *YouTube*, 22 Dec. 2014, https://www.youtube.com/watch?v=lndq2fO_Xx4&t=26s.
Palou, Pedro Ángel. *El fracaso del mestizo*. Ariel, 2014.
Paranaguá, Paulo Antonio. "América Latina busca su imagen." *Estados Unidos (1955–1975); América Latina*, edited by Carlos F. Heredero and Casimiro Torreiro, pp. 250–393. *Historia general del cine*, vol. 10, Cátedra, 1996.
Parks, Lisa. "Flexible Microcasting: Gender, Generation, and Television-Internet Convergence." *Television after TV: Essays on a Medium in Transition*, edited by Lynn Spigel and Jan Olsson, Duke UP, 2004, pp. 133–56.
Peaslee, Robert. "Superheroes, 'Moral Economy,' and the 'Iron Cage': Morality, Alienation, and the Super-Individual." *Super/Heroes: From Hercules to Superman*, edited by Wendy Haslem, Angela Ndalianis, and Chris Mackie, New Academia, 2007, pp. 37–50.
Pitman, Thea, and Claire Taylor. *Latin American Identity in Online Cultural Production*. Routledge, 2013.
Ramírez Berg, Charles. *Cinema of Solitude: A Critical Study of Mexican Film, 1967–1983*. U of Texas P, 1992.
Read, Peter, and Marivic Wyndham. *Narrow but Endlessly Deep: The Struggle for Memorialisation in Chile since the Transition to Democracy*. Australian National UP, 2016.
Reynolds, Richard. *Superheroes: A Modern Mythology*. UP of Mississippi, 1994.
Richard, Nelly. *The Insubordination of Signs: Political Change, Cultural Transformation, and Poetics of the Crisis*. Translated by Alice A. Nelson and Silvia R. Tandeciarz, Duke UP, 2004.
Rinke, Stefan. "The Loss of the Father: Chilean Cinema in the 1990s." *Iberoamericana*, vol. 1, no. 2, June 2001, pp. 185–89.
Risner, Jonathan. "How I Learned to Stop Worrying and Grudgingly Accept Product Placement: Nicolás López, Chilewood and Criteria for a Neoliberal Cinema."

Journal of Latin American Cultural Studies, vol. 25, no. 4, 2016, pp. 597–612.

Rodríguez, Ana Patricia. *Dividing the Isthmus: Central American Transnational Histories, Literatures, and Cultures*. U of Texas P, 2009.

Ros, Ana. *The Post-dictatorship Generation in Argentina, Chile, and Uruguay: Collective Memory and Cultural Production*. Palgrave Macmillan, 2012.

Rosenberg, Robin S. *Superhero Origins: What Makes Superheroes Tick and Why We Care*. CreateSpace, 2013.

Rosenberg, Robin S., and Peter Coogan, editors. *What Is a Superhero?* Oxford UP, 2013.

Rubenstein, Anne. "El Santo's Strange Career." *The Mexico Reader: History, Culture, Politics*, edited by Gilbert M. Joseph and Timothy J. Henderson, Duke UP, 2002, pp. 570–78.

Ruffinelli, Jorge. "De YouTube a la pantalla, de la pantalla a YouTube." *Nuevo Texto Crítico*, vol. 28, no. 51, 2015, pp. 57–68.

Sánchez Prado, Ignacio M. *Screening Neoliberalism: Transforming Mexican Cinema, 1988–2012*. Vanderbilt UP, 2015.

Schatz, Thomas. *Hollywood Genres: Formulas, Filmmaking, and the Studio System*. McGraw Hill, 1981.

Schroeder Rodríguez, Paul A. *Latin American Cinema: A Comparative History*. U of California P, 2016.

Shaviro, Steven. *Post-cinematic Affect*. Zero, 2010.

Shaw, Deborah, editor. *Contemporary Latin American Cinema: Breaking into the Global Market*. Rowman and Littlefield, 2007.

Shouse, Eric. "Feeling, Emotion, Affect." *M/C Journal*, vol. 8, no. 6, Dec. 2005, http://www.journal.media-culture.org.au/0512/03-shouse.php.

Simonsen, Thomas Mosebo. "Categorising YouTube." *MedieKultur*, vol. 27, no. 51, 2011, pp. 72–93.

Slotkin, Richard. *Gunfighter Nation: The Myth of the Frontier in Twentieth-Century America*. Atheneum, 1992.

Soja, Edward W. *Postmetropolis: Critical Studies of Cities and Regions*. Blackwell, 2000.

Steinberg, Samuel. *Photopoetics at Tlatelolco: Afterimages of Mexico, 1968*. U of Texas P, 2016.

Stern, Steve J. *Reckoning with Pinochet: The Memory Question in Democratic Chile, 1989–2006*. Duke UP, 2010.

Suárez, Juana. *Cinembargo Colombia: Ensayos críticos sobre cine y cultura*. Universidad del Valle, 2017.

———. *Critical Essays on Colombian Cinema and Culture: Cinembargo Colombia*. Translated by Laura Chesak, Palgrave Macmillan, 2012.

———. "Decentering the 'Centro': *Noir* Representations and the Metamorphosis of Bogotá." *Hispanic Issues On Line*, no. 3, Fall 2008, pp. 49–70.

Subero, Gustavo. "Gay Pornography as Latin American Queer Historiography." *LGBT Transnational Identity and Media*, edited by Christopher Pullen, Palgrave Macmillan, 2012, pp. 213–30.

Taylor, Aaron. "'He's Gotta Be Strong, and He's Gotta Be Fast, and He's Gotta Be Larger Than Life': Investigating the Engendered Superhero Body." *Journal of Popular Culture*, vol. 40, no. 2, 2007, pp. 344–60.

Taylor, Claire. *Place and Politics in Latin American Digital Culture: Location and Latin American Net Art*. Routledge, 2014.

Taylor, Claire, and Thea Pitman, editors. *Latin American Cyberculture and Cyberliterature*. Liverpool UP, 2007.

Traverso, Antonio. "Dictatorship Memories: Working Through Trauma in Chilean Post-dictatorship Documentary." *Continuum*, vol. 24, no. 1, 2010, pp. 179–91.

Uribe, María Victoria. *Antropología de la inhumanidad: Un ensayo interpretativo del terror en Colombia*. Norma, 2006.

Uricchio, William. "The Future of a Medium Once Known as Television." *The Youtube Reader*, edited by Pelle Snickars and Patrick Vonderau, National Library of Sweden, 2009, pp. 24–39.

Urrutia Neno, Carolina. *Un cine centrífugo: Ficciones chilenas, 2005–2010*. Cuarto Propio, 2013.

Valdés Flores, Euclides. "Pasado, presente y futuro del cine centroamericano." *El Heraldo*, 30 Oct. 2015, https://www.elheraldo.hn/revistas/crimenes/886988-466/pasado-presente-y-futuro-del-cine-centroamericano.

Vargas, Andrew S. "Trailer: Colombia's Afro-Indigenous Superhero 'Zambo Dende' Frees Slaves in New Series." *Remezcla*, 16 Feb. 2016, http://remezcla.com/film/trailer-colombian-afro-indigenous-superhero-zambo-dende-frees-slaves-live-action-series/.

Venkatesh, Vinodh. *The Body as Capital: Masculinities in Contemporary Latin American Fiction*. U of Arizona P, 2015.

———. "Bogotá, Medellín y Cali en el cine colombiano reciente." *La ciudad latinoamericana en el cine*, edited by Gloria Camarero, Akal, 2017, pp. 279–93.

Venkatesh, Vinodh, and María del Carmen Caña Jiménez. "Affect, Bodies, and Circulations in Contemporary Latin American Film." *Arizona Journal of Hispanic Cultural Studies*, vol. 20, 2016, pp. 175–81.

Vernallis, Carol. *Unruly Media: YouTube, Music Video, and the New Digital Cinema*. Oxford UP, 2013.

Vieira, João Luiz, and Robert Stam. "Parody and Marginality: The Case of Brazilian Cinema." *Framework*, no. 28, 1985, pp. 20–49.

Villalobos-Ruminott, Sergio. "Critical Thought in Post-dictatorship." *Journal of Latin American Cultural Studies*, vol. 9, no. 3, 2000, pp. 229–34.

Villoro, Juan. "Haz el bien sin mirar a la rubia." *¡Quiero ver sangre! Historia ilustrada del cine de luchadores*, edited by Raúl Criollo, José Xavier Návar, and Rafael Aviña, Universidad Nacional Autónoma de México, 2013, pp. 14–19.

Wilde, Alexander. "Irruption of Memory: Expressive Politics in Chile's Transition to Democracy." *Journal of Latin American Studies*, vol. 31, no. 2, May 1999, pp. 473–500.

Wilt, David. "El Santo: The Case of a Mexican Multimedia Hero." *Film and Comic Books*, edited by Ian Gordon, Mark Jancovich, and Matthew P. McAllister, UP of Mississippi, 2007, pp. 199–220.

———. *The Films of El Santo*. http://terpconnect.umd.edu/~dwilt/santo.html.

Zeller-Jacques, Martin. "Daddy's Little Sidekick: The Girl Superhero in Contemporary Cinema." *International Cinema and the Girl*, edited by Fiona Handyside and Kate Taylor-Jones, Palgrave Macmillan, 2016, pp. 195–206.

Zubieta, Rodolfo. "Tendrá Kalimán su serie." *El Mundo*, 6 May 2017, https://www.diarioelmundo.com.mx/index.php/2017/05/06/tendra-kaliman-su-serie/.

Index

1968, 18, 61–66, 225nn6–7, 231n65. *See also* Tlatelolco
3 *Dev Adam*, 25, 226n23

adaptation, 2, 10, 13, 27–31, 48, 51, 54, 58–59, 68, 123, 126, 153, 162, 215, 218, 228n32, 230n55, 241n17
affect: associations, 22, 124, 142, 198, 238n43; economy, 137–43, 238n44; intensity, 12, 137–38, 142–43; reaction, 103, 139, 179, 205
Aguasaco, Carlos, 3–4, 63–71, 231nn68–69
Aguila Descalza, El, 66–71
Aguila Solitaria, El, 2
Ahmed, Sara, 138, 143, 238n44. *See also* affect
Alambrista, El, 15, 214
albur, 8, 69
Aldama, Frederick Luis, 3
aliens, 23, 44–47, 57, 63, 215, 230n53, 232n9
Allende, Salvador, 111, 116, 128–29, 235n12, 237n30
amnesty (Chile), 112–13, 238n38
animal, 55, 152, 225n8
anime, 201, 203, 243n24
Appadurai, Arjun, 224n2
Atacan las brujas, 34–38
Avelar, Idelber, 120, 236n22, 237n36

Avengers, the, 171, 189, 241n3; *Age of Ultron*, 241n3; *Endgame*, 223n1, 241n3; films, 1–2, 207, 241n3; *Infinity War*, 8, 25, 241n3
Aviña, Rafael. See *¡Quiero ver sangre! Historia ilustrada del cine de luchadores*

banana republic, 149, 181
Barone, Luis, 216
Bartra, Roger, 64, 225n7
Batgirl, 51
Batman, 9, 21, 36, 57, 67–71, 90–94, 135–37, 143, 152, 194, 218; movies, 51, 72, 139, 234n9; television series, 32
Batman en Chile, 234n2
Blue Demon, 3, 10, 16, 27, 31, 41–42, 51, 55, 73, 229n46, 231n64
Brinkema, Eugenie, 138–39
Brown, Jeffrey, 92–93, 97, 194
Buffy the Vampire Slayer, 226n20
Bukatman, Scott, 179
bureaucracy, 24, 71, 98, 186, 217
Burke, Liam. *See* comic book: film adaptation
Buscando a Miguel, 83–87, 232n6

CAFTA (Central American Free Trade Agreement), 149

Caña Jiménez, María del Carmen, 101–102, 149–51, 233n16, 238n43, 240n8
cape, 8, 15, 30, 38, 60, 79, 98, 128, 143
capitalism, 5, 24, 95, 100–101, 189
Capitán Centroamérica, 4, 7, 10, 12, 16, 92, 135, 152–53, 163, 170–211, 232n9, 243n21, 243n26
Capitão 7, 2, 215
Captain America, 9, 12, 25, 194, 226n22, 241n1, 243n21; comics, 188–91; movies, 1, 171–72, 241n3, 243n18
Cardona, René, 48, 51
Caruth, Cathy, 123, 236n24
Castillo, Debra, 174
Catholicism, 35–39, 229n47
Cavallo, Ascanio, 106, 114–15, 129, 234n4
centrifugal cinema, 107
centripetal cinema, 107
CGI, 1, 28, 102, 178, 192–94, 198, 201
Chanoc, 27, 53
Chapulín Colorado, El, 2, 4–9, 11, 15–19, 25, 62, 75, 88, 94, 138, 152, 213–20, 237n34; animated series, 73, 214; television series, 2, 10, 16–19, 63–73, 110, 152, 172
Chicago Boys, 195, 235n12. *See also* neoliberalism
Chinche Man, 4, 12, 15, 144–70, 173, 175, 180–82, 196–200, 233n12, 239n6
churros (films), 17, 59, 62, 227n25, 228n33
cine chileno: nuevo, 106; novísimo, 106
Codex Espangliensis: From Columbus to the Border Patrol, 224
Cold War, 8, 24, 47, 61, 102, 182, 188–89, 231n64

colonial era, 27, 38–43, 220, 232n4
colonialism, 220, 231n63; post-, 54, 96
comic book: film adaptation, 27, 31, 58; film style, 153–54, 157, 192, 241n17; print, 2–3, 10, 19–31, 55–56, 60, 67–68, 76, 141, 152–54, 188, 215–18, 223nn4–5, 225n12, 226n21, 231n60
commander, enemy, 91–92
communism, 24, 31, 43, 60, 116, 188–89, 230n55, 235n12
computer generated imagery. *See* CGI
Conley, Tom, 154
Connell, Raewyn, 93–96, 233n14. *See also* masculinity
Coogan, Peter, 22–24, 31, 42, 91, 139, 159, 226n18, 232n9, 233n10, 238n42
Correa, Julián David, 75–76
Cortez, Beatriz, 151, 197, 211, 240n8
Cotter, Robert Michael, 3, 18, 25–32, 43, 228n36, 229n46
Criollo, Raúl. *See ¡Quiero ver sangre! Historia ilustrada del cine de luchadores*
Cuevas Molina, Rafael, 150–51, 174, 240n7
Currie, Lauchlin, 81, 232n5
Cybersix, 215

Dalton, David, 26, 231n66, 231n70
damsel in distress, 23, 28–29, 48, 62, 141
DC Extended Universe, 1, 4, 25, 137, 143, 225n5
década perdida, 64, 72
del Toro, Guillermo, 2
Denison, Rayna. *See Superheroes on World Screens*
desaparecidos, 112, 237n35, 238n38
diaspora, 10, 12

Díaz Espinoza, Ernesto, 11, 105–109, 123, 129–31, 144, 233n1
Díaz Ordaz, Gustavo, 18, 231n69
dictatorship: Argentina, 217; Central America, 172, 182, 188–91; Chile, 4, 11, 105–35, 233n2, 235n11, 236nn15–22, 237nn27–35, 238n40; villain, 92
DINA (Dirección de Inteligencia Nacional), 116, 123, 130
Dirty War, 217
Disney, 45–47, 226n21
Doomsday, 218
Dorfman, Ariel. See *Para leer al Pato Donald*
Doutrinador, O, 3, 215
Douzet, Pablo. See Cavallo, Ascanio

Echeverría Álvarez, Luis, 18, 65
Eco, Umberto, 5, 24, 97, 241n20
Ecologista Universal, 21
economic *reconquista*, 217
El man, el superhéroe nacional, 4, 11, 15, 35, 75–104, 110, 144, 195, 216, 232n2, 232n8, 233n16
Elseworlds, 218. See also *Kryptonita*
emotion. See affect
Enchufetv, 6, 67, 166, 192, 240n13
enmascarado de plata, El 19, 30, 48, 228n35
Estévez, Antonella, 106, 113, 235n11
estrategia del caracol, La, 85–87
exploitation cinema, 3, 26, 106, 227n25. See also mexploitation
extraterrestrial, 3, 46–47, 56

Facebook, 6, 12, 170–77, 192, 207
faith, 5, 16, 35, 40–42, 79, 88–89
FARC (Fuerzas Armadas Revolucionarias de Colombia), 75
fascism, 43, 60
feeling. See affect

female superheroes, 48–52, 215. See also Luchadoras, las
femininity, 92, 241n19
Fernández L'Hoeste, Héctor, 3, 36, 54–62, 223n5, 231n60, 231n62
ficheras, 17
Flash, 218
flexible microcasting, 177
football. See soccer
Foster, David William, 3, 54–56, 223n5, 226n21
fotomontaje, 19, 29, 153
fotonovela, 19
Fox, Lucius, 147

García Canclini, Néstor, 72, 223n6
García Riera, Emilio, 225n4
globalization, 65, 95–96, 150–51, 182–83, 186, 223n6, 233n14, 240n11
Golden Age, Mexico, 16–17, 29–30, 37, 225n4, 227n25
Gómez-Barris, Macarena, 120
Gómez Bolaños, Roberto, 62, 66–71, 152, 231n69. See also Chapulín Colorado, El
González Iñárritu, Alejandro, 24
Gotham, 8, 68, 137, 234n9
Greene, Doyle, 3, 18–19, 25–31, 43, 47, 51, 226n16, 227n24, 227n26, 228n34, 229n42, 229n44, 229n48, 230n53
Green Lantern, 218
Guadalupe Cruz, José, 19–20, 28–30
Guttfreund, André, 172, 180
Guzmán Huerta, Rodolfo. See Santo, El

hacha diabólica, El, 29, 37–41
Hassler-Forest, Dan, 234n7
Hawkgirl, 218
healthism, 102, 233n16

Hegarty, Kerry, 22, 26–29, 34, 37, 40, 66, 225n11, 226n15, 227n26, 227n29, 228n31, 228n39, 229n47
Hernández, Juan Orlando, 12, 149, 167–69
Hirsch, Marianne. *See* postmemory
Hite, Katherine, 129, 237n29
horror (genre), 26, 226n24
Hulk, the, 21
Humanón. *See* Kalimán
human rights, 117, 123–24, 129, 182, 188, 235nn11–12, 236n16, 237n27, 240n7
Huracán Ramírez, 30–32
Hutcheon, Linda, 70, 152, 187–90, 241n18, 242n15

Illescas Nájera, Francisco, 21, 225n11, 226n13, 228n40, 229n42
imperialism, 1, 45, 95
indigenous peoples, 41–42, 61–62, 189, 201, 220, 224n8, 229n47, 231n63
Internet, 4, 170–75, 200, 204, 214, 239. *See also* streaming
Iron Man, 1, 21, 137
irruption (of memory), 123–25, 237nn27–28

Japanese culture, 220. *See also* anime
Jeffries, Dru. *See* comic book: film style
Joker, 139, 218, 234n9, 239n45
Justice League, the, 2, 195, 218

Kalimán, 2, 10, 27, 54–57, 160, 230n55, 231n62; comics, 54; movies, 18, 53–54, 56, 59–62, 154; radio series, 53–54; television series, 230n59
Kavoori, Anandam, 175–76
kitsch, 4, 11, 52, 72, 134, 211

Kohut, Miroslav, 24, 140, 226n19
Kokotovic, Misha, 198, 211
Kryptonita, 15, 63, 218

LaCapra, Dominick. *See* working-through (trauma)
Lazzara, Michael, 113, 144
Levi, Heather, 21–25, 32–34, 40, 226n16, 228n30
Lieberman, Evan, 19, 43, 48, 225n8, 225n11, 227n27, 229n43
López, Nicolás, 107, 219, 232n2
López Portillo, José, 64–65
Loreti, Nicanor. *See* *Kryptonita*
luchador, 4, 9–10, 18–22, 26–34, 38–46, 53, 55, 59–72, 214, 224n1, 226n14, 227n28, 228n33, 228n35, 229n50; mask, 12, 15, 147, 169, 239n4
Luchadoras, las, 43, 48–53, 63, 161, 230n54
lucha libre, 19–22, 31, 50, 65, 227n24

machismo, 216
Machuca, 114
martial arts, 55, 89, 108–11, 133–36, 141, 147, 164
Marvel Cinematic Universe, 1, 4, 7, 25, 73, 137, 144, 154, 225n5, 231n61, 241n3
masculinity, 8–9, 39, 92–97, 102, 194, 224n12, 229n43; complicit, 93–94; countertype, 50, 195, 230n56, 233n12, 241n19; hegemonic, 93, 97, 103, 194, 241n19; hyper, 109, 243n22; ideal, 50, 195, 230n56; marginalized, 93–94; stereotype, 230n56; subordinate, 94–95; transnational business, 96, 101
mask, 12, 15, 19, 30, 38–40, 65, 103, 138, 140–47, 225n8, 239n4; unmasking; 40, 52, 103, 133, 199

Massumi, Brian, 137
Mattelart, Armand. See *Para leer al Pato Donald*
Maza, Gonzalo. *See* Cavallo, Ascanio
MCU. *See* Marvel Cinematic Universe
Menganno, 90, 169, 218–19
Metropolis, 8, 68, 226n20
mexicanidad, 41–42, 230n53
Mexican Miracle, 17, 37, 47, 64, 225n6
mexploitation, 18, 25–26, 47, 226n24
Mil Máscaras, 3, 16, 27, 214
mind control, 59–61, 230n55
Mirageman, 4, 11, 15, 102, 105–44, 170, 194–99, 207, 237n36, 238n37, 238n40
Mizsei-Ward, Rachel. See *Superheroes on World Screens*
modernity, 40, 43, 47–49, 56, 61–62, 85, 227n27, 229n44, 230n53
Monsiváis, Carlos, 37
Mujer Meravilla, 21
Mujer Murciélago, La, 51–53, 60, 66
mundo de los muertos, El, 40–42
musical (genre), 28, 63
music video, 80
myth, 5, 8, 24, 97, 159, 226n19, 229n43; of Superman (*see* Eco, Umberto)

NAFTA (North American Free Trade Agreement), 72
Nafta Súper. See *Kryptonita*
Návar, José Xavier. See *¡Quiero ver sangre! Historia ilustrada del cine de luchadores*
Nazis, 67, 188, 215–16
Ndalianis, Angela, 157
neoliberalism, 4, 76, 180, 186, 233n16
Netflix, 144, 173–74, 178, 214, 230n59
Neutrón, 3, 31–34, 43
Noble, Andrea, 225n4, 227n25

orientalism, 54, 56, 231n63
origin: story, 4, 10, 13, 15, 87–89, 180, 193, 199, 214, 225n12, 232n8; moment, 32, 39–40, 57, 60, 89–91, 103, 161
orphanhood, 114–15, 163, 205, 236n19
Ortiz Wallner, Alexandra, 151, 183–87

Padilla, Igor, 154–57, 175–76, 239n3, 239n6; murder, 12, 145–47, 161, 166, 196, 200, 239n2
Palou, Pedro Ángel, 229n49, 231n66
Para leer al Pato Donald, 45, 223n5
Parker, Peter, 109, 224n1
parody, 7–19, 63–71, 75–79, 92–97, 152–53, 171–72, 186–94, 227n28, 240n14, 243n20
postmodern, 242n16
Patoruzú, 2, 23, 215
Pinochet, Augusto, 4, 11, 109–24, 235n12, 236n21, 237n29, 237n35
Plan Colombia, 149
Poblete, Juan, 3, 223n5
pornography, 227n28
postmemory, 131, 237n31
postmodernism, 35, 84, 187, 192, 242n15. See *also* parody: postmodern
Pseudo-Robin, 127, 133
Puyaweb, 12, 171–76, 181, 191–92, 202, 207, 241n2, 243n26

queer, 80, 92, 215
¡Quiero ver sangre! Historia ilustrada del cine de luchadores, 3, 18, 26, 228n35, 229n50

Ramírez Berg, Charles, 17, 30–32, 65, 227n25, 229n45
Ramos, Elmer. *See* Súper H
rape, 11, 96, 109–11, 117–19, 124, 130

religion. *See* faith
remediation, 153–56, 241n17
república maquilera. *See* Cuevas Molina, Rafael
Rettig Report, 112–13, 119, 124, 129, 237n28
Richard, Nelly, 120
Risner, Jonathan, 106–107
robot, 15, 49
Rodríguez, Ana Patricia, 180
Rodríguez, Cecilia. *See* Cavallo, Ascanio
Ros, Ana, 113, 235n15
Rosenberg, Robin, 22, 24, 88, 232nn7–8, 238n42
Rubenstein, Anne, 19–20, 225nn10–11, 229n41, 229n43
rudo, 19, 28, 33, 41, 46, 225n9, 226n16
Ruffinelli, Jorge, 174
Ruvinskis, Wolf, 31

Sánchez Prado, Ignacio, 65, 72, 76, 151, 227n25, 240n9
Santo: animated series, 73; comics, 19, 21, 55, 153, 225n12; movies, 17, 20, 27–43, 47–51, 56, 60, 66, 72, 214, 227nn25–26, 228nn34–38, 231nn64–66; superhero, 5, 10, 16, 18, 25–27, 34, 38, 40, 46; wrestler, 19, 34
Santo contra el cerebro del mal, 30, 32
Santo contra el cerebro diabólico, 33
Santo contra el rey del crimen, 33
Santo contra hombres infernales, 32
Santo contra las mujeres vampiro, 34
Santo contra los clones, 73
Santo contra los zombies, 33, 38
Santo en el hotel de la muerte, 33
Santo en el museo de cera, 36, 38
Santos, 220
Santo y Blue Demon contra Dracula y el Hombre Lobo, 42

Santo y Blue Demon contra Dr. Frankenstein, 42
Satanism, 34–42, 63
science fiction, 23, 32, 63, 178, 216, 226n18
scientist, mad, 27, 31, 48–50, 91, 204, 226n24
secuestro permanente, 238n38
self-reflexivity, 8–10, 45, 106, 152–56, 194, 216, 220
serial (genre), 30–34, 228n34
Shaviro, Steven, 105, 114
Shouse, Eric, 137
smartphone, 4, 170, 175, 214
soccer, 12, 68, 201, 216, 243n2
social media, 2, 12, 167–70, 172, 177, 204–207
Solín. *See* Kalimán
Sombra Vengadora, La, 3, 30–33, 43
Spiderman, 8–9, 21, 25, 67, 90, 107, 152
spreadable media, 13, 176–77, 193, 207, 242n9
Stern, Steve, 112–14, 124
streaming, 2, 6, 13, 29, 151, 172–74, 203, 230n59, 232n2
Suárez, Juana, 76, 80–85, 231n1
SuperAnimal, 21
Superbarrio, 21, 169, 219
Supercifuentes, 2, 233n2
Súper Cóndor, 2, 240n13
Super Drags, 214–15
SuperGay, 21
supergenios de la mesa cuadrada, Los, 63, 66. *See also* Chapulín Colorado, El
Súper H, 12, 15, 167–70, 219
"Superhéroes en Latinoamérica." *See* Enchufetv
Superheroes on World Screens (Denison and Mizsei-Ward), 2, 24

Superhero Origins. See Rosenberg, Robin
Superman, 8–9, 21–24, 33, 43–45, 69–71, 79, 90, 94–98, 107, 137, 166, 194–95, 215–18, 224n8, 224n12, 226n20; comics, 23, 31. *See also* Eco, Umberto
Superniño, 21
Super Sam, 6, 71–73, 172
Superzán, 3, 43–51, 63, 68–69, 230n51
Susana Distancia, 3, 226n14

Taylor, Claire, 174, 239n5, 242n7
technology, 21–23, 43, 46–47, 165, 174, 227n27, 229n43
técnico, 25, 34, 38, 41, 225n9
terrorism, state, 11, 112, 116–24, 243n25
testicles, 216
Tlatelolco, 18, 64, 231n65, 231n69
trauma, 11, 76, 108–109, 113–23, 129–36, 143–44, 215, 232n8, 236n24, 237n36
Trompetero, Harold, 11, 75–79, 82, 90–91, 102–103, 216, 232n2, 233nn15–16
Twitter, 172, 177, 204

urbanization, 4, 11, 17, 37, 64, 82–84, 91–92
Urrutia Neno, Carolina, 106–107

Valdés Flores, Euclides, 148, 151
Valech Report, 112–13, 117–19, 124–29, 237n28
vampire, 3, 15, 31, 34, 46, 63, 226n24

Verduleros, Los, 145–47, 156, 175
video games, 22, 133, 230n59
villain: super, 23–31, 41–42, 59, 68, 91–104, 198, 208, 232n9, 233n10; superior, 210–11
Villalobos-Ruminott, Sergio, 235n11
Villoro, Juan, 21, 28, 225n9
viral video, 2, 176, 241n2

Watchmen, 110
Wayne, Bruce, 92, 109
werewolf, 3, 15, 46, 63
western (genre), 24, 63
Wilde, Alexander. *See* irruption (of memory)
Wilt, David, 19, 29, 53, 225n12, 228n38
Wolverine, 8, 143
Wonder Woman, 214, 218, 224n8
working-through (trauma), 23, 117, 136–37, 144, 166, 236n23. *See also* trauma
World War II, 6, 17, 48, 188

X-Men, 1, 21, 72, 195

YouTube, 2, 6, 12–13, 73, 147, 171–78, 191, 197–99, 202–204, 239n5, 242n9, 242n10, 242n13

Zambo Dende, 3, 220–21, 232n2
Zaror, Marko, 11, 105–108, 126, 133–34, 144, 195, 220, 236n26
Zenitram, 90, 216–17
Zovek, the Incredible, 55

www.ingramcontent.com/pod-product-compliance
Lightning Source LLC
Chambersburg PA
CBHW020643230426
43665CB00008B/297